1995

THE FOLKLORE SOCIETY
MISTLETOE SERIES
VOLUME 14
General Editor: H. R. E. Davidson

The English Mummers' Play

Other titles in the Mistletoe Series

The English Mummers' Play

Alex Helm

With a foreword by
N. Peacock and E. C. Cawte

Published by D. S. Brewer
and Rowman and Littlefield
for the Folklore Society

Published for the Folklore Society by D. S. Brewer, an imprint of
Boydell & Brewer Ltd, PO Box 9, Woodbridge, Suffolk IP12 3DF
and by Rowman and Littlefield, 81 Adams Drive, Totowa, NJ 07512, USA

First published 1981

British Library Cataloguing in Publication Data
Helm, Alex
The English mummers' play.
1. Mumming plays – History and criticism
I. Title   II. Folklore Society
398.2   PR635.F6

ISBN (UK) 0 85991 067 9
(US) 0 8476 7014 7

For my wife
for her toleration of a 'paper fortress' for many years

Photoset in Great Britain by
Rowland Phototypesetting Ltd
Bury St Edmunds, Suffolk
and printed by St Edmundsbury Press
Bury St Edmunds, Suffolk

Contents

List of Figures

List of Plates

Foreword

Born in Burnley, Lancashire, in 1920, Alex Helm died before he reached fifty and before the present work was finally prepared for publication. His introduction to folk customs came through traditional dance, learnt at school and teacher-training college. During World War II he served in the Royal Ordnance Corps in India, attaining the rank of major, and it was there that he met his wife. Back in England after the War, he took up his twin interests of teaching handicrafts and printing, and the study and practice of traditional dance. A chance conversation with Miss Margaret Dean-Smith, then Librarian of the English Folk Dance and Song Society, led him to study the Folk Play, and particularly to examine the papers of Thomas Fairman Ordish. These papers contain material originally intended for use in a comprehensive survey of the occurrence of the Play in the British Isles. The survey was never completed and the papers had remained in the Folklore Society's archives, unexamined, for some forty years, even though at least one 'comprehensive study' of the Play had been published in the meantime. Building on the information in these papers and using his skills in cataloguing and printing, Alex Helm started a geographical index of many customs associated with the Dance and Play. In this work he was aided by many informants and particularly in its compilation, by E. C. Cawte and N. Peacock. The published parts of the Index[1, 2], by their nature, did not include detailed discussion of the connection between the various customs, and it was the purpose of this present volume partially to fill this gap. It is essentially Alex Helm's own work, based upon the experience which he built up over many years of reading and lecturing: the original version of the book was based upon the lectures which he gave at Summer Schools at the University of Keele in the mid-60s.

From the first, the author makes clear what he is about: the discussion of a ceremonial involving death and resurrection, and not a literary curiosity. The classifications and subdivisions are ignored until this point is made. Because the Play has been much discussed in literary terms and the ceremonial elements have been overlooked, numerous misconceptions have arisen. These have had to be refuted at an early stage. Indeed, like the Presenter of the Play, who has often to deny the bad reputation of the players in order to gain their admission, the author has to start by being as much negative as positive in the two introductory chapters.

Of course the classification and subdivision of the types of action cannot be wholly ignored – to do so would be to ignore some of the basic facts revealed by the Index from which this work sprang. Three chapters deal individually with the three main types, beginning with the well-defined ones, the Wooing Play of the East Midlands of England and the Sword-Dance Play of the North-East of England, and concluding with the more amorphous and ubiquitous Hero-Combat Play. The Abnormal Texts discussed in the sixth chapter are often indicative of the underlying primitive ceremonial. The same theme is apparent in the next chapter which deals with the important dramatic aspect of Disguise. Disguise has often lost its significance as the sense of ceremony has been lost in verbal trappings and theatrical diversions, which are most apparent in the Chapbook versions described in the first Appendix.

To expand the geographical theme, the eighth chapter deals with manifestations in other countries. Far from indicating disparity, this shows the one-ness of the ceremony and leads to some explanation of its origins and its relationship to other ceremonials, each of which emphasizes a different facet of the rites surrounding the annual death and resurrection of the primitive god. Finally the wheel comes full circle with a short account of the modern appearance of these different ceremonials in the British Isles and a discussion of the similarities which are still apparent.

The Appendices expand the literary illustrations given in the text, and the visual illustrations, many drawn by the author's daughter, underline the dramatic effects of disguise, which is now one of the few common features of all the ceremonials.

Acknowledgements

The basis of this work is an Index to the Ceremonial Dances of Great Britain first begun in 1955 by Dr E. C. Cawte, Dr N. Peacock and myself. The debt of this book to the parent Index and to my friends and colleagues cannot be exaggerated, since it is true to say that had there not been close collaboration in the compilation of the Index there would have been no material in quantity to permit a detailed examination. I am grateful to my daughter, Alison G. Helm, for drawing the sketches which paved the way to an examination of the costume worn by the performers and opened up a new field of study not yet fully explored. The Council of the Folklore Society freely gave permission for the use of material in the Ordish Collection and the Vaughan Williams Memorial Library gave free access to the library collection. Additionally, many collectors, performers, witnesses and librarians have willingly given assistance and information, and provided photographs, and these are acknowledged by name in the bibliography and lists of Figures and Plates where necessary. I must also acknowledge my indebtedness to Miss Margaret Dean-Smith, who in 1949 first made me aware of the rich field of traditional observance still awaiting exploration and study, and who patiently led me to study and evaluate my findings in a way I would not have dreamed possible twenty years ago.

A.H.

1

Problems and Attitudes

The seasonal round of life in England was once marked by ceremonials performed exclusively by men wearing a 'disguise', not only to preserve their temporary anonymity, but also to mark them as beings set apart from their community. As time passed, ceremony dwindled until only the appearance at the correct time and the disguise remained to mark the ritual which was difficult to understand in the more sophisticated times of recent history. One of the most persistent is the Mummers' play, still surviving in scattered places in the British Isles and, although it is eagerly anticipated by the audiences who gather (often from many miles away), it is almost completely misunderstood by performers and witnesses alike. The performances usually occur during the Christmas period, though they are a feature of the winter months from All Souls to Easter. They take place in the streets as at Marshfield, Gloucestershire, on Boxing Day, or at Midgley, Yorkshire, at Easter. Performances are also given in public houses, dance halls, halls of large houses, &c., as at Uttoxeter, Staffordshire, or Antrobus, Cheshire, or the performers make the rounds of outlying farms as they still do in Ireland. Widely scattered as these survivals are, they still retain elements common to versions long since extinct and to each other. A group of men enter to stand silently in a semi-circle to the rear of where they are to perform. They are disguised either by a poor attempt at dressing in character or by strips of paper or ribbon sewn to their everyday clothes, and hanging from their hats over their faces. They remain silent and immobile until, when it is their turn to speak, they step forward, declaim their lines in a loud voice devoid of any inflexions, and stand back at the conclusion of their speech. The performance only shows lively action when two of the performers fight each other with swords, and even this may be formalised into rhythmic clashing, one is killed and brought to life again by a wonder-working doctor. Following this, other characters step forward and speak their lines, completely irrelevant to what has just occurred. At the end a collection is taken and the performers leave.

This kind of performance, with variations of type to be discussed later, was once a familiar scene of the winter months, occurring as regularly as the season came round. On paper the texts read badly; they are an amalgam of misunderstood words, local allusions, &c., often with garbled passages from reputable literature interpolated without any sign of relevance. The named characters are often mutually anachronistic. Napoleon can, and often does, appear in company with Julius Caesar, the legendary St George accompanies the historical St Patrick, and even Lord Nelson is found in the company of characters who could never have any real life counterpart. Despite these and other absurdities, once the performance begins, all nonsense disappears

and the performers become very different beings from the rather peculiarly dressed individuals they appear at first sight. Without effort they establish a bond between themselves and their audience, so that all are caught up in an atmosphere far remote from the twentieth century. This atmosphere cannot be transmitted on paper, it must be experienced physically during a performance before the sense of age, magic and mystery, all caught up together, can be felt.

A written text cannot transmit any one of these elements, let alone all of them, but paradoxically, one has to rely on such published versions for most of the knowledge of what are unfortunately remnants from the past.[1] The following version from Syresham in Northamptonshire was written down by a baker's man in 1887 and, in some ways, is more coherent than many, since it contains a mixture of a chapbook version combined with what is probably the local traditional text.[2] It has three combats but only one cure, a feature typical of chapbooks. The Doctor's and Fiddler's lines are local nonsense interpolations. The text is as follows:[3]

Enter First Man, called the Fool

Fool
A room, a room, brave gallants! Give us room to sport,
For in this room we wish to resort
And to make our merry rhyme –
Remember, good sir, 'tis Christmas time.
The time to cut up goose pies doth appear,   5
We are come to act our Merry Christmas here
To the sound of the trumpet and the beat of the drum.
Make room, brave gentlemen, and let our merry actors come;
These are the merry actors that travel the street,
These are the merry actors that fight for our meat,   10
We are the merry actors that show pleasant play;
Step in, King George, the champion man, and clear the way.

Enter King George

King
I am King George, from old England I sprung,
My famous name throughout the world hath rung,
And many deeds and wonders have I made known;   15
I've made the tyrants tremble on the throne.
I've followed a fair lady to a giant's gate
Once confined to dungeon deep to meet her fate.
There I resolved with true (*sic*)
To burst the doors and set the prisoners free,   20
When a giant almost struck me dead,

1

And by my valiant arm I cut off his head.
I've searched the world all round and round,
But a man to equal me I never yet have found.

Enter Slasher

Slasher
I am a valiant soldier and Slasher is my name,   25
And with my sword and buckler by my side I hope to
    win the game.
For to fight with me I see thou art not able.

King George
Disable! Disable! It lays not within thy power,
For with my broad edged sword I'll soon thee devour.
Stand off Slasher! and let no more be said,   30
For if I draw my sword I shall surely break thy head.

Slasher
How canst thou break my head?
Since my head is made of iron, my body's made of steel,
My hands and feet and knuckle bones,
I challenge thee to feel.   35

They fight and Slasher is wounded

Fool
And there he lies in presence of you all,
I lovingly for a doctor call.

Doctor enters

O! Here is the doctor. Are you the Doctor?

Doctor
Ten pounds is my fee,
But if thou be an honest man I will only take five of
    thee.   40

Fool
How far have you travelled in doctrineship?

Doctor
O! very far! I've travelled from Itally, Titterley, France
    and Spain,
And safe am returned to cure the deceased[4] in old
    England again.

Fool
And no further?

Doctor
O, yes, a great deal further.   45
From the fireside and the cupboard, upstairs and into
    bed.

Fool
What sort of deseases can you cure?

Doctor
All sorts.

Fool
What's all sorts?

Doctor
I can cure the itch, the pip, the palsy and the
    gout,   50

If a man has nineteen devils in his scull (*sic*) I can cast
    twenty of them out,
I have in my pocket spectacles for blind bumble bees,
    crutches for lame geese,
Pack-saddles for grasshoppers, and plasters for broken-
    backed mice.
I once cured Sir Harry of a nagnail twenty yards long,
Surely I can cure this poor man, so here goes!   55
Here Jack! Take a little out of my bottle,
And if thou be not quite slain,
Rise, Jack! and fight again.
Oh, I see! I can't get him up, I must examine him in the
    mouth.
I see he has got a tremendous large tooth and is suffering
    a great deal of pain.   60
Here, Fool, help me! You pull his feet while I hold his
    head.
I believe it lays in his feet, but well, I will give him a pill.
Here, Jack, take this pill. It will go down like a fussfaggot
    and operate like a forty round ladder.
Those pills of mine are good,
They are not like the pills these quacks take about with
    them, they pick up a few sheep trickling and roll them
    in flour and call them pilacosha pills. Mine are a sure
    cure, they are not the ones that cure for four and
    twenty hours but for four and twenty years.
My grandmother forty years after she was dead,   70
Rose and stood up with her coffin on her head
To tell the people what wonderful cures her grandson
    had done!
Come, Jack, get up!

Jack[5]
Oh! my back!

Doctor
What's amiss with thy back?   75

Jack
My back is wounded,
And my heart is confounded.
To be struck out of seven senses into fourscore,
The like was never seen in old England before.
Hark! Hark! I hear the silver trumpet sound,   80
Farewell, King George, I can no longer stay.

King George
I am King George, that noble champion bold,
And with my glittering sword I won ten thousand
    pounds in gold.
'Twas I that fought the fiery dragon and brought it to the
    slaughter,
And by those means I won the King of Egypt's
    daughter.   85

Enter Black Prince

Black Prince
I am the Black Prince of Paradine, born of high renown,
And soon I will fetch King George's lofty courage down.
Before King George shall be received by me,
King George shall die to all eternity.

King George
Stand off, thou black Morocco dog! or by my sword thou
    shalt die.   90
I will pierce thy body full of holes and make thy buttons
    fly.

2

Black Prince
Draw out thy sword and slay,
Pull out thy purse and pay.
For I will have a recompense
Before I go away.   95

King George
Prince of Paradise, where hast thou been,
Or pray, what fine sights hast thou seen?
Dost thou think no-one of thy age
Dare such a one as thee engage?
Lay down thy sword, take up to me a spear,   100
Then I will fight you without dread or fear,
A battle! A battle! between you and I
To see on the ground which first shall lie.
Guard your eyes and guard your nose,
Or down you go at a very few blows.   105

They fight and Black Prince is slain

King George
Now Prince of Paradine is dead
And all his joys are entirely fled.
Take him and give him to the flies,
And let him no more come near my eyes.

Enter King of Egypt

King of Egypt
I am King of Egypt as plainly doth appear,   110
I am come to seek my son, my only son and heir.

King George
He is slain.

King of Egypt
Who did him slay? Who did him kill?
Or on the ground his precious blood did spill?

King George
I did him slay, I did him kill,   115
And on the ground his precious blood did spill.
Please you, my laws and honour to maintain
Had you been here you would have fared the same.

King of Egypt
Oh! cursed Christian! What hast thou done?
Thou hast ruined me and slain my only son.   120

King George
He gave me a challenge, who now denys? (*sic*)
See how high he was and see how low he lies.

King of Egypt
Oh! Hector! Hector! help me with speed,
For in my life I never stood more in need.
Do not stand there with sword in hand,   125
Come and fight at my command.

Hector
Yes, yes, my liege, I will obey
And with my sword I hope to win the day.
If that be he that doth stand there,
That slew my master's son and heir;   130
If he be sprung from royal blood,
I will make it run like Noah's flood.

King George
Oh! Hector! Hector! don't be so hot!
Thou knowest not what thou hast got.
I can tame thee of thy pride   135
And lay thine anger too aside.
I could inch thee, cut thee as small as flies,
And send thee over the seas to make mince pies.
Mince pies hot! mince pies cold!
I could send thee to Black Sam before thou art three days
    older.   140

Hector
How canst thou tame off my pride?
Or lay mine anger too aside?
How canst thou inch me, cut me as small as flies,
Or send me over the seas to make mince pies?
Mince pies hot! mince pies cold!   145
How canst thou send me to Black Sam before I am three
    days older?
Since my head is made of iron, my body made of steel,
My feet and hands and knucklebones I challenge thee to
    feel.

They fight and Hector is wounded

Hector
I am a valiant knight and Hector is my name,
Many a battle have I fought and always won the
    game;   150
But by King George I received this wound.
Hark! Hark! I hear the silver trumpet spund, down
    yonder is the way.
Farewell, King George, I can no longer stay.

Fool enters

King George
Here comes from post old Ben Bold.

Fool
Master, did I ever do thee any harm?   155

King George
Jack, did ever I take thee for my friend?

Fool
Thou proud, saucy coxcomb, be gone!

King George
Coxcomb! I defy that name.
With a sword thou ought to be stabbed for the same.

Fool
Stabbing is the least I fear;   160
Appoint the time and place and I will meet you there.

King George
Across the water at the hour of five,
I will meet you there if I'm alive.

Fool
Bring the grave-digger!

King George
Bring the undertaker with you!   165

Enter Beelzebub

3

Beelzebub
Here come I, old Beelzebub,
And on my shoulder I carry my club,
And in my hand a dripping pan,
Don't you think I'm a jolly old man?
If you don't believe what I say,   170
Come in, Fiddler, and clear the way.

Fiddler enters

Fiddler
Here comes I who has never been it,
With my great head and little wit;
My head is great, my wit is small,
So I've brought my fiddle to please you all.   175
Now all my dogs, lay down your bones and wimple up
    your ribs and we'll have a jig.

This type of performance was once familiar over large areas of the British Isles. It caused many commentators to whom it was a natural part of their lives, to set their impressions in print. These descriptions are now to be found for the most part in almost inaccessible newspaper files, magazine articles, contributions to *Journals* of learned Societies and in manuscript collections. Almost without exception all of these show that familiarity has seemingly bred contempt. The reproduction of texts has had its own pitfalls. Stage directions, as in the Syresham variant, were added to make sense of who was speaking and who was killed, even though characters neither 'entered' nor made an exit in the theatrical sense. The existence of texts presupposes literary creation; to set them down in dramatic form made it almost fashionable to regard the Mummers as poor relations of the legitimate stage. It is facile to see in the performances of the former, the seeds of early dramatic development, even though the texts reveal neither dramatic form nor content. Of the three fights in the Syresham text, only one has the champion cured, though one might expect the same cure for all three. The entry of Beelzebub and the Fiddler carries the development no further but traditionally they have become part of the Mummers' attempts to make their version more attractive and consequently more lucrative. Early recorders of the custom saw nothing illogical in this; by the time it was considered worth reporting, the observance had decayed to such an extent that it was meaningless. Such students as were attracted to the subject – W. J. Thoms, Thomas Fairman Ordish, E. H. Binney and others – were not of the 'Folk' and tended to equate what they saw or read with their own, more sophisticated, experience.

Students could also be misled by vague accounts which existed from a relatively early date. Where a text and/or a clear description exists of what took place, there is no possibility for confusion, but often accounts are not so specific. Often the same name is used for widely divergent customs. 'Mummers' is the common name for the Play, but it is also applied to the black-faced children who, to this day, sweep the hearths of houses in the West Riding of Yorkshire and south-east Lancashire on New Year's Eve, making a humming sound all the time. In Derbyshire and Staffordshire the performers in the Play were known as 'Guisers'; so were the men and women in Cornwall who changed clothes, blacked their faces and danced in the streets. *Sometimes* the latter also performed a Play independently. 'Morris-dancing', a term normally used to describe the men's ceremonial dance, particularly in the Cotswolds at Whitsuntide, and

elsewhere at other times of the year, is also used to describe a sword-dance in the north-east of England about Christmastime, or simply a Play. 'Pace-egging' can mean either the performance of the Play at Easter or children singing the appropriate song to accompany the collection of eggs, whilst 'Soul-Caking' can mean either the performance of the Play in Cheshire at All Souls or children singing the souling song and begging for 'soul-cakes'. This confusion exists over the whole range of the Play and has become one of its most difficult features to clarify.

The local inhabitant would find no difficulty in understanding what was involved, but these early eye-witness accounts are often vague to us because the writers were describing something familiar to themselves and their readers. Both knew what was involved. The student, many years later, can only guess at the nature of what went on, taking into account the season of appearance, the geographical location, description of costumes, and indeed, any slight clues an account might contain. Even then, it is difficult to be certain without examining large quantities of material and so developing an instinct for what is not 'just right'. Fortunately, more and more information is coming to light so that the observance can be evaluated in a way not previously possible. As study has progressed it has become clear that the custom can best be classified in terms of its internal structure, and that survivals can be divided into three types, the Hero-Combat (of which the Syresham text is an example), the Wooing and the Sword Dance ceremonies. These three types and their inter-relationship will be described and discussed later. Immediately, it is necessary to examine the beliefs and ideas which have developed since the Play was first studied.

Most widespread of these is the belief that the Mummers' performance is all 'St George and the Dragon'. This seems to have its origin in the theory that the texts are derived from the legend as detailed by Richard Johnson in his *Famous Historie of the Seven Champions of Christendom*. He tells how St George, son of the Lord High Steward of England, born, after a Caesarian operation, with the image of a dragon on his breast, a blood-red cross on his right hand, and a gold garter on his left leg, was stolen just after his birth by Kalyb, an enchantress. He was kept by her for fourteen years, when he imprisoned her in a rock and freed the other six champions whom she was keeping captive. After staying nine months in Coventry, the champions set out on their individual travels, George going to Egypt to kill a dragon. This done, he won the hand of Sabra, the King of Egypt's daughter, who was courted by Almidor, Black Prince of Morocco. The rest of the *Historie* is concerned with the adventures of the seven against giants, magicians, dragons, &c., in all of which they are successful, until eventually, at the end of Book II, they die, and Book III, added by a different author, is concerned with the similar adventures of their sons. The constant theme of Johnson's romance is the triumph of Christianity over Islam, to achieve which the champions have all kinds of improbable adventures.

The book is virtually unreadable today, but from its first publication in 1596 it enjoyed tremendous success, so much so that in 1638 it was turned into a five-act play in blank verse by John Kirke.[6] To make it conform to the demands of the stage, Kirke had to introduce new features whilst retaining the most popular features of the prose version. In Act I he recounted, with minor variations, George's early history, introducing a new character, Suckabus, a clown, who ultimately became George's treacherous servant. Later Chorus, in retrospect, told of his encounter with the Dragon, presumably a literary device to overcome the limitations of the stage, and described how he rescued Sabrina, daughter of the King of Morocco. Ultimately, George was tricked into fighting the other champions whom he overcame, but all ended well with a knightly dance of all the heroes. Neither Johnson nor Kirke introduced a theme of death and resurrection, which, as the Syresham text shows, is the crux of the Mummers' traditional performance.

From these synopses it is clear that little about the Seven Champions is relevant, even though only the features which could reasonably claim to have some connection have been chosen. Many Mummers' performances contain a boastful *resumé* by George of his adventures (*ll.* 13–24 and 82–5 of the Syresham version), which summarise very briefly those given in the beginning by Johnson and latterly by Kirke. It seems reasonably certain that the King of Egypt, the Black Prince of Morocco, and St George himself were probably borrowed from Johnson where they occur, but Sabra only has a mention in one line of the Mummers' dialogue (*l.* 85 of Syresham) and otherwise does not normally appear. The prevalence of these characters may be due to the spread of chapbook versions of Johnson's romance, but this does not imply that the George and Dragon theme is the basis of the Mummers' Plays. St George himself need not appear as a character, as he does not at Syresham, though King George need only be a thin disguise for the saint as memory faded. In Ireland, St George is dismissed as St Patrick's boy; in Scotland, out of thirty-five versions, he appears in only one, being replaced by a variety of champions from Robert the Bruce to Hector. It is highly probable that the performers selected names for their champions from their favourite folk heroes, though the absence of Robin Hood amongst the versions is puzzling. He appears in very few versions and then in a very diminished *rôle*. Saint George may have been kept to the forefront of public consciousness when he was belatedly adopted as the Patron Saint of England. Seventeenth in the list of patronal church dedications, he became a very popular figure as the

various mediaeval Ridings and Guild Pageants testify. These would keep him in the public eye until a reasonably late period.

Though the festivals connected with his name always associated him with his traditional opponent, the Dragon, the Mummers never seem to have followed suit. If Kirke found it difficult to include a dragon on the stage, the Mummers must have found it doubly so; to construct a costume which would survive the rough and tumble of many combats as they went their rounds would be beyond their resources, even if he were needed as a character. Such versions as do include a 'Dragon' are peculiar by normal standards[7] or have obviously been brought up-to-date by their promoters.[8] Various arguments have been advanced to show that in St George's opponent, Slasher, the Turkish Knight, &c., the Dragon lurks in disguise. Chambers saw the lines:

> My head is made of iron,
> My body is made of steel,
> My arms and legs of beaten brass;
> No man can make me feel.

as describing a Dragon, offering various literary sources in support of his argument.[9] The Syresham variant of these lines (*ll.* 32–5) is typical, but neither version gives reason for anything but disbelief. The lines could describe an armoured knight which would be more rational in this context as it developed through the years. At Shelford, Nottinghamshire, the 'Plough Bullocks' dragged a plough round the village on Plough Monday, chanting as they did:

> My back is made of iron, my body's made of
> steel
> And if you don't believe it, put your hands
> on and feel. [10]

Here they were describing a plough, and again the lines made sense. Plate 1 shows a fringed paper costume worn by the performers at Sherfield English in Hampshire. This type of disguise has given rise to a suggestion that

Plate 1. Mummer's Coat, Sherfield English, Hampshire.

the design is intended to simulate dragon's scales. If there were any substance in this argument it would be reasonable to expect that only the character portraying the dragon would be thus disguised, whereas all the performers wore similar costumes. No-one would suggest that all the performers were dragons, though if the basic argument of costume were logical, it could be reasonably claimed that they were.

If the Saint is not necessarily a vital character, even allowing for 'Prince' and 'King' variants, and the Dragon is a rarity, much of the foundation for the belief that the source of the texts lies with Johnson has disappeared. One could hardly accept Johnson as a primary source in any event since his book was based on the earlier romance of *Sir Bevis of Southampton* with a considerable debt to the legends of Alexander and the travels of Marco Polo. One would have to push back the basis much further than the Elizabethan author to be consistent, but indeed, the effort would be pointless. The connection between the legend and the Mummers' Play is extremely slight, just as is the connection between the latter and the stage.

The use of the word 'Play' is misleading. The Syresham text shows, despite an attempt at division into speeches, that there is little of dramatic content involved. Two champions fight, one is killed, brought to life by the doctor; two further fights follow, rather unnecessarily, and the whole thing ends with the appearance of two unconnected characters. Any dramatist who attempted to stage a performance on these lines would be doomed to failure on the stage. Furthermore, the use of a stage is foreign to the Mummers. They need a space, nothing more. The space is kept clear by their forming a semi-circle in which the action takes place, and round them are their audience. This could be described as early Theatre-in-the-Round, but nothing more. It is vital to the performance that there should be communication between themselves and their audience, if only for the mundane business of passing round the hat at the close. The audience however, know what is to happen; they are prepared to accept the death as natural, and the dead man need only drop his head to show death[11] or kneel on one knee lest he should damage his costume.[12] These

ingredients occur yearly as a rite, and in a sense, even the modern performers are performing what is left of an ancient ritual. Although the original purpose of what they are doing may be unknown to them, they are nevertheless basically enacting the life-cycle drama, so that fertility of crops, animals and people can be ensured after the dead period of Winter. What they are performing is neither Play nor Farce. It is the remains of what was an urgent magic necessity to ensure that life would go on, and to a primitive society whose future depended on maintaining growth of all things in the summer months, it was necessary to assist the cycle by all means in their power. What began as necessary magic dwindled into a ritual which had become meaningless by the time it was being set down on paper, but its form had been set. The primitive performers who originally took part were probably the medicine men of their community, and their twentieth century descendants, albeit unwittingly, still contrive to give the same impression once the ritual has begun. For the moment, their audience becomes their community, to whom they dispense 'luck', even though originally this was 'fertility'.

If the word 'Play' could be discarded in this context and either 'Ritual', 'Ceremony' or 'Act' replace it, then the way is clear for a better understanding of what the Mummers are about. It can be defined as:

A men's seasonal Ritual intended to promote fertility, expressed basically in terms of an action of revitalisation, in which the performers must be disguised to prevent recognition.

To be recognised broke the luck, and, as Plate 2 shows, the costume is still retained today by performers who continue wishing to be anonymous. The word 'action' has been used deliberately since it is the action which the texts reveal which is important, not the texts themselves. Originally, the action of death and revival was probably mimed and the texts developed as understanding dwindled,[13] and some attempt was necessary to make the inexplicable comprehensible. That the texts only make the understanding worse is paradoxical: as Margaret Dean-Smith said:

Plate 2. Crookham, Hampshire, Mummers, Boxing Day, 1966.

'the Play, and any significance it may have, resides in the action: the text is a local accretion, often both superfluous and irrelevant. The Play can exist in action alone, without a word spoken'.[14]

Although even modern performers are reluctant to write down their texts from a belief that to do so would break the 'luck', it is difficult to explain that it is what they *do* which is important, not what they *say*. It is to attempt to explain what the performers are, or were doing, that this book is written. To do so must involve some conjecture since much detail is missing, and theories or arguments cannot always be supported by facts.

2

Literary Survey

One of the saddest features of the study of the Ceremonial is the inability of the students to find any references to it before the early 1700s. If it can be accepted that the roots of the action probably took hold in primitive times, there is a long gap between then and the first mention in MS or print. It is unlikely that this gap will ever be bridged. We can only assume that there was something before the 1700's which had begun, even by then, to harden off into the form which remains today. There is some value in tracing literary references chronologically. Apart from gaining an impression of contemporary attitudes, there is also an indication of how widespread the observance was.

To date, the earliest known accepted reference is contained in a MS dated *circa* 1800 in Trinity College, Dublin.[1] Its account runs:

'on our new green last evening there was presented the drollest piece of mummery I ever saw in or out of Ireland. There was St George and St Dennis and St Patrick in their buffe coats and the Turk likewise and Oliver Cromwell, and a Doctor and an old woman who made rare sport till Beelzebub came in with a frying pan upon his shoulder and a great flail in his hand threshing about him on friends and foes, and at last running away with the bold usurper whom he tweaked by his gilded nose – and then came a little Devil with a broom to gather up the money that was thrown to the Mummers for their sport. It is an ancient pastime they tell me of the citizens.'

In some ways this source is unsatisfactory. The existing MS claims to be reproducing an earlier one of *circa* 1685 whose whereabouts are now unknown. Whatever took place is said to have occurred in Cork, one of the oldest English settlements in Ireland, and the characters mentioned are clearly those with which we are concerned here. What they actually performed is not described, nor if there was a death and resurrection, or even a combat. The words 'ancient pastime' are used in the same description as the name of Oliver Cromwell, who died in 1658, only twenty-seven years before the account is said to have been written. The events in Ireland which made him hated there took place in 1649, when, amongst other acts of great cruelty, he captured Drogheda and put its garrison to death. From then to the time when he was first mentioned as a figure of fun in this ceremonial was therefore, at most, only thirty-six years, which hardly qualifies as an 'ancient pastime', unless Cromwell himself was a recent substitution in a much older ritual.

Nothing more has come to light between this Irish MS and an account, written in 1738, referring to a performance in Exeter at Christmas.[2] It was not published until 1770 and described St George 'in a (borrow'd) Holland shirt, most gorgeously be-ribboned, over his Waistcoat, etc.', and gives four lines of this autobiographical vaunt:

'Oh! Here comes I Saint George, a man of courage bold
And with my spear I winn'd three Crowns of Gold.
I slew the Dragon, and brought him to the Slaughter.
And by that very means I married Sabra, the beauteous King of Egypt's daughter'.

These same lines, or variants, are still in use today in localities far removed from Exeter, so that it is certain they are at least 240 years old, and obviously much older. Similarly, the same pattern of disguise is still to be seen.

The action was known in the Ludgvan vicinity of Cornwall before 1758:

'. . . at the family feasts of gentlemen, the Christmas Plays were admitted, and some of the most learned among the vulgar (after leave obtained) entered in disguise, and carryed on miserable dialogues on Scripture subjects; when their memory could go no further, they filled up the rest of the entertainment with more puerile representations, the combats of puppets, the final victory of the hero of the drama, and death of his antagonist.'[3]

The performances were likened to the Miracle Plays once performed in the county, and there was a distinction made between the 'gentlemen' who watched and the 'vulgar' who performed.

The distinction was not preserved by John Jackson who gave, in 1793, an account of mummers he had seen in his boyhood.[4] Born in 1742, Jackson spent his youth in Westmorland and Yorkshire. His father held the living at Keighley in the latter county, and the account he gave was very similar to others from the same area at a much later date. The mummers he described were 'Farmers' sons and those of decent tradesmen' who had with them a Clown wearing a patched jacket, 'trowses', and a fox's tail in his cap. There was a wooing scene which involved a father, daughter and two lovers; in this, the Fool won the Lady. The Fool was killed, but no description of a revival was given. The whole was prefaced with a Calling-on Song of 'some thirty stanzas', in which the performers were introduced by the Fool and then followed him round in a circle until all were introduced. The stanza quoted by Jackson:

'My name is Captain Calf-tail, Calf-tail,
And on my back it is plain to be seen;
Although I am simple, and wear a fool's cap,
I am dearly beloved of a queen'.

is familiar in other examples. This is an important account, and although it can only be given the approximate date of *circa* 1750, Jackson said that the ceremony was handed down from father to son. He added:

'as the exhibitors had never been at a play, nor within the walls of a play-house, the originality of the performances must have been with them.'

This comment is interesting for two reasons. First, Jackson made it clear that the performers had not been influenced by the legitimate stage, at any rate up to the time of which he was writing. This supports the argument in Chapter One that to consider the ceremony in these terms is incorrect. Second, it is clear that at some time after he wrote, some interplay between the Folk action and the orthodox drama had begun, for in 1791, John Williams, under the pseudonym of Anthony Pasquin, gave an account of a visit to Bristol Fair in 1770.[5]

Here, he visited Jobson's Booth and witnessed the performance of two plays, one of which, *The Siege of Troy*, included a scene between Hector, Achilles, a Physician and O'Driscoll. Hector was killed in 'a pugilistic combat' by a blow 'to the bread-basket' and revived by the Physician summoned by O'Driscoll. The actual lines spoken have some interest:

O'Driscoll
A doctor, a doctor, ten pounds for a doctor!

Enter Physician

Physician
Here am I.

O'Driscoll
What can you cure?

Physician
The cramp, the gout, the pain within and the pain without.

O'Driscoll
O boderation to your nonsense – take a little of my tip-tap; put it on your nin-nap, now rise up Slasher and fight again.

This is the earliest record of interplay between the Folk action and literary drama, though in this instance the latter was performed in a fairground booth, a poor relation of the theatre. It is impossible now to be certain in which direction this fragment travelled, but it might be suspected that as Jobson's Booth could not have been high in the social scale, the lines were used deliberately because the audience would be familiar with them. They

would be certain to attract good-humoured attention, if indeed, the whole incident were not deliberately interpolated for this reason. This argues that the Folk action was a familiar event to an eighteenth century English audience.

Next in chronological sequence came a chapbook published in Newcastle upon Tyne in 1771 and reprinted in 1788 (see Appendix 1). The former is the oldest complete text known to exist and antedates the Revesby, Lincolnshire, version by eight years. The latter is preserved in a MS in the British Museum[6] and is known to have been performed out of season in October, 1779, despite the Christmas mentioned in its text. So far as is known, it was never performed before this date nor since. Quite unlike any other version, except possibly that from Ampleforth, Yorkshire (see page 25), it has always been something of a mystery and will need discussion later. It is even unlike versions noted at roughly the same point of time, also to be seen in the British Museum, and quite different from a fragment reported from Edinburgh in the 1780's[7] and an Oxfordshire example noted in 1794.[8]

A version described from Boston, Massachusetts,[9] proved that, by 1780, the ceremony had crossed the Atlantic, presumably with the English settlers. The fragment of text and the background detail given, show the pattern to be the same. Again, a letter written on December 15th, 1811, from Halifax, Nova Scotia, to a clergyman in Kent, says:

'in the evening some lads came to know if we would have any rhymes – they had white paper caps on and acted a kind of short piece something about St George and the Dragon and the Holy Land which ended in a sham fight – I cannot find out whence the custom proceeds . . .'[10]

In 1818, George Ormerod, a Cheshire lawyer who never practised, published his only book, *The History of Cheshire*. He had been given a text from Sandbach, Cheshire, which he had intended to include; he found this to be identical with the 1788 Newcastle chapbook and with another version performed on the Welsh/Cheshire border. In the event he decided the Sandbach text was 'too barbarous' for publication and contented himself with printing a few fragments. Examination of the complete text still preserved among his MSS shows that it is far less 'barbarous' than some still performed and its text quite unlike the chapbook. It is true that the characters, First and Second Captains, Sir Guy, etc., are now unfamiliar in the county, though a character designated as the Fool, says, by way of introduction:

'I am not the Prince of Beelzebub'

and then promptly denies the statement by going on with the typical Beelzebub lines. It is also true that the chapbook version to which Ormerod referred did have two passages which would be considered 'coarse' today. In describing his cures, the Doctor said:

'Come in you ugly, nasty, dirty Whore,
Whose age is threescore Years or more . . .'

whilst finally, the King of Egypt insults Alexander by saying:

'The teeth are no whiter than the charcoal,
And thy Breath stinks like the Devil's A-se H-le' *(sic)*

Ormerod's views on the barbarity of the text are the first hint that texts could be edited. As 'good taste' grew, much that had been accepted as normal became less tolerable. How much more illuminating versions might have been, had they been printed as performed, is unknown. Indeed, it is not certain that much was revised. It is known that in some Wooing Ceremonies 'Baby' was often substituted for 'Bastard' when the performance was before polite society. When publishing the Ampleforth dance and play, Cecil Sharp said:[11]

'it has been found necessary to omit several lines that were corrupt and unintelligible, and to amend others. It is hoped, however, that it will be found possible to print elsewhere the whole of the text exactly as Mr Wright gave it me.'

The original version to which Sharp referred has not been preserved, but there used to be a variant in the Vaughan Williams Memorial Library sent by a Mrs Bell. This followed the published version very closely, the main substitutions being of the order of 'First, man' for 'Faith, man', 'Have' for 'I've', etc., though the verse introducing No. 3 in the second Calling-on Song was given as:

'The next he is a sparling lad,
His father is a squire,
For Betsy their sweet chambermaid
He got a great desire.
He huddled her, he cuddled her
Until he made her yield,
But when the truth they came to know
He was forced to quit the field.'

Similarly, when the Doctor described his travels in the published version, he said:

'All the way from the fireside, upstairs, knocked the looking-glass over'

whilst the Mrs Bell version gave:

'. . . knocked the chamber pot over'.

Mrs Bell also gave the Clown four additional lines before the Calling-on Songs are begun:

'Now my Grandmother one of the big-bellied breed
As big as an old gelt in her twang:
She could serve by the tinker at peddling trade
If that isn't a lie I'll be hanged.'

These minor differences suggest that the editorial revisions made by Sharp were, in some instances at least, merely genteel amendments to avoid offending his more prudish readers. In 1949, the present author was told by the leader of a traditional side that his team had two versions, one for performance before polite society, the other to less discriminating audiences. He was not prepared to write down either version. At Goathland, Yorkshire, the Doctor's 'words' 'would not now be tolerated, either for the coarse words, or for the actions',[12] and what form they took still remains a mystery.

There is no doubt that setting down the versions in print would involve some censorship: unfortunately, there is now no way of determining its extent.

Ormerod's reluctance to publish the text from Sandbach in 1818 probably reflects the feelings of many others who published versions. As was said in Chapter One, commentators were observers, and not of the 'Folk' who performed. Only when a text was written down by an actual performer and reproduced exactly as given could it be certain that there was no literary tampering, but these instances were relatively rare at the beginning of the nineteenth century. Bowdlerising must be considered implicit in early accounts. All versions are written largely in metropolitan English which must be far removed from the normal everyday speech of the performers who seem to have stuck to this mode of dialogue.

Ormerod was the first to publicise what he considered 'barbarity', and at the time he was writing, Henry Francis Cary, the translator of Dante, noted that the Tipteers had visited his house in Littlehampton, Sussex, during Christmas, 1817.[13] His comments might have been interesting, but unfortunately a 'sick fit' of his son prevented his seeing them. Although he gave no text for the action, the slight description he gave of Father Christmas, the Turk, etc., leaves no doubt that the ceremony was of the same kind as that described by Ormerod. A version from Keynsham, Somerset, is known to have existed in 1822 (see page 34); others are reported from Abbotsford[14] and Falkirk,[15] Scotland, in 1825. A further chapbook was published in Whitehaven, Cumberland, in 1826. Though no original appears to have survived, Hone published the text in his *Every-Day Book* (see page 57), with the four offending lines already quoted, omitted.

The action is mentioned sporadically from then on until 1849 when W. J. Thoms, coiner of the term 'Folk-Lore, or Lore of the People', began to edit *Notes and Queries*, a serial publication ultimately full of antiquarian jottings and literary notes, still being published today though with not quite the same focus of interest. Thoms' interest in Folk-Lore was brought about by his interest in Shakespeare's plays, and his intention, though so far as is known largely unfulfilled, was to extract references to Folk-Lore from the plays in which he was primarily interested.[16] *Notes and Queries* published many versions and comments on the dramatic action in its pages; furthermore, its immediate success caused it to be widely copied by local newspapers up and down the country. The end product was to produce a large portion of the material now available for study.

Round about 1890, the subject attracted the attention of Thomas Fairman Ordish, a civil servant with an interest in drama, who began to collect together MSS, printed accounts, etc., which now form the Ordish Collection, housed in the library of the Folklore Society in London. His aim was to study the material he was collecting with a view to publishing a definitive work on the subject: in the event, his death intervened, and apart from two papers contributed to *Folk-Lore*[17] and a third still unpublished, his aim was unfulfilled. His published works show that he regarded the sword dance as the formative basis of the ceremony, but his lack of interest in the choreographic dance led him to ignore its form and method of performance. After his death the collection lay forgotten and unnoticed for more than forty years, but so far as is known, it was Ordish who first had the intention of publishing a critical study on the subject; none of the accounts mentioned above did more than record what took place.

The first critical study, written by Arthur Beatty, was

contributed to the October 1906 issue of the *Transactions of the Wisconsin Academy of Sciences, Arts and Letters* and entitled 'The St George, or Mummers' Play; a Study in the Protology of the Drama'. It was intended as a curtain raiser for a book which was never written and is important because Beatty, ahead of his time, saw the ceremony as an action which he compared with others similar elsewhere in the world. This was a step forward of major importance; not only did Beatty avoid the fashionable literary approach, but he also showed that what took place in England had parallels elsewhere. Unfortunately, his article lay unnoticed for many years, and it certainly received no immediate comment so that its impact was small.

It was certainly not mentioned by R. J. E. Tiddy whose incomplete studies were published posthumously in 1923 under the title of *The Mummers' Play*. Tiddy was more in harmony with the subject than any writer since. He lived among country people and their traditions, though not of them, and was inclined to see the ceremonial in its true perspective. His book contained thirty-three versions of his own collecting: so far as can be seen they were reproduced exactly as collected. The initial essay, admittedly not finalised because of his early death in action during the First World War, shows a dependence on tracing text to literary sources, but hints at the importance of the ceremonial nature of the custom.

He was followed in 1924 by Charles Read Baskervill, who explored a type of action which had so far escaped much comment. His article, 'Mummers' Wooing Plays in England', published in *Modern Philology*, explored the ceremonies to be dealt with in the next chapter. Baskervill saw these as literary relics and was able to trace many lines of text to their literary sources – jigs, stage plays, and so on. He missed entirely their ceremonial content, but was successful in rescuing from oblivion versions which had escaped notice up to then. His work is a masterpiece of literary detection even if it missed the point of the ceremonies. He paved the way for the work of E. K. Chambers, whose book, *The English Folk Play*, published in 1933, remains the only full length study of the subject published to date.

Like Baskervill, Chambers saw the actions as literary remnants, even though his final chapter, 'The Residual Problem', uneasily approached the subject as it should have been undertaken from the beginning. He incorporated the work of Tiddy and Baskervill in his survey and was able to refer to 159 examples in support of his arguments. He failed to include the Ordish Collection which would have added considerably to the versions he could have consulted, and he omitted any mention of Beatty's work which might have led him to make a different approach. His book was consequently out of date before it was written, yet it has persisted as the only standard work on the subject since 1933. Both he and Baskervill did succeed in their self-imposed task of establishing the literary source of passages of texts. Their work was so thorough that it is pointless to attempt to retrace their steps now, even if it were a useful exercise. Since their time much more work has been done in the field and in libraries by a variety of students so that much more material is available for an examination which will permit a different approach.

The way to this was pointed by Margaret Dean-Smith in her paper 'The Life-Cycle or Folk Play' in *Folk-Lore*, 1958. This broke the existing pattern of study, and saw the ceremonial for the first time in terms of its central core, relating it to other ceremonies which had previously been considered separate entities. Furthermore, Miss Dean-Smith showed that the texts on which so much reliance had previously been placed, were really irrelevant accretions, only useful in detailing the action they sought, often unsuccessfully, to explain, and that the three types of action now left are really fragments of something much larger. For the first time in the long history of the ceremony, there was a critical analysis which paved the way for a realistic approach to the subject, and it must be admitted that this present book owes its inspiration to her pioneer article.

Revival of interest in the subject in recent years has led to more examples being collected. In Ireland, the work of the Ulster Folk Museum staff has shown that the ceremony there is still alive in far more places than in England. The amount of material is now such that it has been possible for Dr Alan Gailey of the Museum to prepare a full length study of the Irish Ceremonies.[18] His findings bear out those which it is hoped to develop in this present book, and although all the Irish versions are Hero-Combat actions, they show the same underlying pattern of those in England.

For the first time therefore, there is developing a corpus of material extending over some three hundred years which will enable examination of the ceremony in a more realistic manner. It shows that although the core of the action remains constant, there have been other minor changes. Characters appear and disappear. Some, for example Lord Nelson, were introduced as historical figures who caught public fancy; others appear to be characters of local notoriety. As time went by, Saint George was replaced by a variety of other noble 'Georges'; characters were added or left out at the end according to local whim or the availability of performers. The ceremony shows some changes but its ritual remains constant. Changes are part of the flow of Folk Culture, and presumably have been made as long as the ceremony has persisted. They are relatively unimportant – merely an indication that the performers were keeping abreast of the times they lived in. As long as a character died and was restored to life, the ceremony lived on, and this has resisted all changes however modern the approach may have become. With the possibility of these changes in mind, and accepting them as inevitable, it is now possible to examine the three types of action in turn, to see what, if anything, can be learned from each in elucidation of Chambers' 'Residual Problem'.

3

The Wooing Ceremonies

In the East Midland counties of Lincolnshire, Leicestershire, Nottinghamshire and Rutland, the ceremony took a very distinctive form, best called the Wooing Ceremony. Unlike the Hero-Combat versions which attracted comment at an early date, these seem to have escaped notice. It may be that their survival in only a small area of the country prevented them being better known. Whatever the reason, the earliest known example is from Bassingham in 1823, contained in the Hunter Collection in the British Museum,[1] and commented upon by Professor Baskervill in 1924. The version contains all the ingredients of those existing later in the century. For these, the following definition will serve:

The Wooer of a young 'Female'[2] is rejected in favour of a Clown and enlists in the army. The Clown is occasionally accused of being the father of a bastard child of an older 'Female' which he denies. The action continues with a champion overcoming an opponent who is revived by a doctor. Much of the action is expressed in song.[3] Characteristic performers include: the Recruiting Sergeant, Ploughboy, Lady, Clown and Dame. Appears from Christmas to Plough Monday.

The Branston, Lincolnshire, text,[4] described as a 'Plough Play or Morris Dance', last performed *circa* 1913, is typical of the area. The MS gave not only the text but also costume details, as follows:

'Fool wore a pointed cap and white fustian trousers. Sergeant dressed in scarlet uniform hired from the military. King in peaked cap and gold braid and braided trousers. Ribboner wore coat and trousers of many coloured rags in short strips sewn on to his clothes. Doctor wore frock coat, white waistcoat, white beard (of horsehair) reaching almost to knees. Tall silk hat. Carried satchel containing medicines. Dame in frock with doll as baby. lady -?-. Played at

surrounding villages from before Christmas until Branston Feast Day on Plough Monday. Villages visited: Branston, Heighington, Washingborough, Nocton, Dunston, Metheringham, Potter Hanworth.'

Fool (at door of farmhouse)

Good evening Ladies Gentlemen all.
Hope you won't be offended at me being so bold as
    make you a call.
I hope you won't be surprised at these few words I've
    got to say.
For theres many more pretty boys and girls to come in
    this way.
Okum, Spokum, France and Spain,   5
In comes our Sergeant all the same.

Sergeant

In come, recruiting sergeant, (*sic*)
I've arrived here just now with orders from the King
To enlist all that follows horse cart or plough.
Tinkers, tailors, pedlars, nailors, all at my advance,   10
The more I hear the fiddle play, the better I can dance.

Fool

I'm a fool come to see you dance.

Sergeant

Pray, father, if you dance sing or say,
I'll soon march away.

*Fool (Sings: Free version of Trad. Air. 'God rest you merry,
gentlemen')*

Ribboner

Behold you now, I've lost my mate
My drooping wings, hangs down my fate,   20
Pity my condition, It's all along of a false young maid
Who's led me in despair.

All good peo-ple give at-ten-tion and lis-ten to my song;

I'll tell you of a nice young man be-fore the time is long;

He's al-most bro-ken heart-ed, the truth I do de-clare:

His love has been so tire-some, she's drawn him in a snare.

Fool
Cheer up, cheer up, young man, don't die in despair,
For in a very short time, our lady will be here.

Lady (sings as above)
In comes the lady bright and gay   25
Misfortune and sweet charms
So scornful I've been drawn away
Out of my true loves arms;
He swears if I don't wed with him
As you shall understand   30
He'll list for all a soldier
And go to some foreign land.

Sergeant (sings)
Come all you boys thats bound for listing
You shall have all kinds of liquor
And likewise kiss the pretty maid;   35
Ten bright guineas shall be your bounty⁵
If along with me you'll go;
Your hat shall be all decked with ribbons
Likewise cut the gallant show.

Ribboner
Now kind sir, I'll take your offer,   40
Time along will quickly pass;
Dash my rags, if I grieve any longer
For this proud and saucy lass.

Lady (sings)
Since my love enlisted, and joined the volunteers
I neither mean to sigh for him   45
I'll have him for to know,
I'll get another sweetheart
And with him I will go.

Sergeant
Now madam, I desire to know if I am the man
The pleasing of your fancy, I'll do the best I can.   50
I'll give you gold and silver
All brought from India's shore,
And I'll for ever love you
Pray what can I do more?

Lady (sings)
What care I for your gold or silver,   55
What care I for your house or land,
What care I for your rings or diamonds,
All I want is a handsome man.

Fool (takes Lady by the arm and dances)
A handsome man will not maintain you
For his beauty will decay;   60
The finest flower that grows in the summer
In the winter fades away.

Ribboner
Now madam, I desire to know whether I shall be the
    man,
The pleasing of your fancy, I'll do the best I can.
I'll bring you silks and satins, all brought from India's
    shore,   65
And I'll forever love thee, Pray what can I do more?

Lady
Pooh, Pooh, young man. You can't be of your right mind
Give me the man with the ragged trousers
Who takes a girl in a sly corner.

Fool
Ah! Ah! Now you see, this fair lady took her chance   70
Please strike up the music and we'll have a dance.

Enter King

King
In comes I, King George, noble champion bold
With my bright sword in hand.
I've won 10,000 pounds in gold
I fought the fiery dragon   75
And brought him a slaughter
And by these violent means and schemes
I gained the Kings eldest daughter.
I'll turn myself round to see if any man may dare face me
I'll hash him and dash him, the smallest of flies   80
And send him to Jamaica to make mince pies.

Sergeant (to King)
Hold hard Jack, don't be too hot
Thou little knows what thou hast got
A man to entertain thee of thy pride.

King
You! Entertain me of my pride?   85

Sergeant
And lay the anchor by the side
For my head is made of iron
My body is guarded with steel
My legs and arms are made of the best beaten brass
and no man can make me feel.   90

King
Your head is not made of iron
And your body is not made of steel
Your arms and legs are not made of the best beaten brass
And I can make you feel.

Sergeant
Stand out, stand out, you proud and coxsey come⁶   95
I'll make thy buttons fly,
I'll fill thy body full of hills and holes
And by my hand and sword thou shalt die.

Fool
Stir up the fire and shine the light
And see the gallant act tonight;   100
The clock has struck, and the time has come
For this battle to go on.
If you don't believe what I've got to say
Please move your chairs and move away.

Sergeant (to the King)
Draw out thy sword in haste   105
For thy ribs I will abase.
Thou silly ass, thou feeds on grass
Thou knows thou art in danger
Thou lives in hopes to guard thy coat
And keep thy body from all danger.   110

Sergeant here prods the King with the sword and down he goes
The King of Egypt is dead and gone⁷
No more of him you'll see
His body's dead and his soul has fled
What will become of me?
He bore me out and challenged me to fight   115
And this I don't deny

I only stripped one button off his coat,
And made his body die.

Fool
Dead, Dead to be sure
Five pounds for a doctor   120
This dead man to cure.

Sergeant

Ten pounds for him to stay away.

Fool
Fifteen pounds, we must have him.
Doctor, doctor!

Doctor
In comes I the Doctor.   125

Fool
You're the doctor?

Doctor
Yes Sir, I am the doctor.

Fool
How came you to be a doctor?

Doctor
I travelled for it.

Fool
Where did you travel?   130

Doctor
England, Ireland, France and Spain
Over these hills and back again
From fireside to bedside
Where I had many a piece of cold pudding
Made me such a fine man.   135

Fool
Fine man, like me doctor. What pains can you cure?

Doctor
The itch, the pitch, the palsy gout
Pains within and pains without[8]
Get a tooth, draw a leg, and cure the pains within the
    head.
If this man has nineteen pains in his head, Sir   140
I can draw twenty one out.

Fool
You must be a clever doctor
You had better try your skill.

Doctor
Thank you sir, and by your leave and so I will.
Hold my horse boy, while I feel of the man's pulse.   145

Fool
Is that a mans pulse?

Doctor
Yes sir, the strongest part of a working man
Is backwards in the head.

Fool
I expect you know best doctor.
Is this man dead?   150

Pointing to the King

Doctor
No, he is not dead, he's in a trance
He's been trying a new experiment,
He's been living nineteen days out of a fortnight[9]
By mistake: he swallowed our donkey and cart
And choked himself with a pillow, poor fellow.   155
I'll give him a drop out of my bottle
And team it gently down his throttle
It will heal his wounds, and cool his blood
And I hope it will do his soul some good.
This man can dance if you can sing   160
So arise young man, and lets begin.

Fool
Hey, hey, whats the dancing and jigging about?
Here's the tight lad to dance
I can dance half an hour on a barley chaff riddle
Neither break nor bend or spell   165
I'll ask you all to me and my wife's wedding[10]
For what you like best, you must bring with you
I know what me and my lady likes
And what we likes best we shall have.

Doctor
What's that? Ragden.[11]   170

Fool
Go and look greasy chops.
I've always tried to please
A long tailed cabbage
A pickled sameritt
A liver and lights of a cobblers laps   175
And half a gallon of buttermilk to relish it down.

Doctor
We shall have a feed.

Fool
Thank you sir.

Old Dame Jane
In comes I old dame Jane
Head and neck as long as a crane   180
Dib, dab over the meadow.
Once I was a blooming young maid
Now I am a downed old widow.
I travel from door to door
Since all my joy was asked   185
Since you called me what you did
Tommy, take you bastard.[12]

Fool
Bastard, Jinny? It's not like me and none of mine.

Dame
Its nose, eyes, and chin as much like you as ever it can
    grin.

Fool
Who sent you here with it, Jinny?   190

Dame
The overseer of the parish, who said I was to bring it to
    the biggest fool
I could find, so I thought I'd bring it to you.

13

Fool
You had better go swear it to the parish pump.

Dame
That's all I've got to thank you for.

Fool (sings)
Now, madam, as I crossed over yon dell   195
One morning very soon,
Dressed in my best apparel
Likewise my clouded shoes.
To thee I come a wooing
To thee my bucksome Nell   200
If thou love me as I love you
Thou lovest a person well.

Dame
If you love me, tell me true.

Fool
Yes, and to my sorrow.

Dame
When shall be our wedding day?   205

Fool
Tommy, love, tomorrow.

All (sing)
And we'll be wed in wedlock, dear,
So brave old Nelly and I.
Good master and good mistress
As you sit round your fire   210
Remember us poor plough boys
Who ploughs the mud and mire.
The mire it is so very deep
And the water runs so clear
We thank you for a Christmas box   215
And a pitcher of your best beer.

Dame
Hey, hey, and a bit of your pork pie.

Fool
Your allust[13] hungry!

Dame
And your allust dry.

Fool
That's it, Jinney, scrap about.   220

All sing
Here's to the master of this house
The mistress also
Likewise the little children
That round the table go.
We hope they'll never come to want   225
While nations do provide
A happy home and plentiness, and a tender fireside.

We are not the London actors
That acts the London part,
We are the Branston ploughboys   230
We are not the London actors
We've told you so before
And we've done it as well as we can, me boys,
No men can do no more.

Pass round Tambourine and collect beer and pork pies
Good master and good mistress   235
You see our fool has gone
We make it in our business
To follow him along.
We thank you for your civility
And what you've given us here   240
And we wish you a merry christmas
And a happy new year.

This version, reproduced exactly as given in the MS, is remarkably complete even at the late date to which it survived. It contains lines, or variants of lines, which are to be found in the Hunter Collection versions, even though they are not necessarily spoken by the same character. The same feature is apparent in the next text from Plumtree, Nottinghamshire,[14] where the action remains the same, but the combat is between Beelzebub, who is omitted from the Branston version, and Dame Jane, instead of between the more martial characters of the Sergeant and King George. The version is a good example of how texts from the same area and type can appear different on the surface and yet follow the same basic action.

Tommy
Good evening, ladies and gentlemen all,
It's Plough Monday makes Tommy so bold as to call;
I hope you won't be offended
In what I have to say,
For I've a lot more boys and girls to come this way,   5
At your consent they s'all come in.

Tommy wears old white shirt with patches on. Top hat whitewashed one side.

Enter Sergeant and says
In comes I, the Recruiting Sergeant;
I've arrived here just now
I've had orders from the King
To 'list all jolly fellows   10
That follow horse, cart or plough.
All these are to advance,
The more I hear the fiddle play,
The better I can dance.

Fool
You dance?   15

Sergeant
I can either dance, sing or say.

Fool
If you begin to dance, sing or say
I shall quickly march away.

Sergeant – *then sings*
Come ye lads that is bound for 'listing,
'List and do not be afraid,   20
That old hat shall be trimmed with ribbon
Likewise kiss the pretty fair maid.

Farmer's Man with whip
In comes I, the farmer's man,
Don't you see my whip in my hand?
As I go forth to plough the land   25
I turn it upside down.
I go so straight from end to end,

14

And to my horses I attend
Gee! Whoa! Back!

Lady (dressed smart)
Behold the lady bright and fair,
Sweet fortune and sweet charms,
So unfortunately I've been thrown away
Right out of my true love's arms.
He swears if I don't wed with him,
As you all understand,
He'll 'list him for a soldier,
And go in some foreign land.

Sergeant
Do you want to 'list, young man?

Farmer's Man
Yes, to my sorrow.

Sergeant
In your hand I'll place one shilling, 40
And on your hat I'll pin this ribbon.
Ten bright guineas shall be your bounty,
If along with me you'll go.

Farmer's Man
Dash to my wig if I'll grieve any longer
For that proud and saucy lass. 45

Lady (sings)
But since my love has 'listed,
And joined the volunteers,
I neither mean to sigh for him
Nor shed one single tear.
I'll get another sweetheart 50
And along with him I'll go.

Tommy
Have ye any love for me, my pretty maid?

Lady
Yes, and to my honour.

Tommy
When shall be our wedding day?

Lady
Tommy, love, tomorrow. 55

Tommy
We'll make banns and we'll shake hands,
And we'll get wed tomorrow.

Old Dame Jane
In comes I, Old Dame Jane,
With a neck as long as a crane.
Once I was a blooming girl 60
Now I'm a downright old maid.

(To Tommy)
Now I've caught you,
Long have I sought you.
Pray, Tommy, take your baby.

Tommy
My baby, Jane? It's not a bit like me; 65
What is it, a lad or a boy?

Jane
A lad.

Tommy
Mine's all boys. Take it and swear it to the town's pump. 30

Beelzebub
In comes I, Beelzebub.

(Wears old sack stuffed with straw; carrying sock stuffed, tied on end of stick) 35

On my shoulder I carry me club, 70
In my hand a whit leather frying pan,
Don't you think I'm a funny old man?
Is there any old dame that dares stand before me?

Jane
Yes, I dare.
My head is made of iron; 75
My body's made of steel;
My hands and shins are knuckle bone,
And you can't make me feel.

Beelzebub
If your head is made of iron,
And your body's made of steel, 80
Your hands and shins are knuckle bone,
I can make ye feel.
I'll slish you and slash you as small as a fly,
And send you to Jamaica to make mince-pies.

Hits her with club. She falls down

Tommy
O Belzy, O Belzy, what hast thou done? 85
Thou's killed Old Jane and her only son.
Five pound for a doctor.

Beelzebub
Ten to stop away.

Tommy
Fifteen to come. O, doctor, you must come to a case like this.

Doctor (enters)
In comes I, the Doctor. 90

Tommy
You, a doctor?

Doctor
Yes, me a doctor.

Tommy
How became you to be a doctor?

Doctor
By my travels.

Tommy
Where have you travelled? 95

Doctor
England, Ireland, France and Spain,
Now come back to cure the diseases of England again.

Tommy
What diseases can you cure?

Doctor
Hipsy, pipsy, palsy gout,   100
Pains within and pains without,
Draw a leg and set a tooth,
And almost restore dead men to life again.
I'll tell ye a little anydote[15] as I did last week about a
    fortnight ago. I cured an old lady, she tumbled upstairs
    with a half teapot full of flour and I set that.   105

Tommy
Very clever, doctor. Ye'd better try your experiment on
    this old girl.

Doctor
So I will. I'll feel of the old girl's pulse.

Feels back of heel

Tommy
Pulse lie there, doctor?

Doctor
Yes. Where would you feel?

Tommy
Back o' the neck; softest part about a man.   110

Doctor carries a bottle with coloured water
This old lady's not dead, she wants a bottle of my
    medicine.

Makes to give her a drink

And a box of my pills, take one tonight and two in the
    morning, and swallow the box at dinner time. If the box
    don't cure ye, the lid will.
This old lady's not dead, only in a trance
Come rise up old girl, and let's have a dance.   115
If you can't dance, we can sing,
So rise her up and let begin.

Good master and good mistress,
As you sit round your fire,
Remember us poor ploughboys   120
Who plough through mud and mire,
The mire it is very deep
The water runs so clear,
We thank you for civility,
And a jug of your best beer.   125

Tommy
Steady with that beer, Belzy! I've nothing in this box yet.

Beelzebub
What do you want in the box?

Tommy
A lump of pork pie. I'm as bad hungry as you are dry.
I can eat as big as a brick and our old Dame can eat a
    piece as big as a gravestone.

Clown goes out first. As they go, they sing

Good master and good mistress   130
You see our fool has gone;

We take it in our business to follow him along.
Good night and thank you very much.

Go out in same order as they came in.

These two versions have a difference in length, the
Plumtree version being shorter by some hundred lines.
To achieve this the text has been rationalised whilst
maintaining the basic action. The Ribboner, a character
rare in Nottinghamshire, but common in Lincolnshire,
has disappeared, along with King George, but a
Farmer's Man has been added. The Fool, who apparently wooed both the Lady and the Dame at Branston,
has only one wooing at Plumtree, with the Lady. Much
of the missing text is the purely literary part, for example
lines 195–202 of the Branston version which are an
adaptation of Young Roger of the Mill.[16] The bastard is
described more politely as the baby, though 'bastard'
was dropped at Branston when performing before polite
society. The Fool's invitation to the wedding has also
disappeared and, generally speaking, the omitted
passages are those which elaborate the basic action, but
which, in themselves, carry it no further. Both in sense
and form, lines 72–161 in the Branston version and lines
69–117 in the Plumtree version are a complete Hero
Combat action as shown in the Syresham text in Chapter
One. The latter has more than one combat, a feature
which never seems to occur in the Wooing Ceremonies.
The characters at Syresham who appeared at the end but
carried the action no further are not duplicated in either
East Midland version, but Beelzebub at least, takes a
prominent part at Plumtree. It is doubtful if this was a
result of shortening the text, but merely that these
characters were not needed in versions which presented
a complete picture.

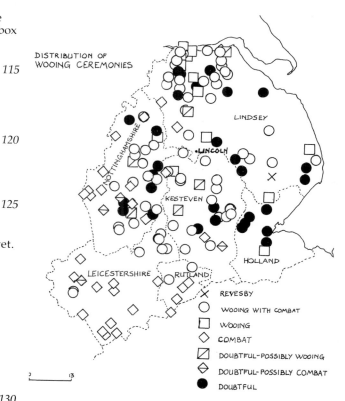

Figure 1. Distribution of Wooing Plays.

Some examples in the area were shortened to a Wooing only[17] with no Death and Resurrection involved. A further sub-type had no wooing, but a combat between named champions, with the typical Wooing Ceremony characters taking part.[18] These present a particular problem as to whether or not they are fragments of the main type or separate entities in their own right. On balance, they must be considered fragments, even allowing for the fact that Wooing actions only are some of the earliest examples from the area.[19] The 'Combat with Wooing Characters' sub-type may have arisen because of a 'cline', a character gradient often seen in zoological studies. The map (Figure 1) shows evidence for this. Moving from east to west across the whole area of distribution, or taking Lincoln as an approximate centre for moving north or south, there is a gradual change of type from Wooing to simple Combat Ceremonies, and this sub-type may have a foot in both worlds.

The preservation of a Wooing theme only at the expense of the Combat with Cure could suggest that the two were separate entities. Chambers considered that:

'it is safest to regard the divergence of the Plough Plays from the ordinary type of Mummers' Plays as due to the merging of the traditional *ludus*-motive of Death and Revival with an independent Wooing Play of later origin.'[20]

He based this opinion on a study of fourteen versions of which only nine had the wooing/combat theme. Now, there are some eighty-four versions available of which sixty-six are of this type. It is true that a wooing theme is one of the oldest literary devices, but it would have been simpler if a single archetype of the Wooing had been used. Instead, as Professor Baskervill showed, this part of the action is a patchwork from all kinds of sources, repeated to a greater or lesser degree in most versions. What is more likely is that the Wooing was considered more important in these versions and consequently persisted longer.

There is some defence for this belief in the nature of the combat as described at Branston and Plumtree, and typical of the area. In the former versions the Sergeant 'prods the King with the sword and down he goes', in the latter Beelzebub hits Jane with a club and she falls down. There is no attempt at the sword play found in the Hero-Combat versions,[21] where it is the most attractive feature. If anything the Wooing versions play down the combat. Its method suggests ritual killing rather than ritual combat. This would accord with the central theme of the actions, that one champion must die for the benefit of his community.

At this point, the 'bastard' incident must be considered. So far, the action has shown a wooing with an implied marriage to follow. There has been a death and a revival. Now comes a hint of a new generation. The incident as it stands is trivial and apparently meaningless. It lacks development, but is persistent in many versions. It was known at Bassingham in 1823 and Broughton in 1824 in almost exactly the same form. It is doubtful if it was understood even at those dates, and even now we can only guess at its purpose. If good taste changed 'bastard' to 'baby' it ought to have suppressed the incident entirely if it were originally as meaningless as it became. The infant completes the Life-Cycle. There are three generations in the action which represent life from the cradle to the grave, and the ceremony is the most unified of all the types because of this. It is un-

fortunate that nothing earlier has emerged to give detail before 1823, but such accounts as do exist are infuriatingly vague.

The Household Accounts of the Monson family at Burton by Lincoln[22] show that Morris Dancers from Nettleham received 2/6d in 1771, whilst those of Lincoln received the same amount in 1781, annually between 1783 and 1788 and again in 1790 'as usual'. The same accounts record annual payments to the 'Plow Men' of Carlton, Nettleham and Saxilby in 1783 and the South Carlton and Burton 'Plow Boys' were similarly rewarded in 1784. Payments are recorded annually to the North and South Carlton Plow Boys from 1786 to 1790. The distinction between Morris Dancers and Plow Boys is not clear. Either or both could have performed the ceremony under discussion. In 1775, nine teams visited a household at Grantham, six came from Great Gonerby, Barrowby, Manthorpe, Spittlegate, Little Ponton and Old Somerby, the other three being described respectively as 'Mr Rowley's, Mr Grundy's and Mr Crabtree's men'.[23] Texts have survived from Barrowby and Old Somerby but not from the other places, but this does not mean that the men were performing a Wooing Ceremony in 1775, tempting though it may be.

The wide use of different names – 'Plough Jacks', 'Plough Jaggs', 'Plough Witches', 'Morris Dancers', 'Mummers' – in this area to describe performers of the same ceremony is particularly confusing. In 1877 Edward Peacock defined Morris Dancers as:

'Performers who perform rude plays, now much the same as ploughboys, though formerly there was a clear distinction'.[24]

Twelve years later, in a second edition of his book, he altered the last phrase to read:

'. . . though formerly there seems to have been a clear distinction.'[25]

suggesting that his first attempt at a definition was too rigid. At Digby, the man who played Tom Fool said that:

'before the plough play came in they used to go round Morris dancing',[26]

but did not specify the difference between them. Examples of this confusion could be multiplied.[27]

There is also evidence of opposition to the performances in Lincolnshire from 1821 onwards. A correspondent to the *Lincoln, Rutland and Stamford Mercury*, 26th January, 1821, wrote:

'It gave me great pleasure at the last Quarter Sessions at Kirton to hear from the Chairman that the magistrates have determined to visit with exemplary severity the misconduct of persons who appear as Morris-dancers, or Plough Bullocks, *or under other names of a similar character . . .*'

The italics are mine to emphasise that almost 150 years ago, the performers were known by different names. Similar complaints were repeated annually in the same newspaper, and others, until the 1880's.

Such complaints are almost non-existent in the accounts of the ceremonies outside this area. If it can be assumed that they were levelled at the performers of the Wooing Ceremonies as well as those in whatever other ceremonies were implied, there must have been some reason for 'good taste' to be so outraged. It is possible that its cause lay in the nature of the action and in those who took part. A Wooing theme inevitably gives opportunity for sexual by-play and mime. The performers were normally farm-workers, ploughboys, often numerous enough on one farm to make a self-contained gang.[28] The daily working life of these men would make them accept things, intolerable to a more sophisticated town-dweller, as a matter of course. One of the fundamental reasons for the inclusion of a 'Female' is surely that the rest of the gang could behave to her in a way insupportable to a real lady.

The size of the gangs was another typical feature, and their size presented them with opportunities for indiscipline. Often they were 'double gangs' with characters duplicated, triplicated, and sometimes quadruplicated. (See Plate 3). It was the practice for such gangs to divide up in a village so that they could work more quickly on each side of the street. They would gather together at the best and likeliest houses for a consolidated performance.[29] No description has survived of the manner of dividing up, nor any of the performance once they joined together again. It might be assumed that once divided, the performance was 'normal', but how duplicate characters with the same lines performed is not at all clear. There was dissension between the double gangs and the normal-sized ones; neither could accept that the other was possible.[30]

All the double gangs had at least one hobby-horse, usually two, a character missing from the texts already quoted. The Burringham gang had two, a white and a grey; unfortunately, no text has survived to show how these horses were used here. There must have been some significance in the colour. The absence of any concrete detail concerning any of the hobby-horses makes their function obscure in terms of the action, but

their purpose was quite clear to performers and audience even at a late date. They were intended to bring 'luck' and onlookers stole hairs from the tail so that they could preserve the luck for themselves for the ensuing year. To prevent this, the performers had an old piece of leather covered with tacks in the tail so that would-be thieves would prick their fingers in their attempted theft.[31]

Plate 4 shows the general appearance of the Lincolnshire hobby-horses. Its basis was a sieve frame worn round the performer's waist and suspended from his shoulders. Between his legs was a scythe shaft, the front of which had a simulated horse's head with moveable lower jaw, and the rear end a tail. Both lower jaw and tail were made to move when the performer pulled a cord. Over these was thrown a cloak, covering the man and hanging at least below the knees. Occasionally, the covering was thrown over the performer's head also, with corners fastened to represent ears, and slits cut in for eyeholes. Horse brasses were often worn for extra decoration, and at Barrow upon Humber the performer wore a horse's bell topping on his head with between three and six bells and a brush.[32] The horses were confined to the south bank of the Humber, in a cluster of Wooing Ceremonies, with an odd one out on the banks of the Trent in south Lincolnshire. He is the most clearly recognisable among the characters by virtue of his disguise.

The performers took themselves very seriously both in their disguise and time of appearance. The latter was normally, though not always, on Plough Monday, the first Monday after Epiphany. They seem to have resisted the introduction of 'new' characters, preferring to retain those who had become traditional.[33] The fortunate chance of a Bassingham version existing from 1823 until the late 1940's[34] shows the persistence with which the performers clung to tradition. The later version is notice-

Plate 3. Alkborough, Lincolnshire, Plough Jags Double Gang, *circa* 1899. *Back Row:* Sergeant, Lady, ?Beelzebub, ?Indian King, Unidentified, ?Beelzebub, Unidentified. *Middle Row:* Hobby Horse, Hatman, Hatman, Doctor, Drummer Boy, Hatman, Soldier, Hatman, Hobby Horse. *Front Row:* Tom Fool, Besom Bet, Bestom Bet, Lady. This is the only photograph of a double gang known to exist, and it is unfortunate that the original from which it was taken, had been damaged by creasing.

Plate 4. Hobby-horse, Scotter, Lincolnshire.

were two or three hobby-horses drawing a plough.[36] Before 1895 there was a plough taken about at Branston[37] and at Barrow upon Humber there was a ceremony of christening a plough with half a pint of beer in the local public house before they went on their rounds.[38] This plough dragging appears in neither of the other two types of ceremony, but as will be seen it had some relevance.

The overall picture of this particular action is one of insistence on ceremony and lack of change. This is one reason why it must be considered the oldest fragment remaining in England. Not only did it show the primitive conception of the life-cycle in its three generations, albeit in a poor form, but it aroused opposition to its performance in its area. No doubt this was occasioned in part by the high-handedness of the performers, a relic perhaps, of the belief that they were for the period of their action, being set apart.[39] Circa 1898, one of the West Halton team was found frozen to death in the snow, having had too much to drink. This gave the local Squire, also Constable of Alkborough, the opportunity to suppress them.[40] Other teams frightened children because they wore masks and were always drunk.[41] The Isle of Axholme gangs from opposite sides of the Trent used to fight when they met,[42] but more seriously, it was said of the Helpringham performance that 'it wasn't proper for a respectable girl to see it'.[43] Circa 1889, at Wispington, the Rev. J. Conway Walter and his wife withdrew from a presentation in their kitchen as they were disgusted with it, and it was said that the Rabelasian details were dropped when 'cultivated people' formed the audience.[44] Most gangs were found in areas where, up to the agricultural depression, large scale arable farming supported a large number of young farm-workers living in their masters' houses. These gangs were scattered when the large estates which supported them were broken up and the tenants dispersed, breaking the continuity which had hitherto held them together.[45]

These are historical, economic and social reasons for the disappearance of this particular ceremony, and no doubt the opposition already mentioned hastened the end. The more primitive a ceremony the more likely it is to offend a sophisticated society. The Wooing actions were probably the oldest left in England; they showed better than the others the three generations which were essential to portraying the Life Cycle Drama. How they showed it is probably the biggest single factor in their disappearance. For this reason they are probably the most important actions of all in that they contain the key to our understanding of all the ceremonies that are left.

ably shorter. In 1823 the Lady had four suitors – the Farmer's Eldest Son, the Husbandman, the Lawyer and the Old Man. In the 1940's this had shrunk to a wooing between her and a Ribboner. St George and the Fool were the original combatants, but had been replaced by Beelzebub and Dame Jane, George no longer being a character. The passage of time had reduced the irrelevancies, but not the basic action. This is a constant feature throughout the area.

Another permanency in the sense of ceremony was the procession. At Willoughton, the performers moved in parallel plough lines with short sticks between them at intervals. To each stick was a man representing a 'horse'. Then came the Waggoner driving them with a lash with an inflated pig's bladder at the end. Next came a plough without wheels which they trailed.[35] At Somerby there

4

The Sword Dance Ceremonies

The most spectacular of all the dramatic actions is the sword dance, confined, as were the Wooing Ceremonies, to a well-defined area – the north-eastern counties of Northumberland, Durham and Yorkshire (see Fig. 2). It is a mid-winter festival occurring in a period from Christmas to Plough Monday. Two forms have survived, the Long Sword dance of Yorkshire and south Durham and the Rapper dance of Durham and Northumberland. The essential feature of both is that each dancer holds a link – the 'sword' – with the next dancer, a rigid link in the

Figure 3. Rapper Dance Lock.

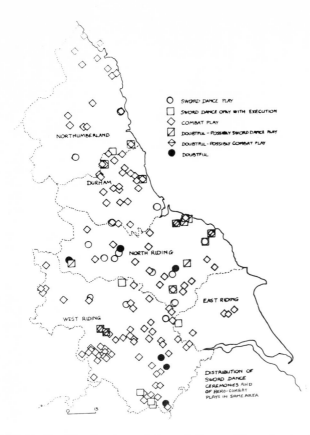

Figure 2. Distribution of Sword Dance Plays (and of Hero-Combat Plays in the same area).

Long Sword, and a flexible one in the Rapper dance. The dancers are introduced by a Leader in song and as each is named, he steps forward with his sword over his shoulder, and follows the Leader round in a circle. On the conclusion of the song, each dancer grasps the tip of the sword in front of him, swords are lowered from shoulders and an open ring is formed. (See Plate 5). This circle is normally maintained throughout the dance.[1] Although the dancers retain their hold, they jump over the swords, either singly or in pairs, or move under them when held overhead to form an arch. The culmination of the dance comes when the swords are interwoven to form either a hexagonal or octagonal shape in the Long Sword dance and a pentagonal one in the Rapper, the shape depending on the number of dancers. (See Fig. 3). It is called a Lock, Star, Rose or Nut according to local inclination. In the Rapper dance it is displayed to the audience by the Leader whilst the dancers 'step' in line. In the Long Sword dance, the Leader holds it vertically above his head whilst he and the dancers continue moving round in a sun-wise circle. It is further used in the latter dance to place over the head of one of the performers, so that it rests round his neck. Finally, the dancers, each taking hold of his own hilt, and, moving in concert, withdraw their swords and the victim drops down as though dead. According to the particular tradition, the victim may be revived in a dramatic sequence, or the action stops there.[2]

This 'Beheading', so far as is known, only applies to Long Sword traditions, where the links are usually about three feet in length. They are made of either wood or metal, and are usually fitted with blocks of wood at one

Plate 5. Linked sword dance team – Handsworth, Yorkshire.

end to form a hilt. The rappers are quite different. They are always made of flexible steel, usually about twenty-four inches long, and are fitted with a handle at each end, one fixed, the other swivelling. Their nature permits a much closer circle and more intricate movements than is possible in the Long Sword dances. Their length makes it difficult to see how the Nut, when formed, can be placed over the head of a victim, not only because the hole in its centre is too small, but also because constant use of the rappers gives them a sharp edge. The description from Earsdon is vague as to how the rappers were locked round the Betty's throat, and sounds positively lethal:

20

'The Bessy, . . . used to wear a hairy cap, and when the Nut was about to be tied, the dancers would sometimes call out 'We'll hang the Betty'; whereupon, Betty would step into the centre of the ring and the swords would be locked tightly around his throat, while the dancers 'stepped' . . .[3]

At Murton, the Tommy, wearing a cap like a policeman's helmet, entered the set and the Star was locked loosely round his neck. As the dancers 'stepped', the Star was raised, then tightened, so as to lift the hat off his head, and the Tommy left the set. The hat was flicked off by a sharp movement of the Star, and the Tommy picked it up again.[4] There is no indication *how* the rappers were locked round the Tommy's neck, but flicking off the hat is more reasonable than tightening the links round the throat.

The Rapper dance seems to be a later, more artistically developed dance than the Long Sword. The spring steel of which the implements were made supports this. Whilst wooden or rigid metal links have always been possible, spring steel could not be made deliberately until 1740 when Huntsman invented his crucible process.[5] The nature of the dance depends upon the flexibility of the implements,[6] but they are nothing like a conventional sword,[7] nor do the performers themselves ever use the word 'sword' in describing their dance. This opens the vexed question of the name 'Sword Dance' for these ceremonies. The performers use various names to describe themselves – as 'Morris Sword Dancers' at Grenoside, 'Morris Dancers' or 'Guizers' at Earsdon, for example. The label 'Sword Dance' is probably nothing more than a convenient means of identification which ignores that not only were the implements nothing like swords, but the performers were not of a naturally armigerous society. There is some evidence for thinking that the so-called 'swords' had some former connection with the trade tools used in the performers' every-day work.[8] The double-ended rappers can be likened to primitive scraping tools once used by miners in their work.[9] The connection between performers and mining has been commented on by many writers, and, although it is not completely established,[10] nevertheless those who did follow this trade may well have used what was once familiar to them in their work.

Whatever the original implements were, their main purpose was to link the performers. This gave the dance its circular shape, and more important, enclosed an area in which a dramatic action could be performed.[11] The choreographic dance had become the dominant feature of the ceremony, so much so that although there had been a revitalisation ceremony with many of the traditions, it had been allowed to wither as understanding of its significance dwindled. There are some who consider the dramatic actions of the sword dancers as merely a remnant of the Wooing Ceremonies. To adopt this belief ignores not only the complex dance but also the important fact that the 'death' is the result of a concerted act by a group against an individual. Like the death in the Wooing actions, this is more of a ritual killing than a ritual combat. Furthermore, there is no wooing as such, but only hints that there once might have been. A general definition of these ceremonies is therefore as follows.

The linked dance is the basis. A man is executed by the links being withdrawn from the Lock around his neck and he is revived by a Doctor, a Clown or a 'Female'.

Characteristic performers include: Clown, 5–8 performers, one of whom is the Captain. Costume: Sometimes latterly quasi-military,[12] previously ordinary clothes with ribbons sewn on.
Appears: Christmas to Plough Monday.

The existence of a dance does not however, presuppose the existence of a dramatic action. There are instances of teams being formed as offshots of a parent tradition; for example, North Skelton, Skelton Green, Lingdale and Boosbeck were offshoots of the Loftus team which was itself formed *circa* 1890. Of these five teams, only three – Loftus, Lingdale and North Skelton – preserved traces of the full ceremony in that the Lock was placed over the head of a victim who 'died'. There was no cure, nor any attempt at one. It seems that offshoots took the dance but little else, and for these, a further classification is necessary:

The Lock is put round the neck of a performer who 'dies' when the links are withdrawn from it. He may fall to the ground. The action is carried no further and there is no revival.

These are the only two ceremonies considered in this chapter. Admittedly, there are dances with no historical evidence of a dramatic action which fall into neither of the above categories.[13]

There are also dances with a Calling-on song only,[14] but in the absence of even a vestigial execution they cannot be accepted as evidence for an action of the type under discussion. The Papa Stour, Zetland, dance has some interest however. It was known to be in existence before 1788,[15] and even then its Calling-on Song was written in metropolitan English not a Zetland dialect. In 1822 it was said that 'Papa Stour is the only island in the country where the ancient Norwegian amusement of the *sword-dance* has been preserved.'[16] The style of the Calling-on Song does suggest an importation, but not from Norway. The characters named are the Seven Champions, making it a unique version, since it is the only one known in the British Isles in which all appear. There is no combat, death or cure; the champions dance a rigid link dance during which each in turn has the Lock (called a 'Shield'), on his head. The whole ceremony could be reminiscent of the knightly dance which formed the climax to Kirke's play. Except for the performance of the dance, the ceremony is not relevant to the present subject.

'New', that is previously unpublished sword dance texts, are difficult to come by. At Greatham, Co. Durham, rigid- and flexible-link dances met. The dance is rigid in form, but the implements are long and flexible. With the dance was a text of considerable interest, as follows:[17]

Rantom Tom
My master sent me here, some room for to provide,
So therefore, gentle dears, stand back on every side,
For if he should come and find no room, he will bind me in his belt,
He will lay me down upon the ground and thrash me like a whelp.
He will make my bones like mice bones, like the ribs of little rats.   5
I once went a-courting to one Susie Perkins
Where the dogs and the cats made such a bow-wowing and barking I forgot what to say.
What the dickens must I say?

Gurn before your nose and see before your eyes,
And if you don't mind, some of these bonny lads will take
   you by surprise.   10

Sings to first tune

They sent me before to knock at your door
To see if you'd let us come in.
Although I'm a Clown they call me a fool,
To please our gallant fine King.
Although I'm little I'm made of good metal   15
I'll scorn for to tell you a lie:
I once killed an urchant[18] as big as myself,
Which made me both lamb and goose-pie.
My coat is made of stand-off, stand-off,
My trousers are made of mohair,   20
My stockings and shoes, they are made of refuse,
And my sword is 'Come strike if you dare'.

He strikes at the air with his sword

So all you young lasses stand straight and stand firm,
Keep everything close and tight down,
For if anything happens is forty weeks' time,   25
The blame will be laid on the Clown.

King (sings to first tune)
Come all you brave gallants and listen awhile,
What makes you so stupid and sad?
There's reasons for maidens be melancholy,
And we'll have them if they're to be had.   30
See how they stand with their sword in their hand,
So boldly they all do appear.
By the sound of my sword, well it makes me afraid,
That the wars they are now drawing near.

Mr Stout (sings to second tune)[19]
Our king he will come in, dressed in his grandery,   35
He'll call his young men in by one, by two, by three.

*King (walks round in a counter-clockwise circle and sings
to second tune)*
Now the first is Mr Sparks, he's lately come from France;
He's the first man on our list and the second in our dance.

*Mr Sparks (follows King and sings as do they all to the
same tune)*
God bless your honoured fame and all your young men
   too:
I've come to act my part as well as I can do.   40

King
The next is Mr Stout, as I do understand,
As good a swordsman he, as ever took sword in hand.

Mr Stout (following Mr Sparks)
I often have been tried in city, town and field,
I never could meet the man that ever could make me
   yield.

Clown
Thou never met me, me lad.   45

King
The next is Mr Wild, he has travelled a good few miles
But I'm afraid the worst of all, these young maids he'll
   beguile.

Mr Wild (following Mr Stout)
If I've rambled the world all over, it's not for any gain,
It is for my true love, that's both well seen and known.

King
The next that I call on, he is a Squire's Son;   50
I'm afraid he'll lose his love because he is too young.

Squire's Son (following Mr Wild)
Although I be too young, I have money for to rove,
I'll freely spend it all before I'll lose my love.

King
The last he is a Prince, he is born of noble fame;
He spent a large estate the wars for to maintain.   55

Prince (following Squire's Son)
Although I be the last, my name I'll not deny,
Although I be the last, my valour here I'll try,
And I'll not daunted be, although I be the last,
For I can act my part as well as all the rest.

1st Clown
Nay, but I'm the last mesel', my name is Rantom Tom,   60
And the lasses you've got here I'll kiss them everyone.

2nd Clown
Gadzooks! I clean forgot that I was one of your crew
If you want to know my name, my name it is True Blue.

All
We are six dancers bold, as bold as you can see,
We have come to dance this dance to please the
   company.   65

They sent me be-fore_ to knock at your door, To see if you'd let us come in. _____

Al-though I'm a Clown they call me a fool, To please_ our gal-lant fine King. _

22

Our dancers are but young, and seldom danced before,
We will do the best we can, the best can do no more.
It's not for greedy gain this ramble we do take,
But what you please to give our clowns will freely take.
You've seen us all go round, so think of us what you
    will;   70
Music strike up and play, we're the lads from Greatham
    still.

FIRST DANCE
THE PLAY

2nd Clown
Here comes I that never come yit,
With my big head and my little wit:
Although my head be big and my wit be samll,
I can act my part as well as you all.   75
So Room! Room! my brave gallants,

Swings his sword round
Listen what I've got to say.
Bold Hector he comes in,
He looks both pale and wan,
With his great beard so long,   80
He's like some collier man.
My name is Bold Hector and I'll clear the way;
Hector, Hector, the banberry bush, me mother's sister's
    son-in-law.
There's great Tom Payne standing staring, swearing at
    the door.
And he winnat come in, he's a poor silly fool like thee. 85

To King
He'll swear more over one inch of candle than thou
    wouldst over a ten pound note burning away.

King
I'm the King of the Conquerors
And here I do advance.

Clown
And I'm the ragged Clown
And I've come to see you dance.   90

King
Dance a dance! Hast thou come to see a King dance?²⁰

Clown
Lord ha' mercy, crack a bottle: if thou was only 'anged in
    t'morn
I'd make a better King mesel'!

King
Thy impudence doth protect thee,
I do both swear and vow,   95
I've been the death of many a man
I'll be the death of thou.

Clown
Wasn't that thou stealing swine the other day?

King
Stealing what?

Clown
Feeding swine, I meant to say.   100

King
Come young men and try your rapiers on this villain or
    he'll stand pranting to me all day.

Prince (to Clown)
There's bad news come to town.

Clown
What bad news?

King
We're going to try you for sheep-stealing.

Clown
Worse news there couldn't be.   105

King
Yes, if we take thy head off.

*The dancers then make the Lock about the Clown loosely, each
man turning clockwise on the spot and standing with hilt
crossed over point.*

Clown
Why! Ye'll give me time to make my will and say my
    prayers?

The dancers assent
My son Basto, I'll leave thee my old spotted cow, and see
    that thou takes good care of her.

All
So I will, Dad!

Clown
My son Taylor, I'll leave thee my lapp-board and shears,
    and see that thou makes good use of them.   110

All
So I will, Dad!

Clown
My son Fiddler, I'll leave thee my backbone for fiddle-
    strings.

to King
And as for thou, I'll leave thee the ringbone of my eye
    for a jack-whistle
So, ladies and gentlemen all, I bid you all farewell.

*The dancers tighten up the Lock round the Clown's neck and
then draw their swords and the Clown falls down dead. King
(sings to 2nd tune)*
Bold Hector he is dead and on the ground is laid,   115
You'll have to suffer for him, young man I'm sore afraid.

Mr Sparks (sings)
I'm sure it's none of I, I'm clear of the crime:
It's 'e that follows I, that drew his sword so fine.

Squire's Son (sings)
Don't lay the blame on me, you dirty villains all;
I'm sure my eyes were shut when first this man did
    fall.   120

Mr Wild (sings)
How could your eyes be shut, when you were looking on?
I'm sure you were with us when first our swords were
    drawn.

All (sing)
Cheer up, me lively lads, and be of courage bold,
We'll take him to the churchyard and bury him in the
    mould.

Prince (says)
Bury him! Bury him! How do you mean to bury him when
    all these people are standing around? If you mean   125
    to save life send for a doctor out of hand.

King
A doctor! A doctor! Ten pounds for a doctor!

Doctor (enters)
Here am I, what is thy will with me?

King
Here's a man fallen upstairs and broken his neck.   130

Doctor
Fallen upstairs and broken his neck! I never heard of such
    a thing.

King
Downstairs I mean, Doctor: Thou's so full of thee
    catches. Where didst thou live, Doctor?

Doctor
I live in Itty-Titty, where there's neither town nor city,
Wooden churches with black puddings for bell-ropes;
Little dogs and cats running about with knives and forks
    in their paws, shouting,   135
'God Save the Queen'.

King
How far doest thou travel, Doctor?

Doctor
From the fireside to the bedside.

King
What, and no further?

Doctor
Yes, the cheese-and-bread cupboard.   140

King
I thought thou was a cheese-and-bread eater.
What is thy fee, Doctor?

Doctor
My fee is £19.19.11¾d, but £19.19.1¾d I'll take of thee.

King
Well! Set to work Doctor, and I'll see thee paid or unpaid
    in the morning.

Doctor
That will never do for me – 'A bird in the hand is worth
    two in the bush', so I'll go home, indeed that I will.   145

King
Nay! Nay! Stay, Doctor, and I'll see thee paid out of my
    own pocket.

Doctor
How long has this man been dead?

King
Just half-an-hour since we took off his head.

Doctor
It's a long time for a man to be dead and brought alive
    again, but however I'll try my skill.

Examines Clown
Here's a leg broken and an arm broken and his wind-
    cutter's loose.   150
No matter ladies and gentlemen, I am a doctor who
    travels far and near, and much at home;
Take these my pills to cure all ills – the past, present and
    to come.
The gout, the itch, the sores, the stitch, the money-grubs
    and the burley-stubs,
All out of this little dandarious box of mine;
Thousands have I erracted and as many more
    distracted.   155
Now is there any young man in this company got a
    scolding wife?
Bring her to me in the morning and I'll give her one pill of
    the sivil that'll send her headlong to the divil.
So I'm a doctor that can cure all aches, pains, cramps and
    sprains,
And take away all wrinkles, hiccough, headache,
    bellyache, toothache and migraine.
I'll make the paper smock to crack, and soon remove the
    pain of love and cure the love-sick maid,   160
The young, the old, the hot, the cold, the living and the
    dead.
I can make the deaf to hear, the dumb to speak, the lame
    to walk and fly.

King
Dame Doctor, you lie!

Doctor
How can I lie when I'm walking on this ground? – I'm
    better than any doctor.
I can cure any pretty maid that goes bow-legged, old
    bones, strange in back;   165
Big stout maids and whisky-jades.
I can make any person or persons fly over nine iron
    hedges,
Such as old Kate Rickerburn, the mother of fifteen dead,
    born alive
Two misfortunes in one night; broke a pot, cut her arm,
And besides that the old lady could crack a
    marble.   170
Now is there any young woman in this company would
    like a little of my ink-a-tink, white drops of life?

Produces a bottle
Look here, when I was late in Asia, I gave two spoonfuls
    to the great Megull, my grandmother,
Which caused her to have two boys and three girls.
She was then the age of ninety-nine, and she swore if she
    lived nine hundred years longer, she would never be
    without two spoonfuls of this excellent cordial of mine
    for a safe deliverance on a cold and frosty morning.   175
Two spoonfuls will cure the cuckle[21] and take away its
    horns.
So my cork I'll pull out, my business to complete:
Soon you will see this young man stand up on his feet.

Gives the Clown a drink
I'll scour him over and over again.   180

Does so
Judge and try, if he die, never believe me more,
But if I find his spirits fail,
I'll blow him up as if the devil was in his tail.

Clown (rises and sings 2nd tune)
Good morning gentlemen, a-sleeping I have been;
I have had such a sleep as the likes was never seen;   185
But now I am awake and alive unto this day,
And now we'll have a dance, and the doctor must seek his
    pay.

SECOND DANCE

This version contains almost all the elements of sword
dance actions known to have existed. Although there is
no 'Female' present, the King calls the Doctor 'Dame
Doctor', which may suggest that there was once such a
character. This omission is rare in the sword dance
actions; even the dance ceremonies with no dramatic
sequences seem to have retained a 'Female' in a non-
descript *rôle*. Nor is there mention of a wooing, and it is
difficult to see any affinity with this particular version and
those of the East Midlands. Alternatively, the attempt to
apportion the blame for the killing amongst the dancers
and the fact that no culprit is found,[22] is typical of the
type. The Clown makes his will in an effort to delay his
death, which occurs in the normal way. From the point
where the King calls for a doctor the version, if anything,
owes more to Hero-Combat actions than anything else,
even though the actual dialogue differs from that of the
typical Guizers' dialogue of Durham. The names of all the
dancers and most of the verses of the Calling-on Song are
similar to those from Bellerby[23] and Gainford.[24] It would
seem that this version represents one which was performed widely over Durham and North Yorkshire, but
whose examples are now rare.

It is not so extended a version as that from Ampleforth, which has been published so often that the briefest
summary will suffice here.[25] The action is divided into
five parts beginning with the King telling his father, the
Clown, that he wishes to get married. On being introduced to the Queen, the King pays her court and the
Clown leaves them. The King decides that he prefers to
remain single and the couple quarrel. The Clown returns
and fights with the King, but the fight is interrupted by
the Queen who, after expressing a preference for the
Clown, takes no further part in the action. The Clown
says he has come to see the King dance, but the latter
tries to persuade him to sing a song. The 'Love Song
about Murder' which the Clown sings does not please
the King who ultimately sings it himself. The dancers are
now introduced by the Clown in two Calling-on Songs,
one following immediately on the other; the dance
follows. At the end of the dance, an outsider in ordinary
clothes enters the ring, the Lock is made round his neck,
and on the draw, he falls down 'dead'. The dancers run
away leaving the Clown alone with the body. The King
returns and accuses the Clown of murder. He, however,
calls in the dancers one by one, but each denies his
responsibility for the crime and No. 6 finally accuses the
King. The latter accepts the blame for killing the 'old
man', but the Clown denies that the victim is elderly
because he is his son, and he, the Clown, is himself quite
young. They all kneel round the victim and sing a mock
psalm ('When first King Henry ruled the land') over him,
the Clown reads the dead man's will and a doctor is
called for. He enters riding on the back of another man,

describes his travels and cures, but fails to bring the
victim to life. Finally, the Clown stretches the dead
man's legs apart, draws his sword down the body from
throat to groin, and the dead man springs to life.

Similar to Ampleforth, but outside the main sword
dance area, is the Revesby, Lincolnshire, version.[26]
Summarising briefly, the Fool introduces his five sons,
Pickle Herring, Blue Britches, Ginger Britches, Pepper
Britches and Mr Allspice. He fights with the Hobby
Horse and 'they spring the Wild Worm', whatever that
might mean. They dance and make a Lock of their
swords, called the 'Glass'. The Fool looks at himself in
this, then throws it down and jumps on it. Pickle
Herring tells him that they have decided to cut off his
head. After playing for time, the Fool eventually kneels
down with the swords round his neck and makes his
will. He falls down and the dancers announce that they
have killed 'our father like ye evening sun'. This brings
the Fool to his feet again. After a dance called 'Jack the
Brisk Young Drummer', all but the Fool, Fiddler and
Cicely go out and the Fool's wooing begins. His sons try
unsuccessfully to woo Cicely, but she chooses the Fool
who is growing younger whilst the sons grow older.

There are many mysteries about this version which are
now likely to remain unresolved. It contains a sword
dance, type unspecified,[27] in an area where no other is
known to have existed unless vague 18th and 19th
century references are accepted.[28] The MS makes it clear
that the performance was given on October 20th 1779,
but the text refers to Christmas. Plate 6 shows that the
MS is written in an educated hand which is itself an
oddity.[29] The performers are listed by name and stage
directions are given throughout. These suggest that the
MS was a 'prompt copy' possibly used by the 'producer'.

Revesby was the home of Sir Joseph Banks, the Presi-
dent of the Royal Society, who was married in March,
1779. October 20th was the date of Revesby's annual fair
when Banks kept open house. On October 20th, 1783, he
wrote:

> 'this is the day of our fair when according to immem-
> orial custom I am to feed and make drunk everyone
> who chooses to come, and I am sure there is no quiet
> in the house all day.'[30]

The MS further contains a note of ownership, on folio 2,
which shows that Sir Joseph's sister, Miss Sarah Sophia
Banks, was sufficiently interested to obtain a copy, but it
has not been possible to identify the handwriting of the
MS as a whole as belonging to anyone in the Banks
family. The most that can be claimed for this version is
that it was based on the traditional and probably compiled for the first time the new Mrs Banks entertained
her guests on the occasion of the annual fair.[31] It is not
necessarily traditional to Revesby or even to the East
Midlands as a whole. Nevertheless, it preserves features
which are present to a greater or lesser degree in all texts
which have survived. Few preserve them to the extent of
Revesby and Ampleforth, doubtful though the former
may be. Most have a Calling-on Song which occurs
normally after a request for room. The two songs of
Ampleforth probably imply an old and a new version as
at Earsdon,[32] whose 'modern' version gives the characters the names of 'Son of' various naval and military
heroes. This was certainly a late introduction presumably as the belief grew that the performance was a
'martial dance'. It is in line with the introduction of Lord
Nelson in the Hero-Combat ceremonies. In some songs

The Fool then calls in his five Sons first Pickle Herring, then blue Britches, then Ginger Britches, Pepper Britches, & last calls out "come now you M^r. Allspice")

They fool it once round the Room, and the Man that is to ride the Hobby Horse goes out, and the rest sing the following Song ———

Come in come in thou Hobby Horse
And bring thy old Fool at thy arse
Sing Tantera day sing Tantera day
Sing heigh down, down with a Derry down a

Then the Fool and the Horse fights about the Room, whilst the following Song is singing by the rest

Come in come in thou bonny wild Worm
For thou hast ta'en many a lucky turn
Sing Tantera day sing Tantera day
Sing heigh down, down with a Derry Down

The wild Worm is only sprung 3 or 4 times as the Man walks round the Room, and then goes out of the House & the Fool fights again whilst the following Song is sung

Plate 6. Folio from Revesby Play MS.

the characters are given trade descriptions as the Merchant at Escrick,[33] Sailor and Tailor at Sowerby or Pitman Bold at Earsdon.[34] Others have purely folk characters like the Clown at Greatham and Bold Robin Hood at Sowerby. A further set is given no name but merely a description such as the man of 'much milder blood' or the one who is as 'cruel as cruel can be' at Kirkby Malzeard.[35] Whatever its form, the song persisted where the dance either lost or never had a dramatic action.

The verbal formulae here and in the main body of the texts show similar constant features; the making of the will, the denial of responsibility and the lapse into Hero-Combat dialogue in the Cure, even though the fragments left do not have each and every one present. The constant feature is the Lock and the way in which it is used to bring about the death. Any variation lies in the victim who may be the Fool, the Queen, the Betty or an Outsider.[36] The resulting Cure may be performed by either a Doctor, a Clown or a 'Female'[37] and its method also varies. The Doctor in all versions is probably a rationalisation of a later date, introduced when the nature of the ceremony was forgotten, and therefore the lock of swords once had a greater connection with the cure than is now apparent. As a means of execution it is both inept and clumsy, even though this is clearly its significance to performers of any known date. If the rôle of the Lock could be inverted, it could be looked upon basically as a means of restoring life rather than taking it.

In this way it could be a symbol of the female principle placed over the head of a male performer to complete the union. In Germanic examples of the ceremony, similar Locks were used as a platform to hoist notable characters as well as their Leader.[38] Similar hoistings were known in Provence,[39] at Buonopani in Ischia,[40] and in Spain at Arexinaga.[41] At Fenestrelle in Piedmont, the dancers hoisted the Fool three times: on the third time they withdrew their swords and he fell to the ground, landing on his feet.[42] Not all of these ceremonies had a dramatic action but many had a Calling-on Song. Whether the former had been lost is unknown now, but it seems clear that the Lock had a different significance on the Continent of Europe. Unfortunately, no early description of the ceremony has survived in England. The well-known account by Olaus Magnus in 1555[43] is often quoted, frequently without acknowledgment, as applying to a particular location, but the earliest reliable English description was written by John Wallis, a curate in a Northumbrian parish, in 1767.[44] Neither of these accounts, nor any subsequent one, suggests that the Lock was used for any but the familiar purpose, and indeed, Wallis does not even mention it.

The details of the Cure which follows the execution suggest that it has been amended. The comment on the Goathland cure has already been noted[45] and at Bellerby, the Bessy simulated all the pangs of childbirth in her progress to recovery.[46] She was finally cured by the medicine 'oakum-pokum pennyroyal'. Pennyroyal is well-known as a supposed abortifacient[47] whose significance was obviously clear to the performers. The Ampleforth method, where the sword is drawn down from throat to groin is apparently meaningless. It may be an unpleasant suggestion, but the method might make more sense if the sword had been used in the opposite direction and thrust rather than drawn. *Circa* 1870 at Askham Richard, Besom Betty cured the victim when the Doctor failed, by brushing the dead man's face with her broom.[48] She may be performing her original function of sweeping away evil. There is more variation in the manner of cure in the Sword Dance actions than in either of the other types, and the implication seems to be that there was more crude by-play, which was subsequently watered down.

The Cure may have some bearing on the significance of this particular type. There are obvious affinities with the Wooing versions but the Bastard incident is missing. The Fool, first seen as an older man whose sons are the dancers, is the pivotal character round whom the action revolves. The relationship in the Ampleforth version is supposedly between the Clown and his son, the victim, and here the former insists he is a young man. The father and son relationship establishes two of the three generations essential to the Life-Cycle drama. The third generation is more difficult to see, though the method of revival at Bellerby may point to a possible one. The Fool at Ampleforth dies and is revived; there is a suggestion that before this he had successfully courted the Queen. At Escrick there were two couples, the Fool and his wife, Madam Sylvester, and a King and Queen who contributed nothing to the action.[49] The latter can be regarded as an Old Couple, the Fool and his wife as a Young Couple, and, although it is not said at Escrick, the dancers here could be the third generation. The three generations are certainly not clear cut, but there is a killing and a cure, so that revitalisation is implicit.

This action is therefore a distinct variant of those that are left, with recognisable Hero-Combat and Wooing ceremony affinities. Its unique feature is a choreographically complex dance, which may once have existed in the East Midlands also. This dance contained, paradoxically, the seeds of perpetuance and decay. In the Rapper area in particular, the dance survived because, at times of economic difficulty amongst the performers, whenever there were strikes, lock-outs or unemployment, it was customary for them to dance to augment their income. The same was probably true of the miners in Yorkshire and south Durham. This kept the dance alive. It was the most attractive feature, capable of more performances in a shorter time than the dance-cum-dramatic action. Gradually the dramatic action was dropped save on its rarer ceremonial appearances until eventually it disappeared from public performance entirely. It is ironic that early collectors of the dramatic action saw no importance in the choreographic dance which was not considered of interest until Cecil Sharp investigated it *circa* 1910, but it was the dance which outlived the drama.[50] Fortunately, the latter lingered in the memories of the old performers to whom it is entirely due that we still have examples to study today.

5

The Hero-Combat Ceremonies

The most widespread of the actions is the Hero-Combat, known in Scotland, southern Wales, the English speaking settlement areas of Ireland and across the Atlantic in America and Canada. Figure 4 shows that it was most common in England south of a line drawn from the mouth of the Dee to the mouth of the Humber. It spreads into the areas of both the Sword Dance and Wooing ceremonies, often existing side by side with them in the same village. Where this occurred, the Hero-Combat actions were often performed by children who were excluded from the ceremonies of their elders. Its basic theme is revitalisation, expressed in the following terms:

In a combat of champions, one is killed and revived by a doctor. Occasionally the combats are multiplied. Characteristic performers include St George, Turkish Knight or Black Prince, 'Female', Doctor, Jack Finney, Devil Doubt, Big Head. These names, however, are subject to endless local variations. Some named characters, amongst them the last three mentioned, do not carry the action further.
Costume: Latterly to correspond with character, but formerly, according to area, strips of paper or ribbons worn over ordinary clothes. Faces blackened, raddled, or covered with headdress.
Time of Appearance: From All Souls to Easter.

This description cannot be as precise as those given for the ceremonials already discussed because local variations appear endless.[1] A typical text from Syresham in Northamptonshire was given in Chapter One; the following, from Burntwood, Staffordshire,[2] is an example of the diversity.

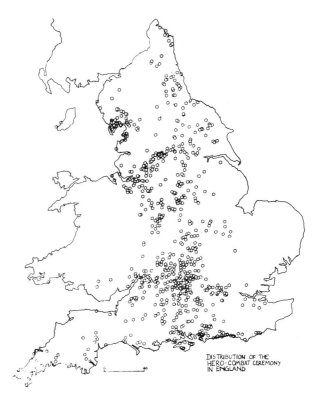

Figure 4. Distribution of the Hero-Combat Ceremony in England.

Enter in
I open the door and enter in
The greatest favours fought to win.
Whether we rise, stand or fall
We do our duty to please you all.
Room, room, gallant room, 5
Pray give us room to rise.
We mean to show you Gia's act
Upon this Christmas time.

We are not of a ragged set
But of a loyal trim. 10
If you don't believe the words I say
Step in, Bold Guide, and clear the way.

Bold Guide
Here am I, Bold Guide's my name,
To England's town I sprang again.
I've searched this wide world round and round – 15
To fight King George, I'll give ten thousand pound.

Enter In
King George, King George stands at the door
And he swears he will come in.
With sword and buckle by his side
He swears he'll tan thy skin. 20
Step in King George.

King George
Here am I, King George,
A noble champion bold.
With my bright sword in hand
I've won three crowns of gold. 25

Bold Guide
What three crowns?

King George
Effia, Sheffia, amma roceo.[3]
'Twas I who fought the fiery dragon
Through and through and brought it to the slaughter.
By means of this and that[4] 30
I won the King of Egypt's daughter.
Stir up these bars and make a light
And watch these two jolly actors fight.
The hour has come, the clock struck one,
It's time this battle had begun. 35

They fight

Enter In
O King, O King, what hast thou done?
Thou hast fought and slain my only son.
Five pounds for a doctor.

Doctor (outside)
No doctor for five pounds!

Enter In
Ten pounds! 40

Doctor (enters)
Here am I, a noble doctor.

Enter In
How came you to be a doctor?

Doctor
By my travels.

Enter In
How far are your travels?

Doctor
From the fireplace to the cupboard. 45

Enter In
Any farther?

Doctor
From the top of the stairs to the bottom.

Enter In
Cure me this man!

Doctor
Here Jack, take a drop out of this bottle and let it run
down thy throttle, and if thou feelest well, rise up and
fight again. 50

Enter In
That's not cured the man.

Doctor
I have another bottle in my inside outside jacket
waistcoat pocket, containing heathercome, smether-
come, oakum, Spain, which brings dead, men to life
again. Here Jack, take a drop out of this phial, open
thy mouth and oil thy dial. And if thou feelest well,
rise up Bold Guide and fight again. 55

Bold Guide
Oh, my back.

Doctor
What ails thy back?

Bold Guide
My back is wounded, bad and sore,
I feel I cannot fight no more. 60
If you can't believe the words I say
Step in Black Prince, and clear the way.

Black Prince
Here am I, black Prince of Paradise,
The Black Morocco King.
And all the woods I travel through, 65
I'm bound to make them ring.
If you cannot believe the words I say,
Step in, Old Girl, and clear the way.

Old Lady Be-elzebub
Here am I, old Lady Be-elzebub,
Under my arm I carry my club; 70
Over my shoulder my dripping pan,
Don't you think I'm a jolly old girl?
Rink, jink, jink, and a sup more drink,
Would make the old kettle cry clinkety clink.
Now, ladies and gentlemen, if you are able 75
Put your hands in your pockets
And think of the ladle.
The ladle is dumb and never yet spake,
There's six so stout and six so bold
Could eat a plum pudding before it's half cold. 80
And if your plum pudding chanced to be pale,
We could drink a good jug of your old Christmas ale.
And if your old Christmas ale is chanced to be strong,
We accommodate you with a jolly good song.

All (sung as a round)

This version, as all of the type, can be divided into three main parts, the Presentation, the Combat with Cure, and, following Chambers, what has become known as the *Quête*.[5]

The Presentation introduces the action by asking for room in which to perform, the most usual lines being similar to *ll.* 1–12 of the Syresham version. Father Christmas often acts as Presenter, as he does rather belatedly in the Iping version (*ll.* 28–34).[6] Sometimes the Fool is used, as at Syresham. Very often, as in the Burntwood text above, anonymous figures with functional names – First Man,[7] First Speaker,[8] Head Man,[9] Open the Door[10] or Roomer[11] – are used. Characters in the Pace-egg and Souling versions are introduced in song,[12] but their names in song are not necessarily those of the main action. A Presenter was essential for purely functional reason. It was often necessary to have a large character

28

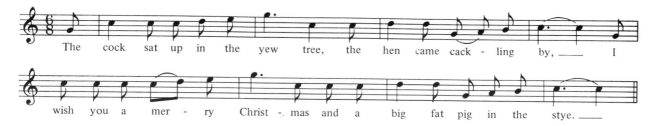

The cock sat up in the yew tree, the hen came cack - ling by, _____ I
wish you a mer - ry Christ - mas and a big fat pig in the stye. _____

who could insert his foot in a closing door, and because of the traditional disguise and absence of scenery it was conventional to have some means of explaining to the uninitiated what was taking place. 'In comes I . . .' is another useful means of identifying an otherwise anonymous character. The champion thus introduced now launches into his vaunt which is countered by that of his opponent. At Burntwood this is brief, but at Minehead it is more extended (ll. 69–115).[13] The vaunts provide the excuse for the combat immediately following. This and the Cure form the crux of this particular ceremony. Together they became its most attractive feature, often developed out of all proportion as a means of inducing higher financial gain.[14] This was achieved by the champions staging a display of sword fighting, sometimes with sticks, very often with military relics from old campaigns. (Here, the implements are clearly Pyrrhic, quite unlike the sword links discussed in Chapter Four). For added attraction there was often more than one combat as at Syresham and Minehead. This multiplication is meaningless; only one death and revival is needed to complete the revitalisation ceremony. The elaboration of the fight is clear evidence of lack of understanding of the ceremony.[15]

Fortunately, the majority of versions avoided complications and the second part of the action was a straightforward fight and death,[16] after which came a Lament.[17] In the Cheshire versions this was spoken by a 'Female', often called Martha or Mary,[18] but elsewhere, the King of Egypt was widely used.[19] The text of the Lament makes it clear that the dead man is the son of the Lamenter, thus establishing two of the three generations essential for the Life-Cycle drama.

The Lamenter also calls for a Doctor who enters after somewhat nonsensical dialogue about his fee, describes his travels in lines reminiscent of the *Land of Cockayne*, a fourteenth century anti-monastic satire,[20] and his cures in lines borrowed from *The Infallible Mountebank, Or, Quack Doctor, circa* 1750.[21]

The nonsense of this dialogue is only equalled by the way in which the cure is brought about. Every cure is a larger-than-life version of the way in which a conventional doctor treats his patients. The Mummers' Doctor has surgical instruments more common in a workshop than in a doctor's bag. After hammers, pincers, saws, &c., comes a bottle which contains the infallible cure. (At Basford, Nottinghamshire, it was discovered during a performance, that the doctor had forgotten his bottle. The cure could not proceed until an old Worcester Sauce bottle had been borrowed from a spectator. This was said to have produced the fastest cure on record, for, unknown to anyone, the bottle was not empty and the 'dead' man took a good swallow before it was realised.)[22]

The doctor's part shows a clear attempt at a parody of a real doctor's work. It adds to the attraction of the combat, it allows the streak of comic inventiveness on the part of the performers to develop; most important of all, it argues a rationalisation of a later date. Since, in sophisticated times, a dead man could not be expected to cure himself, a doctor became necessary. Whether he was always there is debatable.[23]

In the Cotswolds he often appeared riding a 'horse'. This was not a hobby-horse as discussed in the Wooing actions, but almost certainly a relic from the days when country doctors made their rounds on horseback. The 'horse' was usually another man, always mute, who was left outside. Again, in the Cotswolds, an unwilling assistant, Jack Finney,[24] often came with him and always insisted on being called 'Mr Finney'.[25] The character is an enigma. He was the reluctant assistant who brought the 'instruments' required by the Doctor. He sometimes helped in the cure, he sometimes performed it, but apart from adding to comic effect, his introduction has no apparent purpose. Douglas Kennedy saw him as a character budded off from the doctor and a rationalisation of the hobby-horse. He supported the latter theory by tracing the name 'Finney' or 'Pinney' from 'Pony'.[26] This seems unlikely if the doctor's 'horse' was intended to be a real horse. At Long Hanborough, Oxfordshire, Finney dressed as a clown and carried a bladder attached to a long piece of string,[27] part of the normal apparatus of a Cotswold Morris Fool. He is more likely to have his origin in the Fool. His reluctance to carry out his assigned tasks until pressed, suggests this more strongly than a hobby-horse ancestry. He could have developed into a Folk version of the Elizabethan stage fool.

He also took part in cures where a tooth was extracted from the dead champion, though more often these were secondary cures with a 'Female' patient as at Islip (ll. 75–82). The customary method of extraction was to form a line of performers each grasping the one in front round the waist. When the tooth was extracted, the line of performers collapsed and the tooth, usually belonging to a horse or a cow, was exhibited to the audience. The episode is quite irrelevant. It carries the action no further when it is used as a secondary cure and has the appearance of an interpolation. In Suffolk, *circa* 1849, a similar operation was performed during harvest feasts:

'A rustic drama is usually acted on these occasions, which greatly increases the merriment; one of the revellers, habited as a female, feigns to be taken with violent toothache, and the 'doctor' is sent for. He soon appears mounted on the back of one of the other men (the 'horse' has a milking stool to bear his hands upon to keep his back level);[28] the 'doctor' brings with him the tongs which he uses for the purpose of extracting the tooth; this is a piece of tobacco pipe placed in the mouth; a fainting takes place from the violence of the operation, and the bellows are employed as a means of restoring the pretended sufferer.'[29]

As far as present knowledge goes, the dramatic action of the mummers was unknown in Suffolk; it is unlikely that this account postulates its existence there. The tooth drawing of the Cotswold actions was probably an additional entertainment taken over from the harvest celebrations which had lost their importance.

The action ends with the Cure, the remaining part consisting of the procession of now extraneous characters. At Burntwood these are limited to the Black Prince of Paradise[30] and Old Lady Be-elzebub, both unusual. The latter is normally Beelzebub who, with Devil or Dairy Doubt, appears regularly amongst these now unessential characters. Their number varies. At Netley Abbey, Hampshire,[31] there were ten, but generally two or four were normal. Some had only a regional distribution, as Johnny Jack and Twing Twang along the south coast,[32] or Big Head and Little Wits in the Cotswolds.[33] Still others had a unique local existence like the Snake at Mansfield or the Suffragette at Heptonstall.[34] There is no adequate explanation for these beyond local whim. Their numbers doubtless reflected the availability of performers. As time went by this third part of the ceremony became a convenient means of dropping or adding individuals without disturbing the main action. The longer versions of Minehead, Iping and Dorchester do not have the additional characters; one might guess that all available performers were absorbed in the main action.[35] As ceremony dwindled, the additional characters became those who could provide entertainment to persuade generosity. Cleverlegs at Weston Subedge, Gloucestershire,[36] was probably capable of giving a solo dance after the performance, whilst The Linnet at Belcoo, Fermanagh,[37] probably disguised a performer with a good singing voice.

Chambers in 1933 described this part as the Quête[38] and as it had developed the description was correct. It is unlikely that this was its original function. Thirty years earlier he had said of the characters:[39]

'They are none other than the grotesques . . . that I have attempted to trace to their origin in magical or sacrificial custom',

and recognising that the performers had difficulty in using them, added:

'The simplest and most primitive method is just to bring them in, to show them to the spectators when the fighting is over',

This admitted that their original purpose was more than as the unnecessary figures they had become. The two most persistent still carried implements which had adopted far more utilitarian purposes than originally intended. Beelzebub always carried club and frying pan, symbols of the male and female principles, but the one was useful for protecting the donations which were placed in the other. Devil Doubt had a broom, formerly used to sweep a place clear of evil, but latterly it was a jocular threat to those unwilling to contribute. The characters themselves were the misunderstood remnants of more important figures.

One further feature of this third part needs some consideration. On to the basic action were often grafted regional features, which, like the tooth extraction sequence, appear irrelevant. The best known of these was the Cheshire Wild Horse, constructed differently from those of the East Midlands. The head of a dead horse or donkey, boiled to remove the flesh, skull painted and varnished, was mounted on a stick, given bottle tops for eyes, and decorated with horse brasses and other appurtenances.[40] The performer carrying the

head stooped down and grasped the stick, and had a horse blanket thrown over him (see Fig. 5). He was accompanied by a Driver who played a prominent part in the begging by requesting money to help the horse.[41] Another 'horse', similarly built, appeared in the Dorset versions as Tommy the Pony, and played a more prominent part in the action by being killed and revived.[42] At Symondsbury, after his revival, he became oracular and was able to sniff out the young lady who kicked off her bed-clothes whilst dreaming of her young man.[43] With the paste-eggers[44] at Hindley, Lancashire, was a further hobby-horse type. There were two kinds of paste-eggers, the whites and the blacks. The whites visited during the day as well as the night and were decorated with ribbons, but the blacks visited only after dark, had black faces and were dressed as hideously as possible. One in each band wore a stuffed horse's head and was covered with a horse-cloth.[45] There was more significance in the hobby-horse than is now apparent.[46] In Cheshire, when rival gangs met, they fought, and each tried to capture the other's horse, the victors carrying off the captured head with them.[47] In some Cheshire villages when the performance was over for the year, the head was buried, a mock funeral service held over it, and it stayed in its grave until the next year when it was dug up and used again.

Figure 5. Cheshire Hobby Horse.

This is probably the best known regional characteristic, but others include the Calling-on Songs of the Pace-egg and Souling versions of the north-west of England.[48] In Sussex, the performances often concluded with the 'Hip, Mr Carpenter' dialogue pirated from the Ombres Chinoises, a once popular puppet play.[49] In Dorset, the ceremony ended with the Singing of the Travels[50] and occasionally with the ceremonial tying of a bow of ribbon to the Christmas Holly Bough carried by the performers.[51] These are all embellishments to the basic theme which remained constant in all examples of these versions. The Hero-Combat type appears to have been of tougher stock than the other two, for not only did it persist widely in England, but was the only type known to have been taken with them by emigrants from the country.[52]

The bulk of these emigrant versions is to be found in Ireland in areas of English settlement (see Fig. 6), where the ceremony is still a living tradition.[53] The Lislaine text given in Appendix II is typical of south-east Antrim, though, as in England, regional variants are common. The most widely divergent of these is from Co. Wexford where historical characters – Napoleon, Emperor of Russia, Dan O'Connell, Julius Caesar, Wellington, &c., – join the familiar St Patrick, Prince George and the Doctor to perform a version which contains a revitalisation, but only after very lengthy turgid lines. It seems clear that this version was deliberately composed after the Napoleonic Wars, possibly in the 1830's to judge by the O'Connell lines. Another feature of the Wexford versions is the performance of a 'sword dance', Droghedy's

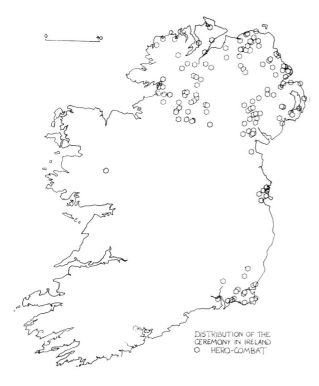

Figure 6. Distribution of the Hero-Combat Ceremony in Ireland.

March', quite unlike the linked circular dances of the north-east of England. It has more affinity with the Cotswold Morris Stick dances.[54] This dance became the focal point of another Wexford type probably composed this century by a priest who wished to keep the spirit of nationalism burning, but who misunderstood the ceremony he was altering. He gave national colour to the heroes by naming them Brian Boru, Robert Emmett, John Kelly of Killane, &c., but omitted the essential revitalisation.[55] In Co. Wexford mumming competitions are held regularly; these keep the ceremony alive but shift its emphasis to disguise and texts.

In Scotland, the actions appear to have been dead for many years. Texts are comparatively short as the Hawick version in Appendix II shows, and they are obviously influenced by the versions of [north-east] England. The earliest mentioned, at Edinburgh in the 1780's,[56] and the last, at Leven, Fifeshire,[57] in 1930 have the same pattern. In the latter place the performance had dwindled to children merely reciting their lines for coppers. Almost all Scottish versions have Galatians as the defeated opponent,[58] but the victor is generally some historical figure like Robert the Bruce or William Wallace, with whom the performers were familiar. The names are unimportant, particularly as the action remains constant.

The North American examples show a similar pattern; they are clearly exports from the British Isles with the names of some of the characters changed. In Newfoundland, at St John's *circa* 1840, characters included St Patrick, Alexander the Great, the Czar of Russia and Dan Donnelly; the text owed something to both Wexford and Ulster versions. Here, the action must have travelled in two steps, first to Ireland and from there to Newfound-

land.[59] In America, the custom has either died or entirely changed its character. In Philadelphia it has become a carnival parade with little resemblance to the dramatic action.[60] An historical survey of the custom given by Alfred L. Shoemaker[61] shows how the performers had introduced American champions, George Washington, Cooney Cracker, &c., although Beelzebub was as prominent as ever. The three versions from Kentucky,[62] one noted at a special performance on Christmas Eve, 1930, and the other two collected as its result, are a problem. They are clearly the ceremonies with which we are concerned in this book, but it is difficult to understand how they existed in isolation. Enquiries made since have produced nothing further, nor any recollection of the three concerned. They are sufficiently distinctive for it to be said that they are not copies of versions previously published.[63]

The fact that actions did travel so widely is evidence that they were an accepted feature of the performers' seasonal life. Although they retained the basic pattern, what has emerged finally is a version which owes something to its place of origin and something to its new surroundings. This may be expressed simply in the 'new' names of the characters or in the traces of other, formerly indigenous customs which remain. The Wren in some Irish versions[64] is one such example. It almost certainly came from the 'Hunting the Wren' ceremonies which in some places showed traces of an independent revitalisation. Also in Ireland, the Strawboys, so-called from their disguise, appeared at weddings, danced with the Bride, and generally set out to bring luck to the newly-weds. *Circa* 1850 at Carlow, these performers had names, there was a fight between the champions, Sir John and St Patrick. The latter always won and Sir John recanted and swore allegiance to the Church.[65] The 'Sir Sop' and 'Building the Fort' ceremonies also show a strong resemblance to the Hero-Combat actions. Off the Scottish coast at Eriskay in the Hebrides there was a Punch and Judy dance, 'Carlin of the Dust', in which an old man and an old trembling hag fought with sticks, dancing all the time. The hag was killed and lamented by her partner, who finally cured her.[66]

If these are accepted as indigenous revitalisation ceremonies they are evidence that the same beliefs which drove English performers to perpetuate the Hero-Combat actions must have been shared elsewhere, even if not expressed in the same manner. One can only argue that the English manifestations had a former, respectable acceptance, whose identical fragments of dialogue suggests that somewhere was a common archetype. It was a pattern which certainly had Victorian approval. When Mrs Ewing published a version suitable for nursery performance,[67] she had copies distributed to the local performers. This killed the local traditional version.[68] What is left of the Hero-Combat versions is emasculated, but here and there are traces of an older ceremony. At Coxwold, Yorkshire, there were memories of a Bride, who wore a lace curtain,[69] and at Kirtlington, Oxfordshire, all the characters were referred to as 'Molly's six children',[70] a Hero-Combat variant of the Lincolnshire Fool and his sons. The Lament establishes two of the generations necessary to the Life-Cycle drama, but there is little evidence of a third. Johnny Jack in Hampshire versions carried dolls on his back to represent his wife and family, possibly a bowdlerised version of the Lincolnshire bastard. At Midgley, Yorkshire, Tosspot still carries an effigy known locally as his 'tally-wife', the local name for a common law wife (See

Plate 7). The extended versions of the West Country have Father Christmas and Dame Dorothy who are clearly an Old Couple whose sons were the combatants. If a third generation existed it must have disappeared in deference to the growth of 'good taste'. Whether or not some of the characters' names had some significance is now unknown. Why Age should defeat Activity in the Thenford version[71] is not clear unless it is a half-forgotten memory of the Fool who maintains he is a young man. Anno Domini at Islip[72] and Old Almanick at Potterne, Wiltshire, may be less obvious contrivances to suggest age.

Plate 7. Midgley, Yorkshire, Tosspot and Tally-wife.

One can only guess at the reasons which prompted the adoption of these and other names, just as one can only guess at the original form of this particular type. Its common inclusion in both Wooing and Sword Dance actions suggests that it is a fragment of the whole, just as the other two are themselves fragments of something much larger. There is a vestigial wooing in the Minehead version (ll. 390–424) followed by a 'Calling-on Song' whose third verse (ll. 434–7) corresponds almost exactly to ll. 52–3 of Greatham and ll. 100–3 of Bellerby (Appendix 2), whilst its general style accords with most Sword Dance Calling-on Songs. The Minehead version is unfortunately an oddity no longer performed, although some Hero-Combat versions still are performed in England and many more in Ireland. The ceremonies which continued into our times are but a few of those which once existed and are now, for a variety of reasons, dead. Not the least of these reasons was the First World War, from which many of the performers failed to return. The

process of attrition had begun before then, however, and was due in part to the changed nature of the ceremony. It had altered from ritual to begging and, by analogy, at a reasonably early date. In 1716, Lady Fermanagh wrote to her husband:

'We have Whisen ayls all about us, which brings such A bundance of rabble and the worst sort of Company round us that I wish noe mischiefes Happens . . . I can't help given the Morrises monny when they come for they tell me everybody doing it is the best way to send them going . . .'[73]

Although this refers to ceremonial dance more than ceremonial drama, it is probably typical of attitudes to similar customs. There is no doubt that begging has been a driving force behind traditional observances in recent times, partly in response to a genuine need as was noted in the Sword Dance ceremonies, and partly to augment income at a seasonal time of the year. Once times improved and the need to beg disappeared, the impetus was removed and the customs faltered. It was said in Staffordshire in 1954 that the miners had too much money and could afford to buy their own beer, but a depression would bring the Play to life again.[74] The difficulty is that if the gap between prosperity and hardship were long enough, there would be insufficient performers with memory of the tradition to bring it back to life again.

The financial aspirations which brought the performers out also contributed to the change. The ceremony became entertainment, with not only the combat and cure playing a large part, but also the post-action diversions of songs and dances. To some extent Dame Dorothy's beating Father Christmas in the Minehead version comes under the same heading, as do the songs in the Dorchester text. After the action the songs need have no connection with what had preceded them, they were simply songs which the performers knew, and could be the popular songs of the day as well as the Carol-type in the Iping version. The dancing mentioned in some versions was often a broom dance, a solo performance of individual dexterity. In Ireland the dances could be reels in which performers and audience took part. This reduced the ceremonial characters to song-and-dance men, and robbed the ceremony of its true character.

Despite this, it was extraordinarily persistent. Why it lived in some areas and not others is still unsolved. Its main area appears to correspond to an area of England where resistance to enclosure of the common land was strongest.[75] This also corresponds to the area where the Anglo-Saxon two and three field systems were found[76] and to an area where the people do not sound their h's.[77] Why the latter should be so is not clear. Characteristics of this area were large villages, large, stable agricultural communities and a system of inheritance which preserved estates intact. Although the dramatic ceremony was known outside the area, where it existed it took forms which were departures from the norm.[78] The features inside the area argue an innate conservatism, which would keep ceremonial alive. Once this way of life was broken as it eventually had to be, there was nothing to maintain custom.

Decline of the Hero-Combat Play can be attributed, therefore, not only to increasing prosperity but also to lack of understanding. Where it still survives, the performers observe such ceremony as is left by maintaining the disguise and appearing at the correct season of the year. Their aim is still collecting – the 'luck' in reverse – but it is unlikely that any performers for the last 250 years at least have had any other consideration but self-gain in mind.

6

'Abnormal' Texts

One further group of versions needs examination before discussion of the types of action can be concluded. This group contains the versions which do not fit comfortably into any of the three preceding types. Although basically Hero-Combat in form, they have elements which suggest something more primitive. It is true that almost every version of every type has a feature peculiar to itself, even though it may only be a character's name or a line of text which does not occur elsewhere. These minor divergences are not the concern here. Chambers saw there were abnormalities amongst the versions available to him;[1] indeed, the title of this chapter is taken from his work. Unfortunately, the material he examined was insufficient for him to form any conclusive opinion. Furthermore, only one of the examples he gives, from Thame in Oxfordshire, can now be considered abnormal in the true sense of the word. His other examples, three from West Dorset[2] and the texts which include Robin Hood from the Cotswolds,[3] are fairly typical Hero-Combat actions, showing only regional variations from the norm. We must look further for abnormalities, since they do exist, and endeavour to assess their place in the pattern of the action as a whole.

Such versions cannot be defined generally and must be considered individually before an assessment can be made. Minor oddities, such as are found in the Chiswick, Middlesex, version[4] where a character called Swiff Swash and Swagger says:

'Once I courted a damsel,
She's often in my mind,
But now alas! she's proved unkind'

may indicate that Hero-Combat versions once possessed a Wooing element, but if they did, it has long since disappeared. The best known of the abnormal versions from Thame[5] was taken down in 1853 'from the lips of one of the performers' and had been seen performed in the Hall of the Old Vicarage, Thame, in 1839. The performer from whom the text was noted had performed at Brill in 1807 and his father had done the same at Thame Park in the previous century. Although its contributor to *Notes and Queries* found that its 'coarseness' was not to his taste, and he could not understand its purport, he certified that nothing had been added or altered in his printed version. He had furthermore been assured by 'Mr Lupton, a local antiquarian and a gentleman of excellent taste and high character' that 'the dialogue was purely traditional and handed down from father to son'. There appears to be no reason, therefore, to doubt the authenticity or age of the text.

It contains almost none of the verbal formulae normally associated with the ceremony, nor are its characters those whom one might expect. The lines are in rhyming couplets throughout and some, if not all the dialogue was sung, though the music is not given. Fairly full stage directions are given and it is clear that the text has been worked over by a practised writer at some stage, but, assuming the historical data is correct, this must have occurred reasonably early. The mummers came in singing, walked round in a circle, then stood to one side. From this position they came forward, declaimed their introductory lines, then returned to their place. King Alfred and his Queen, arm in arm, appeared first. They were followed by King Cole, King William, Giant Blunderbore, Little Jack and St George. Introductions over, a stage direction said:

'Morres-men come forward and dance to a tune from fife and drum'.

The dance was followed by King George striking the Dragon who had so far not appeared, and who roared, demanded meat, turned a 'summersault', then stood on one side. The drum and fife sounded again, all the characters fought each other and ultimately fell down. Old Doctor Ball entered, described his cures[6] and gave each a pill. This cured everyone but the Dragon who died in convulsions. Father Christmas appeared last, stopped the others from fighting again, and asked for contributions whilst one of the performers went round with a hat.

This action can only be classified as Hero-Combat even though it is not typical. The Queen does not speak, her appearance arm-in-arm with the King is, however, indicative of a Couple, but whether an Old or a Young Couple cannot be determined.[7] There is an affinity with both the Sword Dance and Wooing versions in that the action is expressed in song, but here the resemblance stops. Were this the only version to present unusual features it could be dismissed as an oddity, but in many ways it is the least unconventional of the type under discussion.

A less well-known example was performed at Castle Cary in Somerset.[8] It is unusual in that, like the Revesby version, the *dramatis persona* are listed together with the names of those playing the part. More unusual still, some of the performers were women, a very rare occurrence, though it was said of the North Skelton, Yorkshire, team, that:

'an old gentleman and an old lady accompanied the 'gang'. A real lady, mind you, not a man dressed as a woman'.[9]

This must be taken as a sign of decadence, for the men were usually very jealous of their customs and women were not allowed to take part.[10] This jealousy does not seem to have existed at Castle Cary where the text shows again some literary hand had been at work, unless the anonymous contributor had edited it for publication. Unfortunately, the text is printed only in fragmentary form, so that a complete picture cannot be drawn. It is not divided into Acts and Scenes, but is described as consisting of four plays of which only the first is given in full.

This was introduced by the Leader, who was followed by Father Christmas with his usual patter, and described as 'acting much like a Clown throughout the whole performance'. He was followed by King John and a Traveller who said that a Turkish Knight was outside ready to fight St George. King John summoned St George, told him of the Turkish Knight who entered at George's summons, and they fought. During the fight, according to a stage direction, 'the Turk blunders and is wounded. He falls on his knees'. This concluded the first play and the performers danced as they did after each to separate one action from the next. Of the second play only the speech of the Valiant Soldier was given. This contained the typical 'My head's not made of iron . . .' lines, but there was no indication as to how the plot developed. Only three characters were mentioned, the Valiant Soldier, Queen Anne (played by a woman), and King John. The absence of a doctor suggests that again there was no cure, but the boast of the Valiant Soldier normally precedes a fight. The third play was described as that of 'the Shepherd' and whose characters were a Shepherd and Shepherdess (played by a woman), but no indication was given of its development. The last Play concerned a Drunkard, a Doctor and Musicians, one of whom, a woman, played the tambourine, whilst her father played the fiddle.

This particular version is exasperating because of its omissions. One might guess at the structure of the third play by analogy with the Keynsham version performed on December 27th, 1822,[11] itself an abnormal version. Both Castle Cary and Keynsham are in Somerset within easy reach of each other. Regionalism amongst versions has already been noted so that it is fair to assume that the two followed the same pattern roughly. At Keynsham, after a normal Hero-Combat action involving Father Christmas, King George, who was killed, Slasher, also called the Valiant Soldier, a Doctor and Thomas, the Doctor's Man, Father Christmas called in the Shepherdess who claimed to be lost. A Prince entered, addressed her as 'Moll', and said that his parents had agreed they were to be married. To this, the Shepherdess replied:

'I will never marry with a clownd, but I will have a handsome young man to lie in bed with me'.

This is reminiscent of lines in the Sword Dance and Wooing dialogues. The action stops at this point and it is not clear if it ever developed beyond it.

Similarly, at Lydiard Millicent[12] and Highworth[13] in Wiltshire, a normal Hero-Combat action was followed by a wooing between St George and the Tinker, addressed again as 'Sweet Moll', and expressed in song. Again, the theme was not developed and Wooing dwindled into a Little John/Robin Hood dialogue. In the same county at Cricklade,[14] a fragmentary dialogue, following the Keynsham one fairly closely but in rather more literary style, occurred between a Shepherd and a Maiden. Here the wooing was poor, but nevertheless present. None of these wooings is like those of the East Midlands, and all appear to have some literary style. Whether they were sophisticated amendments to an earlier, much cruder passage is problematic.

From Broadway in Worcestershire comes the most unusual of all these variants. First published in 1909[15] in fragmentary form, the full text has since been published[16] despite the fact that the last performance was *circa* 1874. It was as follows:

Father Christmas
In comes I, old Father Christmas,
Christmas or Christmas not,
I hopes old Father Christmas
Will never be forgot.
Christmas comes but once a year   5
And when it comes it brings us here.
Roast beef, plum pudding and mince pie
There's nobody at Christmas likes better than I.
A room, a room, brave gallants! Room!
And give us room to reign –   10
We are come to show our activity
On a merry Christmas time.
If you don't believe what I do say,
Enter St George, and clear the way!

St George
In comes I, St George, St George –   15
The man of courage bold,
With sword and spear all by my side,
Hoping to gain a crown of gold.
'Twas I that slew the fiery dragon
And brought him to the slaughter,   20
So by those fairy means I hope
To gain the King of Egypt's daughter.
Seven years was I shut up in a close cave
And after that cast into a prison where I made
My sad and *grievious mourn*.   25
I saved fair Zipporah[17] from the snake.
Which n'other mortal man could undertake.
I fought him most courageously
Until I gained the victory.
Show me the man that dares me!   30

Turkish Knight
I am the man that dares, the Turkish Knight,
Come from native Turkish land to fight.
I'll fight St George, the man of courage bold,
If his blood's hot, I'll quickly make it cold.

St George
Art thou the man the reckonings give?   35

Turkish Knight
I am the man the reckonings give
And I'll maintain my honour while I live.
Draw out thy sword and fight,
Pull out thy purse and pay,
For satisfaction I will have   40
Before thou goest away.

They fight

Father Christmas
A room, a room, ye gallants!
Room!
And let the gallant soldier in!

Soldier
In comes I, the valiant soldier,
Cut and Slasher is my name.
Straight from the German wars I came
'Twas me and seven more
That slew eleven score,
All brave marching men o' war
Many a battle I've been in
I'll fight St George, the noble king.

They fight

Father Christmas
A room, a room, ye gallants!
Room!
And let the English Lady in.   55

English Lady
Here am I, the English Lady.

St George
Madam, to thee I humbly bend.

English Lady
I think you not to be my friend.

St George
For why, madam?
Did I ever do you harm?   60

English Lady
Yes, you saucy coxcomb!
Get you gone!

St George
'Saucy coxcomb'?
Madam, that word deserves a stab.

English Lady
A stab from thee the least I fear.   65
Appoint a place: I'll meet thee there,
I'll cross the water at the hour o' five
I'll meet you there, if I'm alive.

St George
I'll cross the water at the hour o' ten
And meet you with a hundred men.   70

English Lady
Halt, halt, St George!
Why not have me for a wife?
See what a beautiful lady I am!

St George
That word from thee deserves a stab.
I'll draw out my knife   75
And end thy worthless life.

Kills English Lady who falls in Father Christmas' arms.

Father Christmas
Doctor, doctor, where bist thee?
Five pound for a noble doctor!
Ten pound for a noble doctor!
Fifteen pound for a noble doctor!   80

Doctor
In comes I a doctor, a doctor sure and good,

With my sword I'll staunch the blood;   45
And I'll be bound by a fifty pound bond
If she doesn't arise and come to me.

She gets up

To the Turkish Knight
Drop of brow, drop of heart,   85
Rise up Jack and do thy part.

He gets up

To the Soldier
Drop of brow, drop of heart,
Rise up Jack and do thy part.

He gets up

Frenchman
In comes I, the Frenchman bold,
And I've sworn by the blood of man   90
That I'll never be controlled . . .
I'm here tonight to plant my tree
To plant my tree of liberty.

St George
Thou Frenchman dog, I'll cut thee down
And give thy flesh unto the groun'.   95
Foully thou hast challenged me
Stand forth thou figure of a tree:
We'll see who gains the victory!

Frenchman falls

Father Christmas (having felt the Frenchman's knee)
Doctor, doctor, where bist thee?
This man's wounded in the knee!   100
Doctor, doctor, play thy part!
This man's wounded in the heart.
Five pound for some noble doctor!
Ten pound for some noble doctor!
Fifteen pound for some noble doctor!   105

Doctor
In comes I, a doctor, a doctor pure and good,
And with my glittering sword I'll staunch his blood.
If the man don't rise and come unto me
I'll be bound in a fifty pound bond
Never to call myself a doctor again.   110

*Touches with his sword the Frenchman who gets up, and both
walk out. Sweet Moll comes in*

St George
Sweet Moll, sweet Moll, where art thou going,
So early and so soon?
I've something to say
If yet thou canst stay.

Sweet Moll
What hast thou got to say to me?   115
Pray tell it to me now;
For I am spending all my time,
And that I cannot tell how.

St George
Thy folks and mine could well agree
That married we should be,   120

So pray pull down thy lofty looks
And fix thy love on me.

Sweet Moll
Think I would wed with thee, thou clown,
And lose my maiden head,
When I could get a handsome man   125
To lie with me in bed?

St George
Ain't I as handsome as you, Sweet Moll,
With my dandy leathern breeches,
And a band all round my middle so small?
Pray give me a few more twitches!   130

Sweet Moll
I must have a little tweeking page
That speaks a peevish tongue,
And a pair of silver buckles
Which ladies oft have on.

St George
Sweet Moll, Sweet Moll, thou hast no need   135
To talk o' suchlike things,
As was never bred up in a palace
Among the lords and dukes and kings.
The little thou hast learnt thereof,
Thou hast almost forgot,   140
And if thou wilt not marry me
Then thou shalt go and rot.

He stabs her. Doctor is then called in with speeches as before

Little Dick Nip
In comes I poor little Dick Nip,
With my big head and little wit;
My head so large, my body's so small   145
Yet I'm the biggest rogue of all.
My forehead's made of brass,
My heart is made of steel,
My trousers touch my ankle bones,
Pray, father, come and feel.   150

Father Christmas feels

Little Man Thomas
In comes I, little man Thomas.
I hope all you good people
Will give me what you promise,
And if you will endeavour
To save man Thomas' life,   155
Then out with your bread and cheese
And here's a pretty knife.

Throws a large knife on the floor

Beelzebub
In comes I, Beelzebub
On my shoulder I carries my club,
In my hand my dripping pan,   160
Don't you think I'm a jolly old man?
A drop of your big vat
Would make us merry and sing.
To have your shillings in our pockets
Would be a very fine thing!   165

All form up in a line and salute

Up to *l.* 54 the version is a normal Hero-Combat action, but diverges at *l.* 55 when the English Lady is called in. *ll.* 57–76 are now better known as the Children's Games 'The Lady on Yonder Hill', 'Sir John and the Lady' and 'The Jew from Spain'[18] which have blended together. After the English Lady is killed *ll.* 77–110 revert roughly to a Hero-Combat sequence although the dialogue diverges slightly. The 'Sweet Moll' passage which follows (*ll.* 111–142) again appears to be an interpolation,[19] similar to those of the Wiltshire versions already mentioned. *ll.* 143–165 are virtually the *Quête* even though Little Dick Nip's last four lines (147–50) rightly belong to a champion's vaunt.

Broken down into episodes in this way the version might appear patchy, but the reverse is, in fact, true. One episode follows on the next as logically as can be expected from any version. The wooing seems more important than the combats, as in the East Midlands, but it is poor by comparison. It is tempting to equate the English Lady and Sweet Moll with the Lady and the Dame of the East Midlands, but there is no valid reason for doing so, particularly as St George rejects them both. One might have expected the Sweet Moll passage to have been sung as it was at Lydiard Millicent and Highworth, but this is not stated. If it were, the parallel between this version and the Wooing versions would have been closer.

It is difficult to decide now the place of folk song in the dramatic actions. It was an integral part of Sword Dance and Wooing versions, but not of the Hero-Combat actions. The problem is to decide whether or not the songs were originally an integral part of the actions, or alternatively, if they were put in for added attraction. If the texts can be said to be meaningless accretions, and the original ceremony was a mime, then if one goes back far enough the song has no place unless it developed from a rhythmic accompaniment to any dancing of the primitive performers. The songs can and do exist separately from the dramatic action: where this is so it seems likely that they have been divorced from their natural setting. For instance, in the Midland Counties there once was a 'Poor Old Horse' action whose dialogue was very similar to the Wild Horse passages of the Cheshire texts. Part of this was sung, but the 'Poor Old Horse' song did exist independently of its action and here it made very little sense by comparison with the action as a whole. It is probably true to say that the songs which are embedded in the mummers' dramatic action really did belong there, and those which have them still are the most complete of all. Even so, the Sweet Moll passage is not a very plausible interlude like so much of the ceremony as it exists now.

It is, however, a trace of a wooing which occurs in more than one isolated example and this distribution may be part of the regionalism already noted. This could argue that more examples could be found in the same area if one knew where to look. It may be that they should be taken as evidence of older versions which collectors were able to note before they disappeared entirely. Why they should have existed in this one corner of England is difficult to understand, especially as there are no visible links with the area which formerly supported the Wooing Play proper.

One final example remains to be noted. Its location was in Kent, but nothing more definite than this is known. At first sight it is anything but a dramatic ceremony, but was described as a 'Mummers' Play' by is collector.[20] There are three characters, A, B, and a

Doctor. B is clearly a 'Female' and her dialogue with A follows *ll.* 57–73 of the Broadway version almost exactly.[21] After this, the remainder runs:

B
. . . But stay, sir, do you not want a wife,
To speak English, Scotch and French.

A
Before I'd take you for my wife
I'd take a sword and end my life

Stabs himself

B
Oh, doctor, doctor, is he dead?

Doctor
Not dead, but in a trance,
Arise, and let us have a dance.

All seize hands and dance around

Comment on the similarity between these lines and the Children's Games has already been made. As a dramatic action it could not be shorter, but it contains all the in-gredients necessary for the ceremony – Wooing, Death, Revival and Dance – even if oddly expressed.

There remains the inference to be drawn from these examples. There is no doubt that they existed and were performed. Consequently they cannot be ignored, but it is debatable if 'abnormal' is the correct word to use in describing them. If all the types already discussed are part and parcel of one manifestation, each of which has gone its own separate path for some reason, then these 'abnormal' versions could be the connecting link be-tween them all. Although the Wooing is undeveloped by comparison with the East Midlands' versions, it is never-theless present. It could well be that the typical Hero-Combat version is the real abnormality and that the versions discussed in this chapter survived, for the most part, the bowdlerisation imposed by 'good taste'. They may be relics of an older, more robust ceremony which failed to succumb to the intervention of well-meaning editors. They show more clearly the existence of two couples than any Hero-Combat version, but there is no evidence for a third generation. Instead of the Fool being the pivotal character, the Broadway version has St George, in whom it is difficult to see any vestiges of the Fool. He has the typical St George lines found elsewhere and these bear no relationship to those of the Fool. The saddest feature of these so-called 'abnormal' texts is that they merely point to a solution; in themselves they solve nothing.

7

The Disguise

Detailed examination of the disguise worn by the performers has so far been deliberately avoided. In accordance with its importance it is worth separate consideration, for even in survivals the sense of cer-emonial is best preserved in the time of appearance and the efforts made to prevent recognition. As already indicated, it was a fundamental necessity to preserve anonymity, for to be recognised broke the 'luck'. Even though the disguise may consist of nothing more than a blackened or raddled face, it was sufficient to prevent recognition. Once the action was over the luck-bearers could, for the moment, discard their *rôles* as community medicine men and become their normal selves before passing on to their next calling-place to repeat the magic. Speaking generally for the moment, the disguise, though often showing regional variations, consisted chiefly of strips of material fastened over ordinary clothes so that, in the better examples, almost the whole of the body was concealed (see Plate 8). The headdress was often tall and again covered with strips of material hanging down over the face, so that anonymity was maintained. It was the most important part of the dis-guise which was invariably the last to disappear. In Hampshire, where the costume was best preserved, the strips of paper were often arranged to hang in fringes so that the whole effect appeared 'tiered'. (Plate 9). This type could conceivably be the one which suggested dragon scales. The passage of time brought decline in the disguise particularly in the north of England, where dressing in character became the rule, but even here, knots of ribbon or paper rosettes were often fastened to the costume. Here, too, blackened faces were common, but it cannot be ignored that latterly the performers considered the Turkish Knight's black face as dressing in part.

The anonymity made the performers entirely different beings, remote from their everyday lives. Even in modern survivals there is still an air of ceremony and dispensing magic. It is still considered a breach of eti-quette to recognise a real person as a young American Quaker girl found to her cost.[1] Her recognition of the mumming character of George Washington as the real life Isaac Simmons was a lapse of manners and con-sidered socially incorrect. Evidence of the steps taken to preserve the costume from damage has already been given. At Forkhill, Co. Armagh, the performers took off their disguise after each performance and carried it with them till their next one when they re-disguised them-selves.[2] This kind of evidence underlines the necessity of the disguise, and coupled with its persistence, illustrates its importance.

The flowing strips seem to have been an early feature. The 'most gorgeously be-ribboned shirt' at Exeter in 1737 is a familiar part of any description at any date, even if exactly the same phraseology is not used. Inevitably, the passage of time brought sophistication into what must

Plate 8. Shrewton, Wiltshire, Mummers 1936.

have been originally a crude representation of whatever the performers were trying to represent. The word 'ribbons' is probably a simplification, often used when strips of cloth were meant.[3] In the early accounts it is the strips which were important, not the material of which they were made. The ribbons themselves must have replaced something else used before the narrow fabrics were woven; one can guess that rags or bunches of cloth (fastened in some way to ordinary clothes), were their immediate predecessors. Expense must be reckoned in assessing the material used. Gradually, accounts slip into descriptions of strips of paper or wallpaper. The Marshfield Paper Boys still use a costume made up of strips of newspaper (Plate 10), but it is doubtful if this sort of disguise could be used generally until the middle

of the last century. This was a question of availability and cost; it is certainly doubtful if wallpaper, for example, could be widely used before 1851 when it could be obtained in England for one shilling a roll. Before then it was the prerogative of the wealthy and far beyond the reach of ill-paid traditional performers. Although wallpaper was known in 1509 it was not in general use; one may assume that by 1712 it had become more popular since it was in that year that Queen Anne taxed it at the rate of one penny a square yard. This tax was raised to three halfpence in 1714 and the levy was not repealed till 1836. This must have placed wallpaper beyond the reach of the performers, even though in 1799 there was a French invention for making it in continuous rolls. In 1839, Harold Potter of Darwen patented an improved machine, but even so it took a further twelve years before the price fell considerably.[4] Presumably, if costs had not gone down, dressing in character would have come earlier once the original intention was forgotten by everyone.

The 1823 version from Bassingham shows signs of dressing in character even though ribbons are mentioned:

'Fool drest in cap and trowsers. Lady drest in womans close. Eldest son drest in ribons. Farming man drest in cloth coat boots spirs. Old dame jain, old fashned bonet and bed gown. Old man drest in old fashned hat and long coat. grey hairs. Saint George drest in ribons. Doctor drest. black coat and trawsers white hanchief.[5]

The characteristic disguise in the East Midlands persisted until much later in the century, but there were still oddities. At Ashby, *circa* 1862–1872, one man was blacked and dressed all in yellow with a yellow hat, curved in shape like a horn, with the curved end pointing over one shoulder.[6] Although the character was unnamed, this might have been a representation of Beelzebub who, at Carlton-le-Moorland was described as having a black face and wearing a horned hat and stuffed coat.[7] At South Scarle, Beelzebub wore his working clothes covered by an inverted sack with slits for head and arms pulled over. The sack was stuffed thickly with straw which a string run round the bottom kept in place.[8] These descriptions suggest an attempt to portray a devil (Fig. 7),[9] and the padding may have been protec-

Plate 9. Netley Abbey, Hampshire, Mummers, *c.* 1892.

Plate 10. Marshfield Mummers ('Paper Boys'). Note the mat, on to which the victim falls in order to keep his costume clean.

tion when he was struck by anything. This is dressing in character, not a characterisation of a scapegoat as has been popularly suggested.

Disguise of other performers is more interesting and shows two distinct types. An account from an unlocated place in Lincolnshire[10] describes the Fool as 'combining the Wild Man and Jester in one'. He wore a conical cap covered with shreds. Other characters were described as being covered with bunches of gaudy coloured ribbons. Presumably, the Fool's conical cap represented his jester

half and the shreds the Wild Man side of his character. According to an account from Kirton in Lindsey,[11] the Wild Man feature predominated, for there it was said that he should be dressed in skins or snippets of brightly coloured rags. The description of the Fool at South Kelsey in 1896 is interesting.[12] He wore:

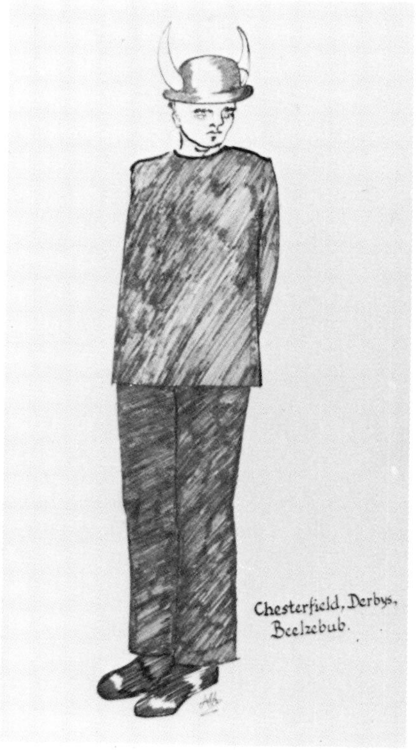

'A Clown's dress; right leg of trousers rings of red, white, blue and black – red at ankle; left leg rings of black, blue, white and red – black at ankle; smock, one sleeve red, one sleeve white; front blue and black; back white, decorated with broad arrow in . . .; dunce's cap about 2' 6" tall with rings of red, white, blue and black and a bell at the point; face painted, moustache, long shepherd's crook in his hand and a collecting box. The fool collected the money.' (Fig. 8)

The rest of the performers of this version were dressed in character, but the Fool's costume showed an elaboration formerly common. It was an exaggerated attempt to portray the parti-coloured Fool with one foot in each world.

This particular costume cannot really be said to be typical of the area where the performers relied heavily on ribbons, giving one character at least the name 'Ribboner'. The Branston coats[13] and Messingham smocks[14] were certainly decorated with ribbons. The latter 'smocks' were, in fact, white shirts worn over ordinary clothes, but the smock was the basis of the second type of disguise familiar in the area. To it were often appliquéd the cut out shapes of farm animals and implements; a motif repeated in the Fool's trousers at Branston.[15] The best example of this disguise was at Cropwell, Nottinghamshire, where the smocks were made of unbleached Holland with appliquéd farm animals. Here, the animals were interpreted widely and included not only the higher farm animals but also the farm dog, a mouse and, for some unexplained reason, the farmer's daughter.[16] In its lowest form this type of disguise was an old white shirt with patches sewn on.[17]

The East Midlands headdress reached a standard of

Figure 7. Beelzebub, Chesterfield, Derbyshire.

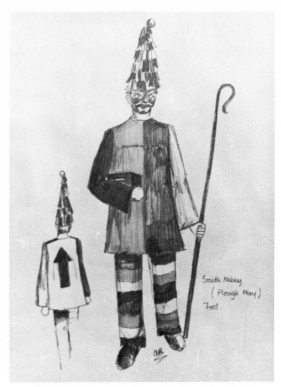

Figure 8. South Kelsey Wooing Play Fool.

excellence not seen elsewhere. The basis was a tall beaver used as a framework for a tube of cardboard. On this were fastened brooches, watches, chains, ribbons, bracelets – almost anything glittering and precious that could be borrowed. These hats were trimmed by the ladies, and once decorated, were so heavy that the performers used to carry them by hand when not performing. At Alkborough, the hats weighed at least seven pounds each;[18] the jewellery here not only decorated the crown but also hung from the brim. It is said that there was as much as five pounds worth of jewellery on one hat, so much indeed, that the 'Female' who wore it did not take part in the rough bits of the action for fear of loss or damage.[19]

The use of bright things as a means of reflecting away evil was widespread, though it did not normally reach such an elaborate degree amongst the Ploughboys and was usually limited to the wearing of mirrors on hats or jackets as in some sword dance teams. Here again, early accounts speak of ribbons plentifully decorating the costume. The Greatham performers wore tunics, often red military ones, plentifully decorated with ribbons, ordinary trousers with a red stripe down the side, and pill-box hats. The King's uniform was more ornate than the others and he often wore a sergeant's tunic instead of a private's. The Clowns wore old patched clothes, had black faces and carried 'toy' swords. The Doctor wore a top hat, frock coat, black trousers and carried a Gladstone bag.[20] The quasi-military dress was common amongst the sword dancers and again it is suggested that this was a late development to accord with what had become thought of as a military exercise. Plates 11 and 12 show this development at Bellerby clearly. Circa 1840, the Hampsthwaite performers wore white trousers and jackets plentifully covered with ribbons,[21] a feature latterly only preserved in the disguise of the ceremony's Fools and 'Females'. At Sleights,[22] the Toms wore loose

tunics of bright patterned stuff with a woollen fringe round the lower edge and yoke, and covered with tags of lace, bunches of ribbons, rosettes, feathers, patches of coloured cloth or silk cut into various shapes – birds and animals of all kinds, squares, stars, circles, diamonds, etc. Sewn to their backs were pictures of ploughs and horses. Their trousers were similarly made and decorated. Their hats were made of straw, very large and completely hidden beneath a pile of artificial flowers, ribbons, coloured crimped paper and feathers. Their faces were blackened, either wholly or partially, and they wore beards made of black, white or red wool. This was done deliberately so that 'no-one might know them'. With these Toms went a King and Queen, walking arm-in-arm, who were treated with respect by the remainder of the performers. Of the Queen at Ampleforth it was said that 'he hadn't had his hair cut for eighteen months, so it was frizzy and long'.[23] There are frequent accounts of the Fool wearing a fox's skin, as at Hexham between 1860–70,[24] whilst at Arkengarthdale in 1869, he wore a robe or cloak of dark crimson tatters, a headdress of the same colour with an appendage like a fox's tail.[25] At Richmond in 1814 he was described as being covered with skins, with again a hairy cap with a fox's tail hanging down his back.[26] The Grenoside captain still wears a cap with a rabbit skin and head on it and, as at Murton, the cap is knocked off by the lock of swords to symbolise the Tommy's death. Similarly, at Escrick, when Woody Garius was executed, his hat was tipped off by one of the dancers and was said to be done expressly to emphasise his death.[27]

The Escrick dancers wore high silk hats decorated with ribbons and artificial flowers, with four sprigs of ivy or holly with gilded berries fixed round the outer edge of the crown, but these were not worn during the performance.[28] Similarly, at Askham Richard, the performers wore top hats with ribbons, but when dancing was resumed the hats were removed and wreaths of artificial flowers worn instead.[29] These two accounts, amongst others, argue the importance of the headgear; it was too important to suffer damage during the course of the dance. This may point to a reason why the Rapper dancers generally do not wear a headdress; the speed and close-knit nature of their dance would make any form of headgear difficult to keep on their heads. Furthermore, the profusion of ribbons noted elsewhere does not seem to exist amongst these dancers. The basis of the costume is generally a white shirt and hoggers, loose-kneed breeches worn by the miners in their everyday work, to which rosettes are pinned uniformly to back and breast, with a sash worn round the waist. This disguise relied more on uniformity than the random fixing of streamers and fringes typical elsewhere.

The pseudo-military uniform must be evidence of decadence. The Goathland performers, with a similar action to Sleights, divided into three sets who wore respectively, tunics of orange, pink and blue, the colours of the local political parties.[30] As the dance became the more attractive feature of the ceremony, the tendency to dress the part more appropriately must have grown. The pink tunics originally worn by the Loftus performers were deliberately replaced by military uniforms because they were considered 'more appropriate'.[31] There was still a desire to 'dress up', to appear in a 'correct costume', or whatever had become correct as understanding died.

This move was, however, resisted by the Hero-Combat performers outside the north of England until a

Plate 11. Bellerby, Yorkshire, Sword Dancers. Old Costume *c.* 1872. (This is one of a pair of photographs which are the oldest ones known of a sword-dance team).

Plate 12. Bellerby, Yorkshire, Sword Dancers *circa* 1926.

relatively late date, and the strips of paper or ribbon continued to be worn on everyday dress until the ceremony died. The blackened or raddled faces were frequent; at Brimington, Derbyshire, the King of Egypt had a copper coloured face,[32] though this probably was dressing in character. At South Cerney, Gloucestershire, the Doctor's face was covered in flour,[33] whilst at Eastwood in the West Riding, a character called Old Oyster Bally wore a beard in addition to having a black face.[34] In places there were vestiges of the disguise worn by sword dancers and ploughboys. At Thenford, Northamptonshire, Beelzebub wore a jacket covered with patches of different colours, and a paper cap, whilst one of the combatants, Activity, wore a fox or hare skin cap and a tippet. His opponent, Age, wore a smock-frock covered with rags and a high cap with a sprig of holly.[35] The effect of a smock could be achieved, as said before, by wearing a shirt over trousers. At Heysham, Lancashire,[36] in an area where a smock had no doubt become an uncommon item of clothing, it was a convenient means of simulating one. Fig. 9 shows a similar disguise from Ireland where the smock was completely unknown; at Ballymore, Co. Armagh, the long shirts were fastened at the waist by a coloured scarf.[37] It is not necessarily a sign of decadence but merely a means of adapting what there was to a common disguise.

The report from Uttoxeter, Staffordshire, of guisers being dressed from head to foot in feathers, like angels in mystery plays, was not substantiated at Christmas, 1964, when the feathers were restricted to a band round a bowler hat, Red Indian fashion, with ribbons fastened to their coats.[38] A simple disguise was merely to wear a coat inside out, a relic of the belief that to do so made the wearer invisible to fairies. This is common in the north of England. At Bramber, Sussex, the performers were dressed like clowns and some had paper or glazed lining costumes,[39] but at Buttermere, Wiltshire, they wore

strips of coloured wallpaper which hid all but their corduroy trousers and heavy boots.[40] In the Hero-Combat actions the hats were still the most important feature, usually being described as 'tall helmets'. The most common type was the tall pointed dunce's cap, as at Guilden Sutton, Cheshire (Fig. 10), or Bagendon, Gloucestershire,[51] where coloured cut-out paper stars were stuck on. The Midgley hats are the most elaborate in the north (Plate 13) and are described as follows:

'. . . a large helmet made of cardboard. The base is from a foot to a foot and a half square with a rim attached underneath to hold on to the head. From each corner arches rise, and cross, these being decorated with coloured tissue paper, as indeed the whole helmet is. Suspended from the arches are one or two bells which tinkle on motion. Suspended from each of the four sides of the square pasteboard are long strips of coloured beads stretching down to the chest.'[42]

These very elaborate headdresses are reminiscent of those worn by the Andover Jolly Jacks which are equally distinctive in their own way. (Plate 14) Here and there are hats suggestive of the elaborate East Midlands variety, for example, at Stockport, Cheshire (Fig. 11), where they were tall and decorated with gold, beads and other trinkets, the rest of the costume being 'somewhat in the style of Morris dancers' – white shirt sleeves and trousers, and red ribbons and handkerchiefs, arranged uniformly. In Cornwall, besides similar shirts and trousers, the pasteboard caps were tall and again decorated with beads, small pieces of mirror and coloured paper with strips of pith hanging from the top.[43] At Bitterne, Hampshire, although unusually for this part of England, the main costume had dwindled to blue trousers and red jackets, the hats were still tall and decorated with flowers and beads in front (Fig. 12).

Figure 9.
Knockloughrim, east county Derry, Mummer.

Figure 10.
Guilden Sutton, Cheshire, Mummer.

Figure 11.
Stockport Mummer *circa* 1890.

Figure 12.
Bitterne, Hampshire, Mummer.

This costume is part decadent, part traditional. Decadence in the Hero-Combat disguise is more obvious than in either of the other types mainly because there are more examples from which to choose. It is expressed in two ways, either by over-elaboration or over-simplification. An example of the former is found in Thomas Hardy's description in *The Return of the Native* where he makes it plain that the womenfolk played their part in dressing the local performers. He says:

'The girls could never be brought to respect tradition in designing and decorating the armour. They insisted on attaching loops and bows of silk and velvet in any situation pleasing to their taste. Gorget, gusset, bassinet, cuirass, gauntlet, sleeve, all alike in the view of these feminine eyes were practicable spaces whereon to sew scraps of fluttering color.'[44]

Although this account was probably somewhat over-written to fulfil the needs of a fictional narrative, there was obviously some feminine disregard for the fluttering strips of paper or ribbon which was more typical. Charlotte M. Yonge gives some support to Hardy's description.[45] In describing the costume of the Otterbourne, Hampshire, mummers, she spoke of bows of ribbon everywhere sewn to white trousers and shirt sleeves and described 'tall helmets made of wallpaper' (Fig. 13). Both these accounts were fiction based on fact, though Hardy particularly carefully stressed in his letters that every ancient superstition used in his works was rooted in truth, no detail being invented to amuse the reading public.[46] His account at least must be accepted. Furthermore, it is historical fact that in the north-west the men danced the Morris but the women dressed the hats ready for the competition for the best dressed hat. This became as traditional as the ceremonial itself.

Plate 13. Midgley, Yorkshire, Pace-Egger.

Figure 13.
Otterbourne, Hampshire, Mummer.

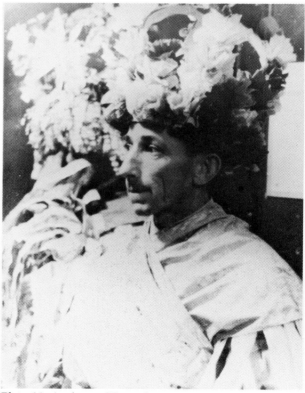

Plate 14. Andover, Hampshire, Mummer. Compare hats with Midgley hats, plate 13.

Simplification on the other hand, led to dressing in character. This is considered decadent, but still denotes some effort on the part of the performers. In the West Country, the disguise reached the elaborate proportions of a costume play on the legitimate stage. The Minehead performers shown on Plate 15 wear costume which could have almost been hired from a theatrical costumier, but two characters, who appear to be combatants, still wear tall hats made of paper with a geometrical design on them. This dressing up is not really exceptional since in Cheshire, the Soulers showed an almost identical degree of outfitting. The Wild Horse's Driver was invariably dressed in hunting clothes and the combatants on ex-military uniforms. This type of costume took the form of anything ready to hand however. Fat Jack, a *quête* character from Chesterfield, Derbyshire, was described as wearing coarse sacking trousers, a much torn jacket and a battered hat, as though he were wearing any old cast-off clothing available (Fig. 14). Often the total effect was anachronistic, a combatant in a 1914–18 uniform could engage an opponent in a Crimean uniform, whilst around them could be a variety of characters dressed in the costumes of any period.

Throughout the whole range of disguise there is evident a need to preserve anonymity, but it is extremely unlikely that later performers understood why even if they insisted on it. The main types of traditional decoration were the streamers worn over ordinary clothes and the cut-out shapes of farm animals, etc., appliqued to a smock or shirt worn over ordinary clothes. By no stretch of imagination could the latter show any resemblance to dragon's scales, nor does it seem likely that the former were used with the same intent by performers not only in this country but also abroad. There must be a much more fundamental belief behind the adoption of this fringed disguise than was obvious to even the performers who wore it. Chambers listed three suggestions which others before him had inferred from the disguise.[47] G. L. Gomme saw it as imitation leaves of trees, T. F. Ordish as dragon scales, and P. H. Ditchfield as a 'strange garb resembling sheep skins'. Of the three,

Figure 14. Fat Jack, Chesterfield, Derbyshire.

Chambers inclined to the last suggestion, because he had formed the same impression from seeing photographs of Hampshire examples. None of the three is entirely satisfactory, though the first and the last may contain some elements of the correct way of looking at the disguise. The commentator who described the Fool's costume in Lincolnshire as being a 'combination of the Wild Man and Jester' may also have had some justice in his comment.

Plate 15. Minehead Mummers.

44

The Wild Man is a familiar figure in art and literature from a very early date. It has been described generally as:

'a hairy man curiously compunded of human and animal traits, without, however, sinking to the level of an ape. It exhibits upon its naked human anatomy a growth of fur, leaving bare only its face, feet and hands, or the breasts of the female of the species. Frequently, the creature is shown wielding a heavy club or mace, or the trunk of a tree; and since its body is usually naked except for a shaggy covering, it may hide its nudity under a strand of twisted foliage worn around the loins.'[48]

This description does not tally exactly with the overall effect of the mummers' disguise, but illustrations of the character show an affinity with the dependent fringes. The Wild Man is known as a character in Folk Ceremonials from an early date. Pieter Breughel the Elder, in a woodcut of the Play of the death of the Wild Man, shows him wearing a costume which could be an art form of the Hampshire disguise. In Switzerland the character is known as a protector of cattle and at Obertsdorf in the Bavarian Alps a Wild Man dance is still performed, with its roots in what appears to have been originally a cattleman's celebration.[49] Frequently, such festivals involved the death of the Wild Man who was brought back to life by a quack doctor. Often, the character is part of the traditional Winter Carnival, though not under the Wild Man name. For example, the *Plaetzlimanli* in the Aargau canton, Switzerland, wears a disguise consisting of small bits of rags sewn on to a garment, and in the neighbourhood of Garmisch, Bavaria, there is the *Flecklegeand*, a man in a patched garment.[50] These two, among many others begin to show an affinity with the English disguise, but it is extremely doubtful that the English performers represented the Wild Man as typified abroad. He appears to be related to Silenus, the Greek God of the wooded mountainside, who, when appearing in plays, wore a close-fitting garment with glued-on tufts to imitate animal fur.[51] The connection between the Wild Man and animals and woods is very clear.

Similarly, the connection between the English disguise and natural surroundings, though perhaps not so obvious, is still present in two varieties. First, the fringed costume, once fairly general over the whole country, and second, the smock, or pseudo-smock, with cut-out shapes of animals, which had a reasonably scattered pattern of distribution. These can be said to express a desire of the performers to be associated with that with which they were most familiar. Individual gangs in the East Midlands were often made up of the workers on one farm; some of whom, if not all, must have had some connection with the farm animals. The appliqued animal costume can be described as a form of 'animal disguise'. Perhaps in its early form the latter would have been made entirely of straw, as it still is in some of the Irish examples. Paper or cloth replaced the straw as it was more tractable to handle and less cumbersome to wear. This disguise could have had as its primary object the fertility of the crops, whilst the animal disguise was directed at the cattle for whom the performers were responsible. Whether or not the tufts of fur or skins which some performers wore in the sword dance ceremonies ever had any connection with the Wild Man character is debatable. If they did, it must have been a long time before the dance became primarily the concern of miners. Nevertheless, these performers could have been carrying the 'luck' to people of more agrarian pursuits and consequently wore a suitable disguise. Whatever the original purpose, the suggestion that dragon scales or armoured knights were intended by the costume is irrelevant. At the same time, there is no doubt that latter day perfomers, probably even those who were recorded in the earliest descriptions, were unaware of the significance of their disguise, but accepted it as part of the tradition they were faithfully observing.

8

Abroad

The interpretation of the fragments left in the British Isles is difficult because they are a confused jumble of local interpretations and misunderstood ceremony. Actions which spread to Ireland and the New World merely underline the tenacity of the ceremony; the form in which they persisted shows them to be variants on the English pattern. It is not generally appreciated that what is found in the British Isles has, or had its counterpart elsewhere, particularly in Europe, and it is these which help to explain what our performers were about. The ceremony was so widespread that accidental development can be ruled out. Its roots must lie in a fundamental belief, long forgotten, but deep-rooted enough to make it persist with a recognisable shape. An individual ceremony of any of the three types taken in isolation, contributes nothing to the understanding of its nature, but by setting them all side by side it is possible to see some pattern taking shape. Even then, what is left in England cannot, by itself, provide a complete answer to what the performers were about. The explanation must be sought by setting the English ceremonies side by side with similar ceremonies known to have existed in the non-English-speaking world.

Some of these ceremonies have already been mentioned briefly. Sword dances are found in Europe, some bearing traces of the ceremony with which we are concerned. Others, like so many of our own, have lost all but the spectacular dance. It is safe to say that our sword dance ceremonies and those of the continent of Europe are of common stock, and the older examples probably had a complete dramatic action as part and parcel of the ceremony. The story of European survivals is much the same as in England; ceremonies have been forgotten, revived, 'improved', parts lost, and parts inserted and amended as sophistication grew, but if fragments are pieced together, a much clearer basic ceremony emerges.

One of the most interesting comes from La Soule in the French western Pyrenees, where the Basque people still perform a version. In La Basse Soule, the companies were sixty to eighty strong, in La Haute Soule about twenty-five. They were divided into Les Rouges and Les Noirs, or the Beautifuls and Uglies. The central figure of Les Rouges was the *Chibalet* or *Zamalzain*, a hobby-horse character, whose construction was a sophisticated version of the East Midlands hobby-horses, but in the horse-and-rider type found most frequently on the Continent. His costume was ornate; the breastplate had gold studs and buttons specially made. Though elaborate, the disguise still retained features preserved in a more primitive form in England. With this character was a *Kantiniersa*, or *La Cantinière*, introduced *circa* 1888 when her predecessor, a *Bohemiènne*, or gypsy girl, was considered too obscene and was dropped. Also present were a *Tcherrero*, or *La Balayeur*, who carried a stick topped by a horse's tail, *Le Chat*, probably the Fool of the troupe, *Porte-drapeau*, an older man and a good dancer, six to twelve *Kullaleros* who danced a simple processional dance, and some shoeing smiths, carrying the tools of their trade and fly-whisks made of horse-hair. There were two couples, one of a man in evening dress and wearing a tall hat who was accompanied by a boy in a clean white frock and wearing a white hat with a veil. The other couple wore dark clothes and carried bullock goads. All these characters were attendants on the horse.

By contrast, Les Noirs were dirty and ragged, with muddy boots and battered hats. Amongst them were Tinkers wearing old clothes and carrying tools and metal utensils, Knife-grinders with stool, wheel and outfit, Gypsies who were the wildest people of the village, and finally, two Gelders wearing leather gaiters and carrying a bag of food and the instruments of their trade.

The ceremony took place in Spring in a period running from New Year's Day to Lent, occurring when parties were invited to visit other villages. On arrival at the village, they were stopped by rope barriers before each of which they danced and finally jumped over. Les Rouges led with Les Noirs behind behaving rudely. This continued all morning; after lunch, all went back to the dancing ground. The Gypsies carried one of their number around who kicked his feet in the spectators' facts to keep them back. There was a great deal of dancing – chain dances, solo dances, and finally, the Wine Glass Dance when each performer danced in turn round a three-inch diameter wine glass half full of red wine, ending by standing on it, except the Hobby-horse who made the sign of the Cross over it.

So far, none of this appears to be relevant, but next a sword was given to the Knife-grinder to sharpen and the master grinder and his man set to work, the latter singing an insolent song about his master who eventually realised what was happening. They fought and the man ran away vowing that he would work no longer.[1] The sword was finally sharpened with the help of an old man. Latterly, the episode died there, but previously it was prolonged. A Barber appeared amongst Les Noirs, and he shaved the Master grinder and finally cut his throat. A Doctor was summoned who gave an account of his travels:

'I have travelled in Armenia and Italy;
In Africa and America.'

and revived the Grinder. The Tinkers mended a pot, not a plough as elsewhere, and the Tinker's wife gave birth to a child on the dancing floor. This incident too, had been censored. The Gelders, assisted by the Tinkers, caught the Hobby-horse and gelded it[2] throwing up two corks in proof. Then they walked it round till it had regained strength enough to dance again. During this dance the horse leaped higher and higher until it was finally hoisted on a 'lock' of crossed hands.[3]

The similarities between this ceremony and the English fragments are obvious. The dance has become dominant and indeed, the Basque performers are justly known for their Wine Glass Dance and not for the action which it once supported. It is significant that the fragments considered obscene have been dropped, but as with most ceremonials, the headdress has been retained. This was complete with ribbons, artificial flowers and mirrors, so that the old magic of disguise had not entirely disappeared. Indeed, retention of disguise was as persistent outside England as it was inside. In Switzerland in Spring, performers wearing a leafy disguise included a Wild Man,[4] who came down from the mountains holding a whole fir tree as a club, to meet characters who were trying to trap him. These included a Fool, a Barber who was also the Doctor, and the Bride. The Wild Man was tempted to drink a glass of Schnapps which overcame him, and he was bound. The villagers put him on trial for the sins of the cold and want of winter and their judgment was death. He died, was lamented by the Bride, revived by the Doctor with his brush, and danced with the Bride.[5] In Bavaria an almost similar Wild Man appeared in an incomplete ceremony. At Whitsuntide the *Pfingstl*, dressed in leaves and water plants and wearing a cap made of peonies, was soused with water, and, in mime, was decapitated.[6] In Saxony and Thuringia, a similar Wild Man, covered with leaves and moss, was hunted in a wood, caught and executed.[7] A lad dressed as a doctor affected a cure by bleeding him.[8] In Swabia on Shrove Tuesday, a 'Doctor Eisenhart' bled a man to death, then revived him by blowing air into him through a tube.[9] The underlying motive of these ceremonies was the constant one of bringing fertility to all, and the leafy disguise of the so-called Wild Men stresses the connection with the Vegetation Spirit.[10]

These few examples illustrate the basic belief that to mime the death of winter and bring the victim to life again as the young Spring would help to speed along the flow of the seasons. In Roumania the purpose was extended to making the performers healers of the sick. Sick children were laid on the ground so that the dancers could dance over them with the object of bringing them back to health and giving them the nimbleness of the dancers themselves. These dancers were the *Calusari*, the little Horse dancers, who used to appear in the remote villages of the country. In the eighteenth century they were described as wearing female clothes, speaking like women, wearing wreaths of flowers on their heads, having faces disguised with white veils and each carrying a naked sword.[11] Their Leader was a flag-bearer who carried a stick with a cloth containing some garlic, reputedly having magical powers. In the company were mutes, comic characters carrying swords or whips, who hit out with them to drive out evil spirits. In some districts the mutes mimed obscene actions with the *Calusari* and were killed and revived. In the eighteenth century they wore masks like stork's heads, whose beaks were worked with string. Near Brasor the death and revival of the mute used to be the principal part of the ceremony, but gradually this was dropped in favour of the dance alone.

By extreme good fortune a performance of the primitive action was filmed *circa* 1939 by a chance visitor.[12] It shows how much of the action was expressed in dance and mime, and how much the disguise had persisted. The mute had a mask made from the skin of a freshly flayed goat, worn bloody side out, with the tail forming the beard. The hats of the dancers were, as usual, spendidly decorated. The action of the ceremony can be summarised as follows. Four men, holding poles horizontally between them, formed a square to represent a castle. Throughout the whole action they 'danced', or rather shuffled their feet. This particular performance was given by two teams and there were consequently two mutes, one of whom brought a cloth and hung it on one of the poles to represent a window. He then took possession of the castle and brought a chair and a piece of sacking for a carpet to furnish it. There was by-play between the mutes as each tried to claim the castle by fighting for it; one began to kill lice with a wooden phallus whilst the other tried to saw off the first's head using his phallus as a saw. One of them took off his shirt to delouse it. Next came a procession led by the Turkish overlord wearing a white dress, a wide red cummerbund and a fez. He was smoking a bullrush soaked in paraffin to represent a pipe, and carried a whip. To let him enter the castle, one of the men forming the walls released his stick which opened like a door. The mutes had to go through the walls. Once inside, the overlord was in possession of the castle, from which he ran out periodically to lash the crowd with his whip and to collect dues and tribute. The mutes took his absences as opportunities to re-enter the castle but left as soon as he returned. Finally, the Turk assumed full occupation and looked for a Bride. She entered in procession, veiled and accompanied by the mutes, bringing with her a distaff with which she was spinning throughout the action. The Turk registered matrimonial conditions with this 'Female', but occasionally left the castle to collect his tribute. Whilst he was away, the mutes returned and tormented the wife. Ultimately, the Turk and his wife were shown as an old settled married couple who went for a walk in the garden of their house. The walk took the form of a gentle dance movement.

Then entered the Russian, an obnoxious character, dressed in red rags roughly bound round him, spitting vodka from a bottle and splashing the liquor over the watching crowd. He carried a whip also. Behind him was a priest of the Orthodox Church riding in a wheelbarrow and dragging his begging bowl behind him. The Russian entered the castle and attacked the wife, being discovered doing so by the Turk. The fight which followed was carried out by their lashing each other with whips and was repeated several times. The Russian was so drunk that he did not understand what was happening when the Turk singed his nose with the hot 'pipe', and he made continuous attacks. By this time the wife had accepted the Russian's advances and the Turk had lost interest in her. The Russian danced with her and forced vodka down her throat, and ultimately, the priest entered and attacked her. The Turk sought revenge for this and drove the priest all round the compound, holding him by the begging bowl and beating him with his whip. The Russian rescued the priest who hobbled off, climbed a nearby roof where, in pantomime, he acted God the Father giving Moses the Commandments.

Whilst the priest was on the roof, a shot was fired and the Turk was killed. The wife arranged the body and covered its face with a cloth. The Russian went over to the Priest and told him to bury the Turk, but the Priest refused. The Russian, now triumphant, spilt more vodka over the wife who was mourning over the body. The mutes again performed an obscene mime with her as she was lamenting. The Priest was brought in in his wheelbarrow but first refused to conduct the funeral. Later, he carried out a perfunctory Christian burial service over the infidel Turk. The Russian again insulted the widow, and finally, in the last details of the burial, sat on the victim's head. The body was then raised by the men who formed the walls, and was borne away followed by the villagers. There was no revival.

This completed the main action on the film which went on however, to show isolated shots of *Calusari* from elsewhere. At Slobozia they were shown preparing their standard by binding on the garlic and kerchief to the pole. The Captain did the binding whilst the members of the team held the post which was raised and brought forward. The mute put his phallus to the pole and the fiddler his bow, thus forming an arch. The team formed a chain, holding their sticks horizontally, and walked round the pole under the arch. Then the dancers lay on the ground and the captain, bearing the pole, and followed by the standard bearer, musicians and lastly the mute, stepped over them. Then followed the bastinado where each member of the team was struck on the thighs and soles of the feet to drive out evil, the mute using his phallus for the purpose. He escaped his own beating with a back somersault but was finally caught and received his beating to conclude the initiation ceremony.

At Falfani the mute was disguised as a bull with horns and led the procession in two instances with a great extended phallus. It was here that the dancers danced over the sick children. At Bukovina there was a New Year's dance of masked village boys. The characters included an old man carrying a broken wheel, a Hobbyhorse and Jew, a Bear[13] and Gypsy, a Bride and Groom, and old men who acted a mime of harvesting. The Bear and Gypsy danced together, the Hobby-horse danced with the Jew and the Bride with the Groom. The old men worked with harvest forks. The Bear died and the Gypsy struck him gently with two sticks in an effort to revive him. He turned him round and tried to pull him up, but the Bear fell again. The Bear took the broken wheel and was finally turned widdershins, which revived him.

The last extract, also from Slobozia, showed the mute with an animal mask and carrying a wooden phallus and crook with a red binding. The main company danced round their standard, the mute turning somersaults and dancing in his own way. He had taken a pot full of water from a house and poured the water over his head, throwing the pot high in the air. This was supposed to kill drought. The dancers formed a three-man high pyramid, holding the posts. This was to represent a good harvest with high stacks of corn and it was repeated twice. The next piece is missing from the film but showed the men dancing on all fours, face down, whilst the mute brought a puppy which he castrated whilst the dance continued. Finally, the poles were thrown on the ground and the men danced with hands on each other's shoulders whilst the mute dragged women from the crowd into the field.

The action revealed on this film took place before the ceremony had declined considerably. The lack of a revival may imply that it had already been lost if it had ever existed. The performers who were filmed were still

47

living in comparatively primitive conditions, and consequently much of the mime, although considered obscene by modern standards, was accepted as part and parcel of the action. The behaviour of the mutes in particular is capable of offence today. Apart from its other features, the enclosure of a space by a ring of linked performers is of special interest when considered in relationship to that of the sword-dancers. The space enclosed by the *Calusari* was clearly intended to represent a marriage-house in which the married couple set up home. The creation of 'doors' and 'windows' leaves no doubt as to what was intended. The links held by the sword dancers are more likely to have been used to enclose some space than to be the representation of swords which the performers were unlikely to have ever owned. Such marriage houses date from the early periods of pre-history. In the early kingdoms of Mesopotamia a sacred marriage, with parts often played by the king and his daughter, took place inside a fragile 'marriage house' or 'bower'.[14] A sacred marriage was also one of the rituals in the annual cycle of Dionysos; presumably the Roumanian example and possibly the sword dance ceremonies had their roots in a similar primitive custom.

The most complete examples of a primitive ceremony were found in the Balkans where they were noted at the beginning of the century by members of the British School at Athens. Individual examples varied, some were more complete than others, but all bore evidence of belonging to the same rite. A ceremony from Thrace was reported by Dawkins[15] as occurring annually before Lent. The two principal actors, *Kalogheroi*, always married men, wore animal skins padded out with straw over their heads and shoulders. Two bachelors were dressed as Brides, and an elderly 'Female', in rags, carried a piece of wood representing a bastard baby. The rest of the team consisted of two or four 'Gypsies', two or three policemen armed with whips and swords, and a bagpiper. The party collected food and money with or without permission and the whole team considered themselves licensed chicken stealers. The 'Female' and one of the Gypsies performed an obscene mime in front of some of the houses. In the afternoon the Gypsies mimed the forging of a ploughshare, the 'baby' grew and demanded a wife and one of the *Kalogheroi* married one of the Brides. This *Kalogheros* was killed by the other, the Bride lamented his death and he suddenly revived. Next, the Brides were yoked to a real ploughshare which they dragged round the village square while seeds were scattered behind it and the performers cried, 'May wheat be ten piastres the bushel! . . . Yea God, that poor folk may be filled', and other similar invocations.

Wace[16] described a similar ceremony in Thessaly and Southern Macedonia which took place on the eve of the Epiphany. In the parties of about twelve performers, there were four main characters and two semi-choruses. While the latter sang, an Arab molested a Bride and then fought and killed her Bridegroom. The Bride lamented the death and there followed a revival by a comic doctor, often brought about by the insertion of a piece of soap in the dead man's mouth. The performance ended with dancing and an obscene pantomime between the Bride and Groom. Similar characters, without dramatic action, were also reported from Skyros in the Aegean. Following the main characters were often duplicate Brides and Grooms who took no part in the action,[17] but who danced, sang and formed a semi-circle in which it was performed.

The performers in these Balkan ceremonies had their faces hidden behind a cloth, modern pasteboard mask or a piece of fur with eyeholes cut in. Around the waist they often had as many as fifty or sixty bells, hung from the shoulders in such a way as to be loose enough to clash as the performers jumped up and down in the dance. A shepherd's cloak, inside out to show the fleecy lining, was worn over head and shoulders; invariably, a shepherd's crook was carried. (Fig. 15). The 'Females' were grotesque and larger than life. The Doctor latterly was dressed to represent a caricature of a medical student in a black coat, collar, black felt hat. In two instances at least, he refused to make his entry unless he had a horse, and the Old Woman had to carry him on her back.

The similarity of these ceremonies to others of Europe and particularly those of the East Midlands is obvious. Their completeness makes them the touchstone for understanding the English fragments. It is evident that in most Continental examples the dance was beginning to assume more importance than the dramatic action, even though its development was not as complete in the Balkans as it was at La Soule. The primitive analogies of the Witchetty Grub ceremony in Australia and the initiation ceremonies of the American Indians given by Beatty[18] contain the same ingredients of the primitive ceremony. They are a representation of the same fundamental belief expressed in terms of a society which had not advanced to even the same degrees as those of Europe. Whether primitive or 'advanced', the central core of the action is the death and revival of a character. Possibly in primitive times the victim was really slain by his successor as in the sacred grove at Nemi.[19] Whether the death is symbolic of the dead year, the rebirth the symbol of the new, burgeoning year, or whether the revitalisation was to benefit the community in other

Figure 15. Masquerader from Skyros.

48

ways does not matter. The rebirth is the sign of hope – imitative magic to increase fertility and bring luck to the community. It perpetuates the life-cycle which could begin again until, after a further year, it was necessary to repeat it to energise the community again.

Death and resurrection of a god is an old and constant recurring theme in religions. The Thracians believed that Dionysos died and was reborn, the Syrians Adonis, the Phrygians Attis,[20] the Egyptians Osiris, the Greeks Hyppolytus, and in modern times the belief is the central doctrine of the Christian Church.[21] Even today, the sophisticated performers of the Thai classical drama still enact the story of Suwannahongs, who was killed, sought by his wife, restored to life, and reigned in his wife's kingdom after killing the king, his father-in-law.[22] All the classical examples, however ancient, are sophisticated when considered in relationship with the funda-

mental belief. They must be considered attempts at rationalisation. Out of superstition grew myth, out of myth grew legend, and ultimately religion, which partly accounts for the worship of Dionysos and the other gods. Wace notice the resemblance between what he saw in Greece and the Dionysos legend,[23] but it would be wrong to assume that this was the ultimate origin. It was more likely an attempt to explain the inexplicable as the society moved away from its primitive beliefs. It is true that the Festival of Dionysos occurred about Epiphany when most of the English examples appeared, but the real point of the similarities is to show that primitive peoples followed the same pattern of belief. The ceremonial in England merely shows that we were once participants in a rite running parallel to those elsewhere in the world. It was so deep-rooted that it persists in many bowdlerised forms to the present day.

9

The Fragmentation of a Ceremony

It seems reasonably certain that all the ceremonies described had the same basic motive – to propagate fertility, later 'luck'. Their development into the present familiar form leaves open the question as to whether they were always essentially the same in form, or whether what is left in England has fragmented even more than is generally appreciated. The revitalisation ceremony has always been performed by men so far as is known, the women who took part in isolated examples can only be considered fortuitous interlopers. Whether this particular manifestation can be considered in isolation from the other men's ceremonial customs is debatable even though it has no visible connection with them and appears to exist as a self-contained entity. The examination of all these ceremonies is best carried out in the method suggested by Dr Joseph Needham in 1936:[1]

'. . . in probing the origin of the various dance-types and their geographical distribution we should pay more attention to their internal structure and less to their names.'

Dr Needham was referring specifically to the ceremonial dance, but the suggestion is valid for all types of ceremony and has already been followed in the preceding pages of this book.

Dr Needham could find no connection between the ceremonial dance and the drama[2] but there does seem to be an immediate connection which is best seen in the sword dance. Here, drama has dwindled in importance and the dance has developed into an art form in its own right. But any dancing in either Wooing or Hero-Combat sequences is either non-existent or undeveloped. Many Hero-Combat and Wooing actions contain a stage direction towards the end of the performance that the characters 'danced around'. By context, much of this 'dancing around' was nothing but heavy-footed stamping about the room either individually or collectively. Some able performer might perform the Broom Dance, but this was

an unusual degree of elaboration. In some Irish versions a reel was specified, in others a Male and 'Female' danced together; where there was room enough the audience was invited to join in. Even this was unknown in England. The essential difference between the Sword Dance and the other two types is that it demanded space for performance which could only be found normally outdoors, whilst the emphasis of Hero-Combat and Wooing ceremonies was largely on performance inside and any development of the dancing here was inhibited by sheer lack of space.

In two instances, both in Oxfordshire, Morris is mentioned in the Hero-Combat actions. The Thame stage direction has already been noted on page 33, whilst at Islip a stage direction read:

'All dance the Morris. Enters Father Christmas. Performers all dance round him . . .'[3]

but no description of the dance was given. The Thame and Islip versions had an eighteenth century date in common but little else. A possible hidden common factor was the fact that the same sort of people performed dance and drama. When D'Arcy Ferris wanted to revive the Bidford, Warwickshire, Morris it was to the existing mummers' team that he turned.[4] Despite this, the word 'Morris' can be misleading since it is capable of different interpretations at different times. Basically, it is a term used to describe any form of Folk Ceremonial activity which involved a 'luck' procession and the wearing of disguise. Argument has raged about the meaning of the word since the days of Cecil Sharp. Its earliest known mention was in 1458 when a wealthy widow, Alice de Wetenhalle, willed her silver cup, 'sculpt de moreys dauns', to her son. This points to a date of existence earlier than the mid-fifteenth century since the dance would have to be fairly well-established to be worth perpetuating in art. Cecil Sharp used the word to identify a particular dance form he found in the Cotswolds, in contra-distinction to the label 'Sword Dance' for the north-eastern linked dances. Investigation since his days has shown the existence of other Morris than Cotswold, more varied in type, but with the common statement that all were performed by disguised men.

There have been many suggestions about the origins of word 'Morris',[5] from it being a relic of a Roman dancing priesthood to the popular derivation from 'Moorish dance', a theory which ignores the fact that nothing like the English dance has ever been found amongst the Moors. Another suggestion is that John of Gaunt's men brought the dances back from their campaigns, whilst still another makes Eleanor of Castille responsible for their introduction into England. The most inspired suggestion was made by E. K. Chambers:

'. . . the faces were not blackened because the dancers represented Moors, but rather the dancers were thought to represent Moors, because their faces were blackened.'[6]

This was an inversion of thought at the time and is perhaps the most penetrating observation made to date. Carrying it further, it would prove more advantageous if the word 'Morris' were regarded as a synonym for 'disguise'.

A close look at some of the Morris traditions may help to underline this. 'Disguise' in its true sense is difficult to see these days since so much of the dress appears to be 'dressing up'. The best known Morris in the Cotswolds which Sharp correctly considered to be the peak of Folk artistic development, is also in some ways historically the most decadent ritualistically. It has developed into a choreographic folk art but in doing so has shed most of its antique features. The only truly disguised character is the Fool. For the dancers, white shirts and trousers, with bells and baldricks of a stylised pattern have superseded the ribbons formerly worn. Even the ribboned hats have begun to give way to jockey or cricketing caps, no doubt because they are easier to keep on during the dance. The rags and ribbons formerly worn can be seen in the Fools' costumes at Brackley, Northamptonshire (Fig. 16) and Bledington, Gloucestershire (Fig. 17). The resemblance is immediately visible when these are compared with any of the older disguises worn by the performers in the dramatic actions. Yet Tiddy notes the actions of the dance Fool and the dramatic Fool as being distinct.[7] The former, he said, always directs his fooling at somebody, usually abusively, whilst the latter normally reels off patter and nonsense. The dance Fool's activity is communally directed but the dramatic Fool's speech is more of an art product. Tiddy's ultimate conclusion:

'The different types of fooling which distinguish the dance fool and the mummers' fool may conceivably indicate a difference of origin, but more probably, I think, show merely two different stages of development in the fool's long passage from ritual to farce.'

is almost certainly the correct one. The two Fools have gone off in different directions, but this does not mean they were not ceremonial characters of one common stock. It also follows that in the dance ceremonies, the dancers attended on the Fool and not *vice-versâ*. Whether the 'Female' ever existed in the Cotswold traditions is uncertain. The costume of the Brackley Fool which included a skirt, is suggestive. Hilderic Friend, describing the costume in 1884,[8] said:

Figure 16. Brackley, Northamptonshire, Morris Fool.

Figure 17. Bledington, Gloucestershire, Morris Fool.

'I am disposed to think this personage had gradually merged in one the two characters of Fool and Maid Marian[9] who at one time figured in the dances'.

This was an unusual piece of perspicacity at that time. If such a character as 'Maid Marian' ever existed, 'she' must have been a casualty of development. Once her function was misunderstood or forgotten, there would be no purpose in her retention.

The Cotswold tradition has become a sophisticated one. Apart from the isolated processional dance to get the dancers on and off the dancing ground, the dances are set dances for six men. They are as highly developed in their own way as the more specialised sword dance. The guide to the antiquity of a dance tradition may lie in the simplicity of its dance pattern as well as in the persistence of the ceremonial characters. For this reason, the processional dance of the north-west and elsewhere in England must be considered as a ceremony whose artistic development has been halted. This could be because of the nature of the places where it was performed. Compact villages with open spaces are uncommon in the industrial towns of the north-west and the dancers performed whilst moving along the cobbled streets. A moving dance does not permit the elaborate figures of one performed on one spot, but it does retain the processional element for bearing round the 'luck'.

Even though the dance did not develop to a great extent, the costume did, but on a traditional basis. The dancers wore a profusion of ribbons as at Lymm (Plate 16) and Godley Hill, Cheshire,[10] or at Royton, Lancashire.[11] Hats were profusely decorated with ribbons, artificial flowers, rosettes, Christmas tree ornaments, almost anything bright and gaudy, but as they were worn during the dance, they could not be so tall or so decorated as those of the Lincolnshire ploughboys with their watches and chains. This particular Morris often accompanied a rush cart,[12] over the front of whose pyramidical load of rushes was drawn a sheet on which the village's valuables – gold watches, silver chains, copper tea-kettles, &c. – were displayed. This almost exactly duplicates the Lincolnshire hats. At Whitworth, Lancashire, up to 1910 at least, the rush-cart was two-wheeled, and space was left in the centre of the pyramid of rushes for a black-faced man who stayed inside during the procession[13] (Plate 17). It is difficult to avoid thinking of the rush-cart as being a bower of the same *genus* as those noted elsewhere, though the Whitworth example was an exceptional one.

The north-western Morris had no Fool, but it did have a leader who controlled the dance, and often a 'Female', as at Lymm.[14] This 'Female' was known locally as the 'Fool' or 'Maid Marian', and, as at Brackley, there may have been some telescoping of the characters. At Staly-bridge, Cheshire, the 'Female' was black-faced and carried a broom to clear a space for dancing. (Plate 18). Why a 'Female' but not the Fool should persist in the north-west is not clear, except that the Leader who controlled the dance was a logical development of the Fool. The old cry of the Cotswold Fool, 'Six Fools and one dancer' may be a justification. The north-western Leader was invariably the best performer just as the Cotswold Fool had to have considerable dancing ability to fulfil his office. Sometimes, as at Royton, there were two 'centres', small boys who danced between the lines. Their purpose has never been satisfactorily explained, but Dr Karpeles, described them thus:[15]

'Whenever possible, young boys were secured to take the part of the two Centres, and this practice was adhered to even at some inconvenience, for the boys when very young used to be so overcome with fatigue that they had to be carried from place to palce. One is tempted to think that the presence of these boys may have some ritual significance, but any such assumption would need further substantiation, before it could be put forward with any confidence.'

No substantiation has yet been found, but if one could see in the Leader and 'Female' the remnants of an Old Couple, these young Centres may have been the relics of a Young Couple. Their age certainly made them a second

Plate 16. Lymm, Cheshire, Morris dancers with 'Female' *c*. 1900.

Plate 17. Whitworth, Lancashire, Morris and Rushcart.

generation, and they certainly had some long-forgotten ceremonial significance.

The Winster Morris of Derbyshire had a complete collection of ceremonial characters (Plate 19). The dance itself was a simple processional. The dancers attended on a King, Queen, Fool and black-faced Witch, who carried a besom to clear a dancing space. According to Sharp,[16]

'The King and Queen took themselves very seriously and were so taken by the dancers, the extra characters, and the spectators.'

They appear to have left any fooling to the Fool and Witch. Here, the Old and Young Couples are clearly shown. Furthermore, the dancers themselves were divided into men's and ladies' sides, distinguished only by their hats. This almost exactly duplicated the dancing processions of Balkan Brides and Grooms. A similar division existed in the simpler dances found along the English/Welsh border,[17] which appeared at Christmas. The costumes were a primitive attempt at disguise; at Much Wenlock, Shropshire, strips of newspaper were worn over pyjama-like material,[18] (Fig. 18) and at Broseley in the same county, the 'Females' were black-faced.[19] At Brimfield, Herefordshire,[20] the black-faced performers wore smocks with a row of bells round the waist (Fig. 19), almost exactly like, but not so elaborate as the Balkan dress. The dance itself was simple, a series of heys with stick-clashing when the performers met. Very little is known of the purely Welsh Morris, though a costume description has survived from Bagillt, Flintshire. There the performers blackened their faces, as they admitted themselves, to prevent recognition. The dancers attended on a Fool, Cadi, or Kate, a 'Female', and a branch-bearer who carried a branch of hawthorn in blossom which was decorated with ribbons.[21] Beatty quotes Mannhardt[22] as describing a Bohemian ceremony where the young girls went to the woods, cut down a young tree, ornamented it, and came back to the village singing:

'Death we carry out of the village,
Summer we carry into the village'.

In Bavaria also, Summer was often represented by a character dressed up in green, carrying a blossom or a little tree hung with apples and pears.[23] In these instances there was a contest between Winter and Summer in which the former was vanquished. A similar contest between Winter and Summer was held in the Isle of Man between the followers of the Queens of Summer and Winter, but no branch seems to have been carried.[24] Although the Welsh and Bavarian ceremonies were different in content, they had the feature of the branch in common.

The most primitive of all the English dance ceremonies occurred in East Anglia where, on Plough Monday, the Molly Dancers appeared wearing their ordinary clothes decorated with ribbons and rosettes, and performed a very simple dance.[25] Sometimes these dancers dragged a plough with them and cracked whips as they went; sometimes the plough was left in the square and made the centre of a round dance as in Cambridgeshire.[26] The dancers wore tall hats banded with ribbons from brim to crown and were often adorned with a plume of feathers. In Yorkshire, Staffordshire and Derbyshire, as well as in East Anglia, the ceremony often consisted of dragging round a plough with no dancing, but sometimes with whip-cracking. There were a Fool and Betty as at Balsham, Cambridgeshire,[27] and Repton, Derbyshire,[28] where they were described as the Fool and his Wife. This is clearly an Old Couple, but there is no dramatic action. Sometimes, as at Hanbury and Longton, Staffordshire,[29] some or all the ploughboys were dressed as women and very often there were performers yoked to the plough who dragged it along. There was no mention of scattering seeds behind it as in the Balkans. Such 'luck' as was involved went to the performers in their collection.

The element of 'luck' to the performers was also sought by the Cotswold Morris dancers who danced round the Maypole before they set off on their rounds.[30] Whether or not the bough carried by the Welsh per-

Plate 18. Stalybridge, Cheshire, Morris.

Plate 19. Winster, Derbyshire, Morris Dancers.
Dancers on rear row – the men's side, with fool holding up bladder.
Dancers on front row – the women's side. King and Queen in centre, witch second from right.

Figure 18. Much Wenlock, Shropshire, Morris Dancer.

Figure 19. Brimfield, Herefordshire, Morris Dancer.

formers was a symbol of luck or whether it was a symbol of summer is unknown, but a similar garland was carried at the Kirtlington, Oxfordshire, Lamb Ale. Amongst the performers here were a Lord and Lady carrying maces (Fig. 20), a Fool called the Squire wearing a dress spotted like a clown's, a band of Morris dancers dressed in the usual fashion and two men carrying 'forest feathers'. These were wooden clubs about three feet long, covered with leaves, flowers and rushes and trimmed with pink and blue ribbons[31] (Fig. 21). The focal point of these ceremonies was a 'bowery', a shed of green boughs set up on the village green, where ale was sold without a license for the nine days of the festival.

Although accounts of the Morris being danced round the Maypole are relatively few in recent times, early accounts of raising the maypole usually mention Morris dancers in the procession formed for the purpose. In Oxford in 1598 there was a riot because the inhabitants assembled with drum, shot and other weapons. Some men were dressed as women, and a woman, decked with garlands and flowers and named the Queen of the May was brought into town. Here again, as part of the procession, were 'Morrishe dancers', who, by their passing mention, played only a subordinate *rôle*.[32] That the Maypole was a symbol of luck persisted as a belief into recent times. In this century it was the practice in Cornwall[33] and Cheshire[34] for one village to attempt to steal another's pole, and there were many fights in the process. This was a deliberate attempt to transfer the 'luck' from one village to another. Indeed, many of the May Day customs had the spreading of fertility as their purpose. Stubbes' account in 1595 makes it clear that before bringing in the May, the country people of his time practised fertility in the woods on the eve of May Day:

'they go some to the woods and groves, some to the hills and mountains, some to one place, some to another, where they spend all the night in pleasant pastimes, and in the morning they return, bringing with them birch boughs and branches of trees to deck their assemblies withal . . . I have heard it credibly reported by men of great gravity, credity, and reputation, that of forty, three score, or a hundred maids going to the woods, there have scarcely the third part of them returned home again as they went.'[35]

About 250 years later the May Day festivities at Hitchin, Hertfordshire, were more decorous. A group, one of many, was described as follows:

'. . . First came two men with their faces blacked, one of them with a birch broom in his hand, and a large artificial hump on his back; the other dressed as a woman, all in rags and tatters, with a large straw bonnet on, and carrying a ladle; these are called 'mad Moll and her husband': next came two men, one most fantastically dressed with ribbons, and a great variety of gaudy coloured silk handkerchiefs tied round his arms from the shoulders to wrists, and down his thighs and legs to his ankles; he carried a drawn sword in his hand, leaning upon his arm was a youth dressed as a fine lady, in white muslin, and profusely decked from top to toe with gay ribbons: these, I understand, were called the 'Lord and Lady' of the company; after these followed six or seven couples more, attired much in the same style as the lord and lady, only the men were without swords. When this group received a satisfactory contribution at any house, the music struck up from a violin, clarionet, and fife, accompanied by the long drum, and they began the

Figure 20. Lady of the Lamb,
Kirtlington, Oxfordshire, carrying the mace.

Figure 21. Forest Feathers,
Kirtlington, Oxfordshire.

merry dance, . . . Mrs J . . . assured me that women were not permitted to mingle in these sports . . .'[36]

Stubbes did not mention these characters, and Hone makes it clear that the dance was a subordinate attraction, only appearing when a contribution had been made. There is a clear analogy between this May ceremony and the Balkan dramatic action in the characters of the Old and Young Couples and the subordinate 'six or seven couples'. About 1850 the same characters were seen at Bampton on May Day, but the ceremony had dwindled to a children's observance.[37] A boy was the 'Lord' and two girls played the parts of the 'Lady' and her 'Maid' respectively. The Lord carried a stick dressed with ribbons and flowers, whilst the two girls carried between them a garland made of two hoops crossed and covered with moss, flowers and ribbons. The 'Lady' also carried a mace (see Fig. 20), a square board mounted horizontally on a short staff, on the top of which were sweet smelling herbs under a muslin, decorated with red, white and blue ribbons. These characters were accompanied by a Jack-in-the-Green. Apart from significant features common to other ceremonies, the resemblance of the mace to the Midgley headdress is quite startling. To a lesser degree, this applies to the Andover headdress also (Plate 14).

Sometimes on the fringe of the May festivities can be seen relics of these characters. At Northill, Bedfordshire, where the Morris played a subordinate *rôle* in 1563 and finally disappeared, a bride and groom, two black-faced characters and Mayers carrying a tutti-pole persisted almost as long as the custom went on.[38] At Lowestoft, Suffolk, two boys appeared each May Day up to 1914 dressed as a bridal pair, with black faces, wearing lace curtains and danced and sang.[39] These antiques persist,

outliving the understanding of performers and witnesses. In Glamorganshire towards the end of the last century, the Fool and his wife were not considered 'proper' and tried to attach themselves to any group of performers – Wassailers, Mari Llwyd, etc., – so that they could not only gain some reflected respectability but also share in the proceeds.[40] They did not always succeed.

Most of the ceremonies discussed in this chapter appear to have no connection with the dramatic action in form, but they do share a common disguise and common ceremonial characters. They also share a common purpose – to bring 'luck', originally fertility, to the places visited. They also appear at some point in the old-style Winter months.[41] The inference is that all these customs shared a common ancestry, and developed their own individuality as they moved further away in time from the primitive ceremony. Essential ingredients of the primitive ceremony must have been the procession of disguised participants, a standard or totem, probably phallic in intent, which developed into the Maypole, and three generations of life represented by an Old Couple, a Young Couple and a third infant generation. Sexual activity, real or mimed, probably originally the former, took place inside a 'bower' and a revitalisation ceremony, again real or mimed, was its central core. Dancing, singing (or possibly chanting in its very early form), was carried on by characters who were not vital to the action, except to maintain a space clear for the performance. The use of a plough obviously depended on its invention, but this would not preclude the mimetic action of sowing and planting by primitive people who were moving from a hunting to an agrarian economy. If these ingredients are accepted, then the dancing procession of duplicates developed into the choreographic

Morris and the linked ring which maintained the space developed into the Sword Dance.

The whole ceremony must have developed gradually from a primitive basic concept. There is a very close connection in savage ceremonies between myth and ritual, the former being a late invention to explain the latter. The intent of ritual is imitative magic to bring about a desired result. The dramatic revitalisation was an attempt to urge on Nature the need for producing large crops and herds as well as to ensure the continuity of the tribe itself. Consequently, this must have been the driving force of the primitive ceremony, but the ceremony persisted long after its need or purpose was understood. It did not prevent the offshoots from taking their own form, but examination shows that all these diverse paths led to the same goal. None of this can be proved; it must remain conjectural. Change in everything is inevitable and the performance of the ceremony becomes more sophisticated. What does not change is the fundamental pattern of the ceremony. As far as the life cycle drama is concerned, a champion must still die for the good of his community and he must be revived. How either death or revival is brought about is unimportant; it is the fact, not the method, which counts. The dramatic fragments of England demonstrate this clearly, and the Wooing Ceremonies in particular show that there was once something more primitive which the performers enacted. The performance can only be understood in their own context of Folk Life and Custom; to attempt to understand them in terms of literature and sophisticated art makes nonsense of them. Further enquiry could well produce more information, but in the meantime it is certain that what is left can throw more light on the dark places of pre-history if the enquirer is bold enough to discard the misconceptions which have grown up during the years.

Appendix 1

Chapbook Texts

In south Lancashire and western West Riding of Yorkshire there appeared texts which were not handed on by oral tradition but by printed booklets. These have become known as the 'chapbook' texts from the form in which they were produced. However, the description is partly misleading since most of the known chapbook texts were printed after the chapbook proper had passed out of use. Chapbooks were the literature of the poor, condensations of much longer works, which were produced at a price within the reach of all but the most impecunious.[1] The price of the play chapbooks qualifies them for the name since they were inexpensive, costing at most only one penny. None of the surviving examples can be the missing chapbook which many people have seen as the archetype of all the Hero-Combat texts known to exist, but the chapbook texts themselves may owe something to it. All the surviving versions are Hero-Combat, and there is no evidence that any other type ever existed. The texts show that they have had some literary adjustment, but whether the similarity of dialogue between printings in widely separated towns is due to the popularity of the version or to good-natured piracy between individual firms is not clear. At the end of this Appendix is given a list of all examples known to exist or have existed. To avoid using the titles repetitiously here, examples are referred to in this text by the numbers shown against them in the list.

The versions fall into seven groups determined by their action and the time of appearance for which they were intended. Since these publications are extremely rare, it is useful to summarise the action of the texts in each group before discussing them further. The three versions of Group I are divided into Acts and Scenes, Act I, Scene 1 being given over entirely to what might be described as a Calling-on Song, spoken, not sung, by Alexander, and introducing a noble King, a Doctor and Dives, a Miser. Of these, only Alexander and the Doctor retain their names in the subsequent action. This begins in Act I, Scene 2, when Alexander calls for room in which to perform, and the King of Egypt and Prince George, also called Slacker,[2] introduce themselves. George has the typical autobiographical vaunt familiar to many St George characters. At the end of the scene all exeunt, and Act II, Scene 1 begins with a combat between Alexander and St George, who is killed. The King of Egypt calls on Sambo for help and is answered by the Doctor in the usual Sambo lines, to the effect that he would help but his sword point is broken and he consequently is unable to do so. When the King of Egypt calls for a doctor, the latter answers in his own *rôle*, describes the diseases he can cure, but not his travels, and restores George to life. Act II, Scene 2 begins with the Prince speaking the first lines after the cure, and then carrying on a nonsensical dialogue with Alexander

concerning the choice of a wife.[3] Ultimately, Alexander and the King of Egypt quarrel and in Act II, Scene 3 they fight and Egypt is killed. There is no cure, nor attempt at one. The Conclusion, with a covert request for largesse, follows and ends the action.

No. 1 is the earliest complete text known to exist, antedating Revesby by eight years.[4] Its division into Acts and Scenes is a clumsy attempt to rationalise a ceremony which even in 1771 was inexplicable. The division is arbitrary with no regard for any suitable point at which the action might be broken, and clearly the text ought to be one continuous whole. The Calling-on Song is a literary form of those associated with Sword Dance, Pace-egg and Souling ceremonies, but is not so elaborate. No. 2 is identical with No. 1 apart from a different arrangement of lines and correction of typographical errors. No copy of No. 3 is known to exist. The arrangement of a typescript in the Manning MSS in the Bodleian library[5] suggests that it was transcribed from an original, but no indication of source is given. Hone reprinted this text as sent to him by a correspondent in Whitehaven, but omitted the four crude lines discussed in Chapter 2. It is difficult to decide if these versions were actually performed, or whether they were examples printed by chapbook publishers to add variety to their lists. Both the places of publication, Whitehaven and Newcastle upon Tyne, were special centres for the chapbook publication, and their dates of publication make them the only ones likely to have been published as chapbooks proper. Brand made it clear that No. 1 was used by local performers in Newcastle upon Tyne, but found that

'. . . the *Stile* of them all is so *puerile* and *simple* . . .'[6]

and Hone's correspondent implied that the Whitehaven version was still in use in 1826. None resembles surviving traditional examples from their areas.

The solitary example from Group II is an oddity. It has a Prologue instead of a Calling-on Song and this is spoken by the Fool who makes no attempt to introduce the characters but simply praises his own learning:

> '. . . I know my letters all by sight,
> Tho' I've by name forgot them quite.
> I know Philosophy in part,
> Can say my Almanack by *heart*.
> And know within an hour or two,
> *What clock is by it*, at first view . . .'

The action follows, beginning with an autobiographical vaunt by George and the entry of Slasher. They fight, Slasher is killed and George goes out. The Fool enters, laments the death of his 'chiefest son' and calls for a doctor. They haggle over the fee, the doctor describes his cures and finally restores Slasher. George returns and the rest leave whilst he delivers a vaunt which provokes a challenge from the Prince of Paradise. In the ensuing fight George is again victorious. The dead man is lamented by the King of Egypt who describes him as his 'son and only heir', but there is no cure. Instead, Hector is summoned to seek revenge, but is wounded by George and leaves. The action ends with George fighting inconclusively with the Fool. Two soliloquies follow, the first 'The Tailor's Soliloquy' and the second 'A Lecture upon Lectures' given by two of the performers. These are attempts at wit far removed from the humour of the traditional performers; for example, in the Tailor's Soliloquy, the performer says:

'. . . Even Kings would be Sans Culottes if I turned traitor, and would not make them breeches . . .'

and in the Lecture upon Lectures:

'. . . the word orattor means jawing; because why? why because no man can speak without his jaws. Now you think I can give you a latin divination of that word; why what's English for oss? why bone to be sure: and the jaws being full of bones, is a fixed proof that the word orattor comes from oss . . .'

Finally, all the performers sing a 'New Song' whose twelve four line stanzas roughly summarise the main action, and although unspecified, they no doubt take a collection.

Only the main action of this version is traditional in characters and action. The literary embellishments show that the compiler thought they were necessary to 'entertainment', but they depart from the original purpose and distort even the faint traces of ceremony which otherwise remain in the most modern actions. Its title, 'The Mummers' Act; or, Morris Dancers' Annual Play of St George . . . for the Amusement of Youth on Christmas Holidays, is in some ways most apt, in others inept. 'Act' is better than 'Play', 'Morris Dancers' reflects the confusion of name, but 'the Amusement of Youth' is an indication of the ceremony's decline.

The three texts in Group III have more familiar characteristics and Nos 6 and 7 show an attempt to attract by illustrations. No. 5 has none, but the other two have two identical ones, a witch riding on a broomstick, on the front cover and a full page wood engraving on page 4 which shows St George thrusting his sword through what appears to be a winged devil. The action of each is virtually the same. Act I begins with the Fool calling for room 'to sport' and St George continuing with a vaunt similar in tone to, but not identical with the one used in the Group I texts. Slasher and George fight, the former is wounded and the Fool calls for a doctor as his 'chiefest son is slain'. The Doctor demands his fee, discusses his travels, details the cures he can bring about and cures Slasher. The Act closes with the return of St George and the departure of the other three characters. Act II begins with yet another autobiographical piece from St George, followed immediately by him killing the Prince of Paradine who is lamented by his father, the King of Egypt. The latter calls for Hector who fights and is wounded by George. In No. 6 only, Slasher returns to fight Hector and takes over the 'My head is made of iron . . .' lines, which the other versions give to Hector. No cure is attempted, nor does the Doctor re-appear. This concludes the action proper and the texts end with Beelze-

bub and Devil Doubt making their usual *Quête* appearance.

Acts I and II in these versions could exist independently of each other since the action is complete in both apart from the omission of the second cure. There is a possibility that this text has been extended to make a lengthier publication. The traditional elements have been retained in the patter of the Doctor and *Quête* characters' speeches, and although there has been some literary tampering, it is not to such an extent as was obvious in the Groups I and II texts.

The ten examples in Group IV show an attempt at elaboration of illustration though the texts, with some additional lines in Act II, remain the same as those in Group III. The additional lines spoken by St George and the Fool, are almost identical with *ll*. 58–68 of the Broadway version (page 34). Apart from this extract, the comments on the texts and traditional elements made on the Group III versions apply equally here therefore, but some consideration can be made on the presentation of the printed form.

No. 9 has the front and back covers printed in pale green, the front cover showing two armoured knights in combat, and pages 1, 3, 5, 7 and 8 having small illustrations at the top to depict the action supposedly taking place on the relevant pages (Fig. 22). Of the others, the page 3 illustration shows a Fool, dressed after the style of a Court Jester in motley, persuading the Doctor, in long, monk-like dress, to cure the fallen champion who sits forlornly on the ground. The last illustration at the head

THE PACE EGG.

Since my head is made of iron,
My body's made of steel,
My hands and feet of knuckle bone—
I challenge thee to field.
    [*They fight, and Hector is wounded.*]
I am a valiant knight, and Hector is my name,
Many bloody battles have I fought, and always won
      the same ;
But from St. George I received this bloody wound.
    [*A Trumpet sounds.*]
Hark ! hark ! I hear the silver trumpet sound ;
Down yonder is the way. [*Pointing.*]
Farewell, St. George, I can no longer stay. [*Exit.*]
    [*Enter Fool to St. George.*]
  ST. GEORGE.—Here comes from post, old Bold Ben.
  FOOL.—Why, master, did ever I take you to be my
    friend ?
  ST. GEORGE.—Why, Jack, did ever I do thee any
    harm ?
  FOOL.—Thou proud, saucy coxcomb, begone !
  ST. GEORGE.—A coxcomb ! I defy that name ;
With a sword thou ought to be stabbed for the same.

Figure 22. Beelzebub from Walker's *Pace Egg*.

58

of page 8, shows Devil Doubt looking like a big-eared elf carrying trident and besom, dancing whilst a knight runs away in the background. This is the only chapbook to attempt relevant illustrations in this group, the others adopting more stereotyped forms. Nos 8 and 10 have identical illustrations, the front cover of each showing a knight in martial pose (Fig. 23), whilst a caricature of Punch heads the text proper. Two further illustrations of armoured knights in stylised martial poses follow, and finally, there is a winged devil with a broom intended to portray Devil Doubt. No. 11 strikes a different note. The front cover has an illustration of a Victorian boy and girl, but of the three illustrations inside, one is of a sailor dressed after the fashion of one of Nelson's men, another is of a Highlander with a battle axe, presumably intended to be St George since it introduces his lines. The final one is of a particularly revolting devil carrying off humans strapped to his back, chest and to the long pole he carries. None has any relevance to the surrounding text. No. 12, rather more ambitiously, has the cover hand-coloured in yellow, black, red, green and brown on a white ground. On the front cover the same illustration of the devil is used as in Nos 8 and 10, but facing the opposite way. The illustrations are smaller and cruder than any other of this group. They attempt once more to portray the action and include Punch, presumably intended for the Fool, a knight with a cross on his breast for St George (Fig. 24), a Victorian gentleman with bottle protruding from his hip pocket for the Doctor, a very crude drawing of a king and knight in pseudo-Greek armour representing no-one in particular, and finally a smaller version of the winged devil used on the front cover. No. 13's illustrations follow those of Nos 8 and 10, but different blocks have been used, the final winged devil being shown sweeping with his besom. The illustrations in Nos 14 and 17 have even less relevance than any so far mentioned and were probably used originally in other chapbooks. No. 17 has a variety ranging from two clearly belonging to *Ali Baba and the Forty Thieves* to others depicting a grenadier or couples dancing in the formal surroundings of a hall.

This particular version (No. 17) is a bridge between Groups IV and V: it owes its text to its own group but its title and final 'Grand Sword Dance' to No. 19 of the next Group. The four texts of Group V leave tradition completely in their search for variety. Nos 18 and 19 have identical texts, their differences lying in their method of presentation. Both have hand-coloured covers, No. 18 being washed in red, yellow, black, brown and green, and No. 19 in blue, green, yellow and orange. No. 18 shows George mounted on a horse killing the dragon and No. 19 shows a convivial male party seated round a table drinking punch. The text illustrations, in black and white, show a variety from a jester performing on a stage and heraldic representations of knights in combat with a dragon, to a conventional Irishman hitting another man on the jaw and a dragoon evicting a man through a window whilst a serving maid looks on. The texts are as follows:

Jester
Good morrow friends and neighbours dear,
We are right glad to meet you here,
We come with Christmas once a year,
And we wish you plenty of good cheer.

Enter all the knights

Figure 23. Knight from cover page of Johnson's *Peace Egg*.

Figure 24. St George from Harkness' *The Peace Egg*.

Chorus (for all to sing, or the Jester to repeat)
May luck attend the Milk Pail,
May ewes yield two and three,
May each blow of the thrashing flail
Produce good Firmity.
Good morrow, masters all,
May the day be fair and clear,
When we wish a 'merry Christmas
And a happy New Year'.

They all follow the Jester round in a circle, he repeating as follows:
We are Mummers blythe and gay,
And come to make you happy;
For these bold Knights, come, clear the way,
And draw your stout Brown Nappy.

Behold St George, a valiant Knight,
Who bravely slew the dragon;
Produce me such another wight,
Him you shall vaunt and brag on:

Britain, renown'd by all the world,
Where'er he glorious flag's unfurl'd,
Renown'd alike by friend or foe,
The land that keeps the world in awe.

Sure I'm St Patrick, from the bogs,
This truth I fain would learn you,
I banish'd serpents, toads and frogs
From beautiful Hibernia.

I flourished my shilelah,
And the Reptiles all ran races;
'Twas devil take the hindmost!
And they've never since showed their faces.

And I'm St Andrew, fra the North,
Men fra that part are men o' worth;
To travel south we're maething loth,
And treat you fairly, by my troth.
The land of oatmeal and the yeuch,
(Laird bless the Duke!) excuse the joke,
Where mony a Ton Brunstane teuk.
Lang may the 'Glorious Haggis smoke'.

Of Taffy's land I'm Patron Saint,
O yes, indeed, I'll you acquaint,
Of Ancient Britons I've a race
Dare meet a foeman face to face;
For Welshmen (Hear it once again)
Were born before all other men:
I'll fear no man in fight or freaks,
Whilst Wales produces Cheese and Leeks.

St George
I challenge all my country's foes.

St Patrick
And I'll assist wid mighty blows.

St Andrew
And you shall find me ready too.

St David
Odds blud! and I, so well as you.

They all follow the Jester round as before

Jester
While we are joined in heart and hand,

A gallant and courageous band,
If e'er a foe dares look awary,
We'll one and all poke out his eye.

Enter Saladin
Don't vaunt thus, my courageous knights,
For I, as you, have seen the sights
In Palestine, in days of yore,
'Gainst prowess strong I bravely bore
The sway, when all the world in arms
Shook Holy Land with war's alarms:
I for the Crescent, *you* the Cross;
Each mighty host oft won and lost.
I many a thousand men did slay,
And eat two hundred, twice a day;
And now, again, I'll try, – and zounds!
I'll try hard, but I'll crack your crowns.

St Patrick
And faith you may try,
For you sing a loud note;
But I'll alter your tune
Wid a hole in your coat.
Come on you 'Man Eater',
I'll wager a groat,
You ne'er eat a Pat,
Or he'd stuck in your throat.

St Patrick and Saladin fight
Cut 1 – Crossing each other
Cut 2 – Crossing each back
Cut 3 – Crossing each other
Cut 4 – Crossing each back
4 Shoulder cuts
St Patrick loses his sword, and falls

St Andrew interposes
Haud your hand, you base Tyke,
Wad you strike when he's down?
Scotsman ne'er saw the like,
So beware you false loon.
I've a wee wittle here,
So for you, de'll may care a:
You'll ken 'what the steer',
Wi' this 'Andrew Ferrara'.

St Andrew and Saladin renew the fight. – Same as before
St Andrew loses his sword and falls

St David interposes
Cots splutter hur nails,
She's a devil to fight,
For the honour of Wales
I'll contend while 'tis light;
And then, when 'tis dark.
Now I'm ready, here goes,
If the daylight won't do,
Then for ayr hyd de nos. [7]

The Grand Sword Dance
Cut 1 – Crossing each other
Cut 2 – Crossing each back
Cut 3 – Crossing each other
Cut 4 – Crossing each back
The fight ends with the same result as the others.

St George interposes
Come take your breath,

60

And try a bout with me,
I'll fight unto the death
Before I'll flee;
When the field I have won,
We'll empty a flagon,
As sure as a gun,
To the Knights of the Dragon.

They fight
St George conquers Saladin

All the characters
Huzza

Saladin rises
Now brave St George, I quit the field,
I need not be ashamed to yield;
I swear by all the Pagan gods,
That four to one's a little odds:
We'll sheath our swords, and end the strife,
And never more, upon my life!
Will I draw the sword for priestly elves,
But let them fight their fights themselves.

The Jester
Now brave St George he rules the roast,
'Britons triumphant' be the toast;
Then let the Wassail Cup abound
Whene'er the Mummers' time comes round:
When Christmas cheer prevails, I trow,
And maids kiss 'neath the Mistletoe,
Let cheerful song and dance prevail,
And Bumpers of October ale.

Grand Sword Dance
Cut 1, and cross
Cut 2, and cross partner
Which is R. & L.
Same back again
The Two Knights at opposite corners R.H. – Cut 1, and cross,
and Cut 2 with the opposite knight
Same back
Which is Ladies Chain
Four swords points up in the centre
All go round – all out 6
And come to bridal arm protect
And round to places
Repeat the first figure
All go round and finish

The only concessions to tradition are the retention of St George and the circular perambulation made by the characters. The Grand Sword Dance is nothing like the linked dances of the north-east. The stage directions are rigid so that there is no latitude for variation, though this is not to say that its performers would necessarily adhere to the instructions. The Doctor is omitted so that there is no revival, and the whole purpose of the ceremony has been lost. No. 20 goes part way to restoring the balance by bringing back the Doctor, retaining the same four champions of Nos 18 and 19, and introducing Sabrina and the King of Egypt, then diverges again by making the opponents the 'representatives of Nations – France, America, Russia, Turkey and Germany', clearly a gesture towards patriotism. The action opens with the Jester to whom enter Saints George, Patrick, Andrew and David, followed by the King of Egypt holding Sabrina by the hand. St George embraces her and by turn, the Knights describe themselves. St Denys of France enters, fights with George and is overcome, but is spared by the latter on the intervention of Sabrina. The five countries enter and quarrel with George. The stage direction for the ensuing fight is as follows:

'St George and the four Powers fight. – St George wounds, and knocks down America and Russia; his foot slips and he falls on one knee; Turkey and Germany rush upon him; when St Patrick, St Andrew, and St David, beat them back. America and Russia, rise and renew the attack, when a mimic battle ensue, – to kept up at pleasure, – Each Saint wounds, knocks down his foe, and retires, leaving St George to finish the combat with America, whom he wounds and knocks down; then rests on his sword looking at them grimly.'

This is a far cry from the slapdash combats of the traditional performers and restricts any attempt at originality or spontaneous action. Finally, the Jester summons the Doctor, and the dialogue which follows clearly owes something to the more robust versions of the ceremonial performers. After the cure, the whole performance ends with the 'Grand Sword Dance' of Nos 18 and 19.

No. 21 is different again. Here, the characters are Seven Champions, St George of England, St Patrick of Ireland, St Denis of France, St James of Scotland, St Thalis of Denmark, St Wanski of Russia and St Pietro of Italy. With them are Guillaume, King of Germany, Rosalynd, his daughter, and Hans Lighthead, the King's Jester. Costume instructions are given: Guillaume should be dressed in 'red double tippet edged with ermine, a crown of gold, sceptre, etc.', whilst the champions were to be dressed according to country of origin, St Denis, for example, with a 'tunic of fleur-de-lys pattern'. The action begins with Hans Lighthead announcing to Guillaume that seven knights wish to be admitted. Rosalynd desires to see them, and after some discussion, the champions are admitted. They make it clear that they have come to take part in the jousts to be held that day. They each boast of their skill and Guillaume decides that they alone shall fight despite Hans' comment:

'No-one else, sire? Oh, blow me tight!
Why, sixty knights are ready drest,
And waiting here to do their best.'

Rosalynd agrees with the king and the fight begins. St George overcomes all but St Thalis who, seeing what happens to the other champions, declines to fight. As a reward, George is given the hand of Rosalynd who, with Hans, brings the performance to a close by asking for contributions from the audience. There is neither Doctor nor cure and the whole is written in very mediocre rhyming couplets. Its action is clearly taken in part from the adventures of St Andrew and the final tournament in Greece where the champions finally overcome all Pagan opposition in Johnson's romance. These versions come from centres where chapbooks of all types were published in quantity and there is more than a suspicion that the publishers added them to their lists more for variety than for action purposes. Despite this, some performers did use them.

The Group V examples represent the nadir of these chapbook versions, and it is a relief to turn finally to No.

22, an unpretentious publication with familiar Irish characters, an unnamed Presenter, St George, Turkey Champion, Doctor, St Patrick, Oliver Cromwell, Beelzebub and Little Devil Doubt. It is a version which fits exactly the Hero-Combat versions described in Chapter Five. There are no stage directions, the speeches are not even preceded by the name of the speaking character, and it could well be a version taken down whilst a performance was in progress. Although published as a chapbook, with a text supported by crude but relevant woodcuts, it is not of the same type as any of the other chapbooks. It had more than one edition since copies exist with different borders round the illustrations, and typographical errors corrected. In 1928 facsimile copies were given free with the *Irish Book Lover*, and in commenting on these, the contributor dated the chapbook from 1850, adding that he bought a copy from the printer in 1913.[8] This gives a span of at least sixty-three years so that it is not surprising that more than one edition was involved.

Group VII contains examples which, so far as is known, have no surviving copies. No. 23 is mentioned in 1846 as being different from No. 2 which is quoted in extenso:

'. . . the Lancashire version differs . . . as any one curious in these matters may see by procuring a copy, a new edition having just been published by P. Whittle, F.S.A., Friar Gate, Preston, at the reasonable charge of one penny.'[9]

The title of No. 24 is taken from an advertisement on the back of No. 11, and but for other evidence would not be considered here. *Circa* 1825–40, there was a description of three types of performers at Failsworth, Lancashire. Very young performers used treadle-pins and carried besoms, an older set with tin scimitars performed the old 'thredbare peace-egg rhymes,' and finally, the oldest –

'the 'don'-set or 'lump-yeds, youths of 10 or 12, with real swords, who fenced three up and three down. They performed the new-fangled 'Robin Hood and his merry men of Sherwood . . .'[10]

Additionally, James Wood, writing from Oldham in 1905,[11] described a performance which resolved itself into attempts by various people to join Robin Hood's outlaw band, success being determined by their fighting and defeating him. If this version could be found, it would almost certainly belong to Group V, if not to a Group of its own.

Very little is known of No. 25. The only copy known to exist was in the Bussell Collection of Children's Books sold at Sotheby's in 1945 to the National Magazine Company. The collection is reported to have been ultimately deposited in a New York library, but exhaustive enquiries have so far failed to discover it. Its date is interesting, making it one of the earliest three known.

It is unfortunate that out of the twenty-five listed, only five have a firm printing date. The problem of dating the others is more complex, though No. 4 has a handwritten note, 'Done in 1840', on its cover. The Group III versions are probably the most recent of all, No. 5 being in use and circulation until the 1914 War and possibly later. On typographical evidence the other two of this Group can be dated *circa* 1890; the firm of Looney and Pilling was in business in Spear Street from 1855–1884, but was

eventually acquired by Abel Heywood at a date now forgotten. The examples given in the List are probably late recensions of earlier copies now lost.

In Group IV, Wrigley, publisher of No. 8, was in business as a 'block-cutter' from 1832–1850. Although a block-cutter normally worked for textile printing, Wrigley must have been a letter-press printer also. It seems reasonable to assume that he cut blocks for his own publications, and the ones he used in the chapbook owe more to theatrical and fictional works than to tradition. The illustrations were followed by Johnson, Carr and Lund, who used the same blocks, or versions of them, the only differences being the individuality of hand-produced work. Johnson set up his business in 1813, continuing at the chapbook address until 1851 when his son took over, moved and expanded the business. Buchan had his business at various numbers in St Peter's Street, Leeds between 1875 and 1897, though it is doubtful if he actually moved premises since street number changes were often caused by extensive building. Wardman was a 'letterpress printer and printing ink manufacturer' in Bradford in 1830. In 1845 he was also a 'worsted spinner', but by 1863 his firm had disappeared. Lund was a 'Bookseller, binder and printer' between 1847 and 1868, whilst Carr only traded from the Hanover Street address between 1840 and 1868. Harkness of Preston began printing broadsides *circa* 1838 and continued to do so until approximately 1885. Unfortunately, after he died, his existing stocks were taken to Blackburn and sold as waste paper. The word 'Annual' on the cover of his chapbook is set in Pica 2-line Open Sans Serif No. 2, which did not appear in the English typeface catalogues until 1844, so that this particular example must date from the middle of the nineteenth century.

It is unfortunate that the firm of Walker's which published the bulk of these chapbook versions suffered two disastrous fires in 1878 and 1904, destroying records which would otherwise have thrown valuable light on the history of their publications. Their version of the *Seven Champions* (No. 21) was certainly performed *circa* 1880 and again *circa* 1905.[12] 'Pagan' on the cover of No. 20 is set in Tuscan, a typeface only available from 1878 and the typeface of No. 18 is also dated from approximately 1885. These Group V versions must belong to the end of the nineteenth century. Of the four publishers listed for No. 20, C. H. Johnson, grandson of the Joseph Johnson who published No. 10, was in business between 1875 and 1912, John Heywood added 'Ridgefield' to his two existing addresses in 1879, and W. H. Smith left New Brown Street in 1884. This version could only have been published between 1879 and 1884, which supports the end of the century dating for this Group.

It is obvious therefore, that these chapbooks belong to a period running from the late eighteenth century to the early twentieth century. This in turn, throws some light on their area of use as shown on the distribution map (Fig. 25). They are a product of the industrial north-west, each of the examples being published in one of the cities of this area. From the cities they spread out into the adjoining villages and towns until they finally suppressed whatever traditional version had existed. They certainly appear to have been unknown as printed versions elsewhere. In 1835 a publisher in Swindon, Wiltshire, reported that every Christmas there were demands for mummers' books which could not be met because they did not exist.[13] At that time they were certainly in use in the north-west of England, but do not seem to have strayed beyond this area. One can only assume that

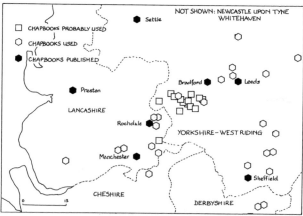

Figure 25. Map of distribution of chapbook plays.

there were reasons for a demand in this area which did not exist elsewhere, and the most likely of these was the fact that new industries were attracting people to towns and factories. The early nineteenth century was a time when poverty was endemic amongst the agricultural workers. Enclosure Acts had turned farm labourers into a landless unemployed. Food prices, aggravated by bad harvests, had risen because of the Napoleonic Wars and farmers failed to keep pace with new methods which could have increased the agricultural yield. In East Anglia additionally, the woollen industry suffered a decline from roughly 1786–1816,[14] and its workers joined in the exodus to the cities. Such conditions forced a drift from the land and from depressed areas; it was inevitable that much of this emigrant population sought work wherever it could be found, even though it was completely different from anything they had previously known. Factory life dulled awareness of the seasonal cycle and there was no need to preserve its annual round. Whether the will to maintain ceremony traditionally was weakened by new surroundings, or whether it could not flourish without an outside stimulation is unknown. Although much longer dramatic actions were kept alive by pure oral tradition elsewhere in the country, the people of the north west depended on printed copies for their versions. Thus, they lost control of the ceremony and handed it over to publishers who were more concerned with profit than with maintaining tradition.

This in itself may be significant. The number of titles which contain the words 'for the amusement of youth' suggests that the ceremony had dwindled to a children's performance, presumably because their parents had lost interest. Brierley makes it clear that the performers of his youth abandoned the ceremony when they reached the age of twelve,[15] though elsewhere in England it was the jealous preserve of young men. Well into this century the performers of the north west must have been children; the Midgley version, probably based on No. 11, is still annually performed by school children. There may be some connection between the appearance of the play chapbooks and the death of the old style chapbooks, which vanished when newer forms of cheap reading material were being produced. Amongst these, *Chambers' Edinburgh Journal*, *The Penny Magazine* and weekly serialisations of novels were a product of the new desire of the working classes for education. This growing sophistication may have turned the adults from the meaningless ceremony. If so, it was fortunate that enter-

prising publishers kept it alive from whatever motive, even if in doing so, they distorted it, made it respectable and handed it on to a different age group of performers.

There is no doubt they misunderstood the material they published. Their illustrations must have influenced the performers to turn away from the ribbons, streamers and patches of elsewhere. The pictures published by Fallow (Plate 20) of the performers he saw *circa* 1880 were wearing a costume with a strong resemblance to the illustrations published by Wardman (Fig. 26), and the mock armour worn by the champions in other versions must owe something to Wrigley's blocks. The publishers were less successful in stripping away other traditional features. They retained the title 'Pace' or 'Peace' Egg, even though they largely ignored its derivation from 'Pasche' – Easter, and published their versions under this style for Christmas also. They seemed unable to make Beelzebub and Devil Doubt disappear. Versions which ignored them like No. 4, appear to have had a short life. Their re-appearance in later texts may be an indication that the performers insisted on their inclusion as being familiar. Assuming that the version seen by Fallow was based on No. 21, he comments that it ended with Beelzebub and Devil Doubt, but examination of the text shows that they are not included in the printed version. One must assume accordingly that the performers added these characters from an older version, just as the Midgley performers retained Tosspot and his Tally-wife. Even though the texts may represent a desire for change, the performers themselves still had memories of the older, traditional characters.

One further point needs consideration even though it presents a problem which so far has no immediate solution. The printed chapbooks, as said, never strayed outside their immediate area, and yet here and there, thoughout the distribution of the Hero-Combat ceremonies, texts occur which are clearly based to a greater or lesser degree on these chapbook versions. The Syresham version given in Chapter One is typical of this oddity, and yet outside the north west, performers insisted that their version was never in print, or they had never seen it printed. Even more surprising, the work of

Figure 26. Illustration from Wardman's *The Mummer*. Compare costume with Plate 20.

Plate 20. Mummers, *circa* 1880, Leeds vicinity. Compare with Figure 26.

Professor Abrahams in the Caribbean has produced at least one version whose text depends heavily on the Groups IV and V texts as well as on traditional lines from elsewhere.[16] This version is performed by the natives of the islands and there can certainly be no question of handing on orally by traditional English performers. Again, *The Philadelphia Sunday Dispatch* in 1866 spoke of mummers going from house to house 'where they enacted a mock play, entitled "Alexander and the King of Egypt" '. No text was given, but the similarity of its title with those of Group I is remarkable. No record of printed chapbooks has survived across the Atlantic, but their small size would make them convenient to carry where larger volumes would be an encumbrance. A possible theory for the appearance of chapbook texts in areas outside the north west of England is that they were imported when the local traditional version was either dying or had died, but no proof exists of this.

Although the publishers had little motive beyond profit in publishing, they obviously played an important part in keeping tradition alive in the industrial North West. Their versions make dull reading by comparison with the lively traditional versions from elsewhere, but they did succeed in maintaining a form of tradition in an area where it was obviously dying. They may have distorted ceremony, stifled its spontaneity and set a new style of disguise, but they certainly established an area for a type which is as distinct in its own way as that of the East Midlands. They also add a footnote to the times, often overlooked that the use of a printed text argues a standard of literacy not normally associated with the early nineteenth century.

Check List to Chapbooks in Appendix 1

Group I

1. *Alexander and the King of Egypt. A Mock Play as it is acted by the Mummers every Christmas*, Newcastle; Printed in the Year 1771.
2. *Alexander and the King of Egypt. A Mock Play as it is acted by the Mummers every Christmas*, Newcastle; Printed in the Year 1788.
3. *Alexander and the King of Egypt: A Mock Play as it is acted by the Mummers every Christmas*, printed by T. Wilson, King-street, Whitehaven, 1826.

Group II

4. *The Mummers' Act; or, Morris Dancers' Annual Play of St. George, with Prologues, Songs, Recitations, &c., for the Amusement of Youth on Christmas Holidays*, New Edition, London. Printed for all Booksellers, and sold by Pearce and Son, Gibraltar-St., Sheffield.

Group III

5. *The Peace Egg, or St. George: An Easter Play*, supplied by Edwards and Bryning, Ltd., Castle Works, Rochdale.
6. *The Peace Egg, or St. George: An Easter Play*, printed for the Booksellers by Looney and Pilling, Spear Street, Manchester.
7. *The Peace Egg, or St. George: An Easter Play*, printed by Abel Heywood and Son, Oldham Street, Manchester.

Group IV

8. *The Peace Egg*, printed and published by J. Wrigley, 30, Miller-street, Manchester.
9. *The Peace Egg. A Christmas Joust for Boys*, William Walker and Sons, Otley.
10. *The Peace Egg*, published by J. Johnson, Bookseller, &c., 42, Call Lane, and 1, Cloth Hall Street (Opposite the Corn Exchange), Leeds.
11. *Walker's Series of Juvenile Plays for Christmas and Eastertide: The Peace Egg*, William Walker and Sons, London and Otley.
12. *The Peace Egg; or, St George's Annual Play for the Amusement of Youth*, printed by J. Harkness, 121, Church Street, Preston.
13. *The Peace Egg*, printed by G. Buchan, Printer, Wholesale Stationer, Dealer in Toys and Fancy Goods, &c., Leeds.
14. *The Peace Egg*, published and sold by J. Roberts, 4 Wood-street, Leeds, 1856.
15. *The Peace Egg or Saint George's Annual Play for the Amusement of Youth*, printed and published by R. Carr, Hanover-street, Manchester.
16. *The Peace Egg*, Sold wholesale and retail by J. Lund, Westgate, Bradford.
17. *The Mummer; or the Wassail Cup. A Romance written expressly for all Mummers, to commemorate the Holy Wars, and the happy Festival of Christmas*, printed and sold by H. Wardman, Chapel-lane, Bradford.

Group V

18. *Walker's New Mummer or the Wassail Cup*, William Walker and Son, London and Otley.
19. *Walker's New Mummer; or, the Wassail Cup. A Romance. Shewing how the Four Brave Patron Saints Conquered the Renowned Pagan Giant Saladin. Written expressly for all Mummers, to commemorate the Holy Wars and the Happy Festival of Christmas*, William Walker, Kirkgate, Otley.
20. *New Mumming Book. The Four Champions of Great Britain, showing how St. George of England; St. Patrick of Ireland: St. Andrew, of Scotland, and St David, of Wales conquered the Representatives of all Nations.* LONDON: J. H. Roberts & Co, 52, Fleet Street, Strand. MANCHESTER: John Heywood, Ridgefield; W. H. Smith & Son, New Brown Street. LEEDS: C. H. Johnson, Publisher, Cloth Hall Street and all Booksellers and News Agents.
21. *Walker's Series of Juvenile Plays for Christmas and Eastertide: The Seven Champions of Christendom*, William Walker and Son, London and Otley.

Group VI

22. *The New Christmas Rhyme-Book*, printed for the Booksellers by J. Nicholson, Cheapside, Church Lane, Belfast.

Group VII

23. Version published by Peter Whittle, Preston, before 1846.
24. *Walker's Juvenile Plays for Christmas and Easter: Robin Hood, Little John and his Merry Men*, William Walker and Sons, Otley.
25. *The Christmas Rime, or, The Mummers' Own Book*, J. Smith, Belfast, *c.* 1806.

Locations of the chapbooks given above are as follows: No. 1, Dyce Collection (D.20, N.1), Victoria and Albert Museum, South Kensington, London; Nos 2, 19, 21, The Bodleian, Oxford; No. 4 is in private possession but a Xerox copy can be seen in the Sheffield City Museum; No. 5 is in private possession; Nos 6, 7, 9–11, 19, 20, 22 are in the Ordish Collection, Folklore Society, University College, London, Gower Street, W.C.1; No. 8 is in the British Museum (1077 g.37 (27)); Nos 12, 13, 18, Vaughan Williams Memorial Library, 2, Regents Park Road, London, N.W.1; and Nos 14–17 are in the Leeds Reference Library, Central Library, Leeds.

Since the above check-list was prepared the enquiries of Dr Cawte have produced an additional version in Group I:

Alexander and the King of Egypt. A Mock Play as it is acted by the Mummers every Christmas, Callander and Dixon, Printers, 3, Market Place, Whitehaven, n.d.

One copy is in the Hutchinson Collection, Whitehaven Public Library, and another copy, identical in text, but with type reset, is in Carlisle Public Library, Jackson Collection, Shelf J169.

Further examples may be found in M. J. Preston, M. G. Smith and P. S. Smith: *An interim Check-list of Chapbooks containing Traditional Play Texts*, History of the Book Trade in the North, Newcastle, 1976.

Appendix 2

Examples of Texts

The texts which follow have been selected on a regional basis to illustrate the 'sameness' and yet the diversity of examples throughout the country. Examples could be multiplied but the ones given show regional characteristics by which to identify areas where unlocated plays might be placed. To use these examples in this way can, of course, be only a rough and ready guide since almost any area has examples which do not follow the norm. This must be accepted in the study of this subject, but fortunately, the majority of examples give particulars of location so that only a few need some detective work to discover where they could have been performed. Despite the differences, more apparent than real, which seem to be brought to light by the juxtaposition of these examples, the fundamental revitalisation is present throughout. The preponderance of Hero-Combat examples is to be expected. Not only did they exist over a larger area of the country and fewer relatively, have been published than either of the other two types. Sword Dance examples are difficult to discover and most of the ones known have already been published. There is more scope with the Wooing Plays. The recent discoveries made by Dr E. C. Cawte in Leicestershire prove that more field work will produce more examples for study, and far from the music being forgotten in these examples, Dr Cawte is proving that the patient collector can find extraordinarily complete versions which are adding considerably to our knowledge.

Scremerston, Northumberland, Hero-Combat version

Ordish Collection

Northumbrian versions are extremely short and confine themselves to the bare action required. There is usually an absence of *Quête* characters, but the actual begging is not omitted as this version demonstrates. The disguise is simple, merely dressing in character, with an attempt at blackened faces, and very often the performers were children. Only three characters are mentioned in this version which would permit them not only to move round the district more quickly but also to have an increased share in whatever collection was taken. The ceremony has largely disappeared from the versions, and the object of begging has become of supreme importance.

Redd[1] sticks, redd stools!
Here comes in a pack of fools,
A pack of fools behind the door,
Step in, Slasher.

Enter Slasher
Slasher is my name!   5
With sword and pistol by my side
I hope to win the game.

Enter Goliath[2]
The game, sir, the game, sir!
It's not within your power.
I'll strike you into inches   10
Within this half an hour.

Chorus
Fight on, fight on, ye gentlemen!
Fight on, fight on with speed!
Fight on, fight on yer warriors,
And slay Goliath dead.   15

Slasher
Is there a Doctor in this town?

Enter Dr Brown
Here come I, Dr Brown,
The best doctor in the town.
From nation to nation I've learnt my trade,
And come to England to cure the dead.   20

Slasher
What can you cure?

Doctor
Coughs and colds, Pox and Scurvy and many things more.
I have a little bottle by my side called Inky-Pinky-[3]
I give this man three drops.

Gives them to Goliath
Rise up Jack and fight again.   25

Goliath jumps up and fights again
Once I was dead but now I'm alive,
Bless the kind doctor that made me alive!
We'll all shake hands and never fight no more.

Each crosses his hands and join hands in a circle, all dance round continuing to shake hands in a circle.
But be as good brethren as we were before.

Health to the master, the mistress also,   30
And all the little children that round the table go.
With your pockets full of money and your cellar full of
    beer,
We wish you a Merry Christmas and a Happy New Year.

Hats carried round during this song.

Costumes
White shirts, smutted cheeks, or corked moustaches,
&c., high paper caps, wooden swords or sticks.

Footnotes to Scremerston Text
1. Prepare.
2. This is a variant of 'Galations' (see p. 31).
3. Elecampane.

Greenodd, Lancashire, Pace-Egg Version. Hero-Combat

Miss Anne R. Burkett: Collection

Pace-egg versions are to be found in North Lancashire,
Westmorland and Cumberland. The action is stereotyped, usually a single death and revival, and a lament,
spoken in this instance by the 'Female', Molly Masket.
The song which should be a Calling-on Song has become
part of the *Quête*, but of the seven characters introduced
in the song, only the 'Female' has any part in the
dramatic action. The Hunchback who complains about
the Doctor's cure was probably Tosspot, but the other
characters of the song, Lord Nelson, Paddy from Cork,
etc., exist where the Pace-egging was confined to
children singing the song only. The large number of
characters involved if all actually appeared would make
this a fairly large company, and the likelihood is that one
performer doubled other parts. The dressing in character
is also typical of the area.

Stir up the fire and strike a light,
And see this noble act tonight.
If you don't believe a word I say,
Step in, King George, and clear the way.

King George steps forward and says
In steps I, King George, a noble champion bold,   5
With my right hand and glittering sword
I won three crowns of gold.

Enter Prince of Paradise
In steps I, Prince of Paradise, black Morocco King,
My sword and buckle by my side and through the woods
    I ring,
And through the woods I ring.   10
I'm brave, lads, and that's what makes us good;
And through thy dearest body, George, I'll draw thy
    precious blood.

King George
If thou be made of Jinnus' race.
I'll make blood sprinkle down thy face;
If thou be made of noble blood,   15
I'll make it run like Noah's flood.

Prince of Paradise
Black I am, and black I be,
Lately come from Africa;
Africa's my dwelling-place,
And now I'll fight thee face to face.   20

They fight and Prince falls

Molly Masket
Oh, George! Oh, George! What hast thou done?

Thou's gone and slain my only son,
My only son, my only heir!
Can'st thou not see him bleeding there?

King George
He challenged me to fight, and why should I
    deny?   25
I'll cut his body in four parts and make his buttons fly.
I've heard of doctors far and near,
I've heard of one in Spain,
I'm sure if he was here he'd bring
That dead man to life again.   30

Takes out his purse
I'll give five, ten, fifteen, twenty-five pounds for a
    doctor.
Is there not one to be had?

Dr Brown
Yes! In steps I, old Jackie Brown,
The best old doctor in this town.

King George
How came you to be a doctor?   35

Dr Brown
By my travels.

King George
How far did you travel?

Dr Brown
From Hip-tip-to, Tallyantic Ocean,
Ninety degrees below bottom,
Where I saw houses built of rounds of beef, slated with
    pancakes;   40
Roasted pig running up and down the street
With knives and forks sticking in their teeth
Crying, 'Here's a living! Who'll die?'
Last night, yesterday morning,
About three o'clock in the afternoon,   45
As I was going through St Paul's churchyard,
The very dead arose crying, 'Doctor! Doctor! Give me a
    box of your ever-failing pills.
It's a pity a man like me should ever die'.
When I was going through town this morning I saw a
    dead dog jump up.
It bit a man's leg and made his stocking bleed.   50

King George
Any further?

Dr Brown
Yes, a little.

King George
How far?

Dr Brown
From my grandmother's bed to the stairhead,
From the stairhead to the chair leg,   55
From the chair leg to the three corner cupboard
Where they kept the bread and cheese,
Which makes any man grow fat and lusty.

King George
I am not talking about fat.

Dr Brown
Neither am I talking about lean.   60

King George
What are you talking about?

Dr Brown
What I can cure.

King George
What can you cure?

Dr Brown
Ipsy-pipsy, palsy and the gout,
The plague within and the plague without.   65
If there's nineteen devils in that man
I'm sure to drive one-and-twenty out.

King George
Drive them out!

Dr Brown
Here I lay down my gold watch,
Points to half past hundred and forty four.   70
I have also a little bottle in my inside, outside, rightside,
    leftside, waistcoat pocket, which my grandmother gave
    me three days after she died, saying, 'Take this, it'll
    bring any dead man to life again'.

King George
Bring that dead man to life again.   75

Doctor gives Prince a dose

Dr Brown
Here, Jack, take a drop of this bottle,
Let it run down thy throttle,
Rise up, Bold Slash, and fight again.

Hunchback, raising a leg of the dead man
As green as grass and as cold as brass.
This man's never stirred a limb yet, doctor.   80

Dr Brown
Perhaps my silly old wife's given me the wrong bottle.

Molly Masket
Thou's a limestone!

Dr Brown
Then perhaps it's my mistake.

Produces another bottle
Here, Jack, take a drop of this my nip-nap,

Let it run down thy thip-thap;   85
Rise up, Bold Slash, and fight again.

Prince of Paradise rises

Prince of Paradise
Oh! my back!

Dr Brown
What's amiss with thy back?

Prince of Paradise
My back is bound,
My sword is sound,   90
I'll have King George another round.

They fight again briefly.

Dr Brown
Stop, stop these swords without delay,
And fight again another day.

Song[1]
So the first to come in is old Tosspot, you see
A jolly old fellow in every degree;   95
He wears a top hat and he wears a pig tail,
And all his delight is in drinking mulled ale.
Fol de la, fol de la,
Fol de diddle di dom day.

In comes I that never came yet,   100
Great head and litle wit.
If my wit be ever so small,
Me and my Pompey'll wallop you all.

So the next that comes in is old Mally, you see,
She's a jolly old lassie as ever you see;   105
She's gold and she's silver and copper in store,
And by coming pace-egging she hopes to get more.

In comes I, old Mally Masket,
Under my arm I carry my basket.
In my basket I carry my eggs,   110
With my eggs I carry my brass,
And I think myself a jolly old lass.

So the next that comes in is Lord Nelson, you see,
With a bunch of blue ribbons right down to his knee,
A star on his breast like silver does shine,   115
And he hopes you will have a good pace-egging time.

So the next that comes in is a jolly Jack Tar,
Who fought with Lord Nelson during the last war;
He's fresh from the sea, old England to view,
And he joins in pace-egging with this jolly crew.   120

So the next to come in is a soldier, you see,
Who's fought against the Frenchmen in a far country.
He's a sword by his side wherever he goes,
To teach all young lasses so and so.

So the next to come in is poor Paddy from Cork;   125
He hails from ould Ireland, he comes to seek work;
He's his scythe on his back, and he comes to work hay,
And then he's off back to ould Erin again.

Here's two or three jolly boys all in a row,
We've come a pace-egging, as you all well know.   130
Spare not eggs and small beer, and you needn't fear
That you'll see us again till this time next year.

Ladies and gentlemen, sit by the fire,
Put your hand in your pocket for all you desire.

Put your hand in your pocket and take out your
   purse,
And give us a trifle, you'll be nothing worse.   135

Costume
Performers were children dressed in adult's clothing.
They also wore crowns, top hats, bonnets and gowns,

morning suits and sailor suits. Wooden swords and a
doctor's bag. Large butter basket for collecting eggs.

Footnotes to Greenodd text
1. The music for the song was not collected, but a
version similar is given in Alex Helm: *Five Mumming
Plays for Schools*, 1965, 37.

Antrobus, Cheshire, Soul-Caking Play. Hero-Combat

Alex Helm: Cheshire Folk Drama, *1968, 13–21*

Of the many versions formerly existing in Cheshire, this
is the only one still traditionally performed. Its time of
appearance is All Souls and the performers dress according to character. Its similarity to the Pace-egg versions,
both in song and text, is noticeable, though here the
characters of the song are reduced to two, neither of
whom appear in the action proper. The main action
largely follows the dialogue of the chapbooks, apart from
the 'Female' lamenter, but when the purely traditional
characters appear in the *Quête*, there is a reversion to the

nonsense lines of the traditional versions. Beelzebub has
the topsy-turvey lines found elsewhere, and after the
Land of Cockayne extract, the Wild Horse's Driver makes
some purely topical allusions. The begging is centred on
the appearance of the Horse, and its purpose is to prepare for his retirement. It is very similar to the Old Horse
Ceremonies of Derbyshire and elsewhere, where the
function was to beg with a similar hobby-horse, but
without dramatic action. The final song was probably
one familiar to the performers of the time as an added
inducement to generosity.

And the next that steps up is a miser you see,
He wears his old rags to every degree;   10
And when he does sell them, he sells them so dear
That no-one will buy them until this time next year.

Letter In knocks on door and enters house or inn

Letter In
Now ladies and gentlemen, light a fire and strike a light,
For in this house there's going to be a dreadful fight
Between King George and the Black Prince,   15

And I hope King George will win.
Whether he wins, loses, fights or falls,
We'll do our best to please you all.

Exit

King George
In comes I, the champion bold,
I've won £10,000 in gold,   20
'Twas I who fought the fire dragon and brought him to
   the slaughter,

And by these means I won the King of Egypt's daughter.
I've travelled the whole world round and round,
But never a man of my equal found.
If you don't believe these words I say,   25
Step in, Black Prince, and clear the way.

Black Prince
In comes I, Black Prince of Paradise, born of high
    renown,
I've come to take King George's life and courage down,
If that be he who standeth there, who slew my master's
    son and heir,
If that be he of royal blood,   30
I'll make it flow like Noah's flood.

King George
Ah! Ah! Mind what thou sayest.

Black Prince
What I say, I mean.

King George
Stand back, thou black Morocco dog! or by my sword
    thou'll die.
I'll pierce thy body full of holes and make thy buttons
    fly.   35

Black Prince
How canst thou make my body full of holes and make
    my buttons fly?
When my body is made of iron,
My fingers and toes of double joints,
I challenge thee to yield!
Prepare!   40

They fight and Black Prince falls dead. Enter Mary.

Mary
Oh! King George! What hast thou done?
Thou's killed and slain my only son, my only heir,
See how he lies dead and bleeding there!

King George
Well, Mary, he challenged me to fight,
Better to fight than to die.   45
Ten pounds for a doctor, five for a quack!
If you don't believe these words I say,
Step in Quack Doctor and clear the way.

Enter Quack Doctor

Quack Doctor
In comes I, who never cometh yet,
The best quack doctor you can get.   50
Here I come from the continent to cure this man King
    George has slain.

Mary
How camest thou to be a doctor?

Doctor
By my travels.

Mary
And where hast thou travelled?

Doctor
Icaly, Picaly, France and Spain,   55

Three times out to the West Indies
And back to old England to cure diseases again.

Mary
And what disease canst thou cure?

Doctor
All sorts.

Mary
And what's all sorts?   60

Quack Doctor
All sorts; the Hump, the Grump, the Ger, the Gout,
The pain within and the pain without.
In my bag I've got spectacles to blind humblebees,
    crutches for lame mice, plasters for broken backed
    earwigs. I've pills and I've powders for all kinds of
    aches, including headache, earache, also cold shakes. 85
    I've lotions and I've motions, also some fine notions
    that have carried my fame far wide over five oceans.

Mary
And what are thy fees to cure my son?

Doctor
Five pounds, Mary, but you being a decent woman, I'll
    only charge you ten.

Mary
Well, cure him!   70

Doctor (to Black Prince)
Here, John, take three sips from this bottle down thy
    thrittle throttle.
Now arise, and fight thy battle.

Mary
Thou silly man, as green as grass, the dead man never
    stirs.

Quack Doctor
Oh! Mary, I quite forgot. I took the right bottle off the
    wrong cork. I have another little bottle here in my
    inside? – no, outside? – somewhere round the backside 75
    pocket, which will soon bring him to life again.

Stoops and gives another drink. Black Prince stirs.

Black Prince
Oh! my back!

Mary
What ails thy back, my son?

Black Prince
My back is broken,   80
My heart is confounded,
Knocked out of seven centuries into fourteen score,
Which has never been known in Old England before.

Quack Doctor
Here, John, take three drops of this down thy thrittle
    throttle,
Now arise and fight thy battle.   85

King George and Black Prince fight again. Enter Letter In.

70

Letter In
Lay down your sword and rest
For peace and quietness is the best.
He who fights and runs away
Lives to fight another day.
If you don't believe these words I say,   90
Step in, Derry Doubt, and clear the way.

Derry Doubt dances in

Derry Doubt
In comes little Derry Doubt,
With my shirt lap hanging out,
Five yards in and five yards out –   95
Out goes little Derry Doubt.

Dances in and out
If you don't believe these words I say,
Step in Beelzebub, and clear the way.

Beelzebub
In comes Be-i-l-ze-bub,
On my shoulder I carry my club,   100
In my hands a dripping pan,
And I reckon myself a jolly old man.
With a rin-tin-tin, I sup more drink,
I'll drink a pot dry with any man.
I've just done six months in gaol for making a whip crack
    out of a mouse's tail.   105
Early Monday morning, late on Saturday night,
I saw a 10,000 miles away a house just out of sight.
The doors projected backwards, the front was at the
    back.
It stood alone between two more and the walls was
    whitewashed black.
If you don't believe these words I say,   110
Step in, Wild Horse, and clear the way.

Enter Wild Horse and Driver

Driver
In comes Dick and all his men,
He's come to see you once again.
He was once alive, but now he's dead,
He's nothing but a poor old horse's head.   115
Stand around Dick, and show yourself!
Now, ladies and gentlemen, just view around,
See whether you've seen a better horse on any ground.
He's double ribbed, sure footed, and a splendid horse in
    any gears.

And ride him if you can!   120
He's travelled high, he's travelled low,
He's travelled all through frost and snow,
He's travelled the land of Ikerty Pikkery,
Where there's neither land nor city;
Houses thatched with pancakes,   125
Walls built with penny loaves,
Pig puddings for bell ropes, and black puddings growing
    on apple trees;
Little pigs running about with knives and forks in their
    backs,
Crying out, 'Who'll eat men?'
He's a very fine horse, he's of a very fine mould,   130
We've got to keep him clothed to save him from the cold.
If you look down this horse's mouth, you'll see holes in
    his socks.
This horse was bred in Seven Oaks,
The finest horse e'er fed on oats;
He's won the Derby and the Oaks,   135
And now pulls an old milk-float.
But that's not all this horse's history!
Oh no! He's as many rinkles and jinkles in his head as
    there are furrows in an acre of new ploughed land. His
    ears are made out of a lady's pocket book, his tongue
    from an old box hat, and his tail from a tachin end.[1]
Stand round, Dick!
As I was going round Frandley Brow the other day, this 140
    horse broke loose, ran into a lady's parlour, broke all
    the glass wheelbarrows, wooden fire-irons, &c. Now I
    ask you all to open your hears to buy Dick a new sprung
    cart. Not one for him to pull, oh dear, no! but for him to
    ride in. If you don't believe these words I say, ask those
    chaps outside there. They're better liars than I am.

Song (Tune – Flanagan's Band)[2]
Oh! for now our play is ended and we can no longer
    stay,
But with your kind permission, we will call another day,
    &c.

(Finishes)
It's a credit to old England and the boys of the Antrobus
gang.

Footnotes to Antrobus text
1. The meaning of this phrase was not clear.
2. The music for this part was not collected, but presumably 'Flanagan's Band' is an error for 'Macnamara's
   Band'.

Islip, Oxfordshire, Mummers Play. Hero-Combat

*P. J. Manning Collection. Bodleian Library MS Top. Oxon.
d.199, f.307–9*

The following version was performed in Percy Manning's presence in 1894. It is one of two versions which are
from this location, the other one being dated, reputedly,
at 1780. In the hundred or so years between the versions,
some changes have taken place. In 1780 a character
called Anna Domino replaced Molly, and the Duke of
Northumberland was the Duke of Blunderland, no
doubt a confused recollection of Jack and the Beanstalk
and Giant Blunderbore. An additional character in 1780

was Salt Peter who had lines similar to those normally
spoken by Jack Finney. King George was obviously a
later substitution, since in 1780, the part was given to
Earl or King Percy. The action has all the typical Cotswold features of fight, combat, cure and tooth-drawing,
and indeed, the latter has replaced the normal *quête*. This
is a typical traditional version with few elements of chapbook examples present.

Enter Molly with broom in hand
In comes I, old Molly, sweeping up.
Merry, Merry Christmas, a Happy New Year,

Pocket full of money and cellar full of beer.
I had six children last night, I bred them up in a tinder
  box.
I had a slice of bread and lard given me the night
  before;   5
I eat all that myself.
Don't you think I'm a jolly old mother to them all?

Shouts
Come in the next man!

Enter Northumberland brandishing sword
In come I, the royal Duke of Northumberland
With my broad sword in my hand.   10
Where's the man that dares to bid me stand?
I would cut him as small as flies
And send him to the cookshop to make mince-pies.
Mince pies hot, mince pies cold,
I send him to the old man before he's nine days
  old!   15

Molly
Come in next man!

Enter King George brandishing sword
Where is that man that dares to bid me stand?
Although he swaggers and swears he'd cut me up as
  small as flies,
And send me to the cook-shop to make mince pies,
Mince pies hot, mince pies cold,   20
And send me to the old man before I'm nine days old;
Battle to battle, betwixt you and I,
See which on the ground first, you or I,
Guard your blows, and guard your nose,
Or on the ground you quickly goes.   25

They fight and Northumberland falls.

King George
Doctor, doctor, I've killed a man!

Doctor's Voice from without
More like a monkey and stole his.

King George
Doctor, doctor, do your part!
For King George is wounded to the heart;[1]
From the heart to the knee –   30
I'll give five shillings for a good old doctor like thee.

Doctor
I shan't come for five shillings or nothing like it.

King George
Ten shillings then.

Doctor
That's more like it!

King George
Come in, Jack Spinney.   35

Enter Doctor
My name's not Jack Spinney.
My name's Mr Spinney.
A man of great pain,
Do more than you or any man again.

King George
What can you do so clever?   40

Doctor
Cure the magpie of toothache.

King George
How should you do it?

Doctor
Cut off his head and throw his body in the ditch.

King George
Come and serve this man the same.

Doctor
In comes I, old Dr Good,[2]   45
Whose hands are never stained with blood.
I'm not one of those quick quack doctors. I come to do
  the good of the country, both to ladies and gentlemen.
I can cure the hip, the pip,
The palsey and the gout.
And if the old man's in that man,   50
I can fetch him out.
I've travelled old England, Scotland, Wales and Spain,
Take one of my soft pills and rise again!

Gives pill and Northumberland rises
Come in next man!

Enter Beelzebub
In comes I, old Beelzebub,   55
On my shoulders I carry my club;
In my hand a frying pan.
Don't you think I'm a jolly old man?
Come in, next man!

Enter Fat Jack
In comes I, old Fat Jack,   60
My wife and family at my back;[3]
My wife's so big, my family small,
I've brought a rattle to please you all.

They all dance round the room. Molly falls down and groans.

King George
My wife Susannah looks very ill.

Doctor
What's her complaint?   65

King George
Toothache, I think.

Doctor
Fetch my horse, Jack.

Fat Jack
I shan't. Fetch it yourself.

Doctor
What? Keep a dog and bark myself? Fetch him this
  minute!

*Fat Jack fetches one of the disengaged characters, and Doctor
tries to get on his back. He plunges about.*
Give us a leg up, Jack! Woa! Woa!   70

72

Doctor is then thrown off
Jack, you give my horse too much corn.

Jack
I only give a bean and a half.

Doctor
That's a bean too much!

Fat Jack
Feed him yourself next time then.

Doctor examines Molly and gets out a pair of pincers
Toothache, you think?   75

King George
Yes.

Doctor
Just come and give a pull then.

Takes hold of nail which Molly has sticking out of her mouth.
Pull! *(Fails to draw it)* That's not got him!
Pull! *(Draws out nail)* That's got him!
Why! Here's a tooth here as long as a two inch nail,   80
And got roots like a poplar tree!
I'll put that in my pocket for a keepsake.
Bring me an old woman that's been dead seven years,
Seven years laid in her grave.

She could rise up and eat bread and cheese
   hearty,   85
Her life I'm bound to save.
I've travelled old England, Scotland, Wales and Spain,
Take one of my pills and rise again.

Molly takes pill and rises

Costume
Molly   Old woman in a sunbonnet, carrying a broom.
King George   Carries a broad sword.
Duke of Northumberland   Carries a broad sword.
Doctor   Blue coat with brass buttons.
Beelzebub   Black face, bludgeon in one hand, frying
   pan in the other.
Fat Jack   Has a large hump on his back and carries thick
stick.

Footnotes to Islip Text
1. There is confusion here. If King George is wounded, Northumberland should be speaking. Possibly the victor varied from time to time.
2. The Doctor has obviously changed his name since his first entrance. It is possible that Jack Spinney was originally a character who was dropped with the passage of time.
3. This character is the equivalent of Johnny Jack in Hampshire.

Minehead, Somerset, Mummers' Play. Hero-Combat

Ordish Collection

The text was collected in 1895 when the play had not taken place for over fifteen years. The words were said to have been derived from a printed book which came from Swansea, 'might be a hundred years ago'. The action shows that some practised writer had worked over the text, and the ceremony has clearly given way to entertainment. A normal Hero-Combat version is buried in the literary text, and there has been attempt at humour, even poor humour of the variety of one character beating another. There appears to be an attempt at a wooing towards the end of the action, expressed in song, for which the music was not given. The interpolation of purely historical characters amongst the traditional, fictional ones is normal of texts from this area. It is difficult to see how many performances could be given with an action as long as this one must have been, and probably there was less dependence in the performances on the collection. In any event, any collection, divided amongst the number of performers needed would be very small. The photograph (Plate 15) shows an unusual elaboration of dress, and it is clear that even by 1880, or whenever the last performance was, the ceremonial content was very small.

Enter Two Mummers

1st Mummer
Gentlemen, ladies, upon my forehead!
It's on my shoulder I carry my sword.

I show my sport, I bend my rhyme,
And now I'm fit for Christmas time.
'Tis now in the merry time of Christmas.   5
And Christmas draweth near,
I hope your pockets are full of money
And your cellars full of beer.
And if you believe not what I say,
Walk in old Father Christmas and boldly clear the
   way.   10

They retire

Father Christmas
Here comes I, Old Father Christmas;
Welcome or welcome not,
I hope old Father Christmas
Will never be forgot.
When, in the midst of summer,   15
The sun it shineth hot,
'Tis then old Father Christmas
Is almost quite forgot.
But now, in the winter time,
When his old grey beard is frozen with ice,   20
And his old bald head is covered with snow,
I hope you'll make him welcome before I go.

Marches round. Enter Dame Dorothy

Dame
Here comes I, old Mother Dorrity,
Fat face and go marity;[1]
Head big and body small,   25
The purtiest little cratur amongst us all.

Father
What say? the purtiest little woman amongst us all?
The ugliest old jade amongst us all –
Can't I never go out to a ladies' and gentleman's party.
But thee art always larripin' after me?   30

Dame
Thee out to a ladies' and gentlemen's party?
All thee dost mind is after the ladies.

Father
And all thee dost mind is after the fellows! So,
There's a pair of us. What dost want me home for?

Beats her

Dame
Come home to supper.   35

Beats him

Father
What's got for supper?

Dame
A good old favourite of thine.

Father
What's got?

Dame
A girt dish of water porridge.

Father
A girt dish of water porridge and a girt long pitching-
    pick to ate it wi'?   40
Porridge is so thin, I do suppose,
I'll have to doff all my small clothes.
And jump in round to catch the bread.

Dame (beats him)
That's good enough for thee, thee old rogue.

Father
What's got for theeself?   45

Dame
Tea, toast and butter; tea, toast and butter.

Father
Tea, toast and butter! Anything is good enough for me!
I tell thee what, old woman,
I'll tell thee a little of thy own.

Dame
What canst thee tell me?   50

Father (leaning forward on his stick)
Dost mind the time when thee was up in Jossy
    Hosegood's fuzzy brake?
When the wind blowed high,
And the wind blowed low;
And the wind blowed puff –

Dame (knocks away his stick and he falls)
And down thee didst go.   55

Father (rising)
Sudden change this from my last wife,

When I had a silver watch in my pocket and a gold guard
    hanging out.
Now I'm walking about with my trousers a-broke and
    my sleeves hanging out.

Dame (beating him round)
Good enough for thee, thee old rogue.

Father
Ah! I tell thee what, old woman!   60
If thee disn't mind my words
Thee shan't be my blowse.
So thee hook it!

Drives her out. Laughing
I've driven the old jade out at last.
Although I'm come, I have short time to stay;   65
Then walk in, St George, and boldly clear the way.
Enter brave champion, and boldly act thy part,
And let the noble company see thou hast a lion's heart.

Exit Father Christmas. Enter St George

St George
Here come I, St George, I've many hazards run,
And fought in every land that lies beneath the
    sun.   70
I am a famous champion,
Likewise a worthy knight,
And from Britain did I spring
And will uphold her might.
I travelled countries far and near,   75
As you may understand,
Until at last I did arrive
In the Egyptian land.
Wherein that horrid fight
With the fiery dragon bold,   80
Did neither overcome, nor kill,
Nor make my blood run cold.
I fought the cursed dragon and brought him to the
    slaughter,
And for that deed did win the King of Egypt's daughter.
And now the tyrant Valentine   85
Has challenged me to fight,
And given his word without delay
To meet me here tonight.
I am for England's right,
And England's admiration,   90
And soon you'll see me draw
This weapon in vexation.
Is there a man that me can stand?
Let him come, and I'll cut him down
With my courageous hand.   95

Enter Valentine, the Morocco King

Morocco King
I am the bold Morocco King, and Valentine is my name;
Thy lofty courage soon my hand shall turn to shame.
For such a fall thou shalt receive of me,
So let us fight it out most manfully.

St George
Art thou the traitor Valentine   100
That led fair Zebedee away,
When I the fiery dragon
For that Egyptian maid did slay?
If thou art he, I'm glad to meet thee here,
And for that thing thy life shall pay most dear.   105

Morocco King
St. George! St George! 'Twere well to yield thy right,
For lo! I am a King, and thou art but a knight.

St George
Oh! thou silly braying ass that feeds on thistles, weeds
    and grass,
Don't offer to abuse a stranger.
For by word I'll buy a cord   110
And tie thy nose unto the manger.
None of thy kingly powers do I mind,
My sword shall answer thee and all thy traitor kind.
Of such a man as thou, I'll never be afraid,
So let us fight it out for the Egyptian maid.   115

They fight and Valentine is killed. Enter Prince Imbridge

Imbridge
As I was rising from my bed,
I heard my own dear son was dead.
Oh! thou cursed Christian, what hast thou done?
Thou'st slain me by the slaying of my own dear son.

St George
He first to me the challenge gave   120
And how could I deny, to see how high he looked
And now how low doth lie?

Imbridge
I see him lying there,
Which makes my heart to bleed;
Distracted I shall run,   125
Was ever greater need?
Help, help, my faithful Sambo,
Avenge my own dear son.
Make no delay, but gird thyself and take thy sword in
    hand
And fight as a royal subject, under thy King's
    command   130
For me, my time is come,
For me, my sands are run;
I'll lie down and die
Along with my own dear son.

Lies down, embraces Valentine and dies. Enter Sambo.

Sambo
Here come I, Sambo, Prince Imbridge's law I do
    obey,   135
And, with my sword in hand; I hope to win the day.
See yonder, he that standeth there,
Hath killed my master and his only son and heir.
I'll try him if he's made of noble blood,
I'll make his body flow like Noah's flood.   140
I'll through thy body make an empty way
If thou hast anything against my tender master, say.

St George
I nothing have to say against thy tender master or thee,
So let us fight it out most manfully.

They fight. Sambo is wounded.

Sambo
Hold! Hold! St George, pray fight no more,   145
For I am wounded very sore.

St George
Rise, rise, and speed thee home to thy own land,
And tell what champions thou hast seen in old England.

Sambo (rises)
I'll rise, St George, pray fight no more,
For I am wounded very sore.   150

*Sambo goes out. St George retires. Two men remain lying.
Enter Dame Dorothy.*

Dame
Oh! the poor dear men! Oh! the poor dear men!

(Repeat ad lib.)
They've a-been in the wars; they've a-been in the wars.

Enter Father Christmas

Father (singing)
Fal-the-lal-the diddle-al-the-way,
Fal the lal, &c., *(ad lib.)*

Dame
Poor men! They've been in the wars.   155

Father
In the wars! In the wars!
So have I been in the wars;
In the battle of pea-soup,
When the soup flied all over my head,
And now I'm bald-headed.   160

Takes off hat

Dame
Thee been in the wars? *Beats him*
See these poor dear men. *Beats him*
I shall get a doctor.

Father
I shall get a carpenter.

Dame
I shall get the doctor.   165

Father
I shall get the carpenter.
They shall have a timmern jacket
That shall last them all their lifetime.

Dame
They shall have a doctor. They ain't dead yet.
Why dissn't feel the pulse of 'em. *(Strikes him)*   170

He lifts Valentine's legs

Father
Here's a fine pair of holds for a sole.

Dame
Why dissn't feel the pulse of 'em? *(Beats him)*

He feels their heads

Father
Why their hair is standing like pounds of rushlights.

Dame Dorrity feels pulse

Dame
I'm going for the doctor.

Father
Is there a doctor to be found,   175
All ready near at hand;
To cure a deep and deadly wound,
And make these champions stand?

Enter Doctor

Doctor
Oh yes, there is a doctor to be found
All ready near at hand,   180
Can cure a deep and deadly wound
And make these champions stand.
I am a learned doctor, lately come from Spain;
I can cure all diseases and raise to life again,
I can cure the itch, the stitch, the palsy and the   185
    gout,
And if the devil's in, I'll quickly drive him out.

Father
Thee call he a Spanish doctor? Looks more like a
    Portugee.

Dame
Insulting the doctor again? *(Beats him)*
Why dissn't ax² him about his fees?

Father *(feels the Doctor's knees)*
Doctor, how's thee knees?   190

Doctor
What meanest thou? My knees are right.

Dame *(beating him)*
Fees! Fees! Thee old rogue!

Father
What's fees, fees?

Dame
What's to pay?

Doctor
Ten pounds in money.   195

Dame
Ten pounds in money?

Father
Ten crocks of honey? I can't carry it.

Dame
Ax him to do it for a farden³ cheaper.

Father
I am a poor old man and have a scolding wife,
Cassn't do it for a farden cheaper?   200

Doctor
You're a fatherly looking man,
And have a scolding wife;
And as 'tis such a rogue as thou,
I'll cure them both for five.

Dame
That's the doctor for me; that's the doctor for me.   205

Father *(beating her)*
Go up top a penny loaf and fall down and break thee
    neck. That'll be the doctor for thee.

Dame
Better ax the doctor to get on with his job. Ax him to give
    'em some pills.

Father
Doctor, cassn't thee give 'em some mills?

Doctor
That's what the miller has to grind the corn with.

Dame *(striking him)*
Thee old rogue! Why dissn't ax him for pills?   210

Father
What dost call they things you stir about in a bucket?

Dame
Apple dumplings, thee old rogue. That's the bolters for
    thee.

To doctor
You'd better go on with your job.

Doctor *(gives pills)*
Here's pills to cure ague;
And pills to cure pain: 215
Here's pills will bring the dead to life.
Rise, Jack, and fight again.

Both men rise and walk round, arm in arm.

Father
Horrible! Terrible! the like was never seen.
A man struck out of his seven senses into nineteen.

*Dance. Father Christmas, Dame Dorrity, Doctor and
Valentine. Enter Turkish Knight.*

Turk
Here come I, the Turkish Knight,   220
Come from the Turkish land to fight.
I'll fight St George, who is my foe,
I'll make him yield before I go.
He brags to such a high degree,
He thinks there's none the like of he.   225
So, here I am, the Turkish Knight,
Come from the Turkish land to fight.

Enter St George

St George
Fight who?

Turk
Fight thee, St George, thou man of courage bold,
And if thy blood is hot, I soon will make it cold.   230

St George
Hold! Hold! Proud Turk! Be not so hot.
In me is one thou knowest not.
To whom dost thou the challenge give?

Turk
To thee, thou English dog!
No longer shalt thou live.   235

St George
Talk not of English dog,
Nor yet of Turkish knight;
Or in one moment's time
I'll make thee for to fight.   240
Draw forth thy sword and fight.
Pull out thy purse and pay,
For satisfaction I will have,
Before thou goest away.

Turk
No satisfaction shalt thou have,
Before I've made of thee my Turkish slave.   245

They fight. The Turk is struck down.

Turk
Hold! Hold! St George, pray, fight no more,
For I am wounded very sore.

St George
Rise! Rise! thou Turkish dog,
Go home to thine own land
And tell what champions thou hast seen   250
In this our old England.
With 30,000 men like thee I'll fight
For to maintain the crown which is the British right.

Turk (rises)
I'll rise, St George, and go my way
God bless the King and all his ships at sea.   255

St George
Where are my champions, brave?
Let them appear.

Enter two Mummers

Mummers
Here are thy champions, sword in hand,
Ready to obey at thy command.

St George
Take that man hence; bind him in chains so
    strong,   260
Cast him into prison, for his time shall not be long.

They take Turk out
God bless the King and all his men of war,
Bold British hearts, the soldiers and the tar.
Shades of British heroes, 'gainst whom none could
    stand,
Now shall rise before us, mighty in command.   265

He waves his sword. Enter Admiral Duncan.

Duncan
Drums beat to arms, trumpets sound to fame.
I am a British hero, Admiral Duncan is my name.
I served my Royal Master with credit and renown,
And won for him the victory at the battle of
    Camperdown.

St George waves his sword. Enter Lord Nelson.

Nelson
Drums beat to arms, trumpets sound to fame.   270
I am a British hero, Lord Nelson is my name.
On the 26th December, that being the very day,
Nineteen sails of line – some struck, some sunk, some
    cowardly bore away.

St George waves his sword. Enter General Wolfe.

Wolfe
Drums beat to arms, trumpets sound to fame.
I am a British hero, General is my name.   275
How many rocks have I climbed,
How many walls have I scaled?
Never haunted nor daunted at all,
Till at last the fiery bullet
Came and struck me in the gall.   280
There on the watery sands I bleeding lay,
Midst the fierce sounds of war's alarms,
Till, from above, a Voice to me did say,
Rise, General Wolfe, die in my sheltering arms.

Dancer. All retire. Enter Giant.

Giant
Here come I, the Giant – 'ugh! 'ugh! 'ugh!   285
Beelzebub's my name – 'ugh! 'ugh! 'ugh!
I come here from a giant race,
Is there a man can look me in the face?
With my long teeth and crooked claws,
Soon will I grind him in my jaws,   290
Here come I, Beelzebub,
Under my arm I carry a club;
Under my chin I carry a pan,
Don't I look a jolly old man?

Enter Little Man Jan.

Jan
Here come I, Little Man Jan,   295
With sword and pistol in my hand.
Where'er I go they tremble at my sight,
No lord or champion long with me can fight.
I've made the French to tremble and the Spanish for to
    quake,
I've fought the jolly Dutchman until their hearts did
    ache.   300
If there's a man will now before me stand,
He soon shall humbly fall by my courageous hand.

*Giant comes forward with a roar. Jan shakes at knees, flies
round stage, pursued by Giant, who strikes at Jan and misses.
Jan dodges round, fires pistol, misses and finally runs out.
Enter Slasher.*

Slasher
In come I, Slasher, the valiant man.
I dare, Beelzebub, to look thee in the face
And soon will send thee off unto another place.   305

Giant (comes forward with a roar)
Who is the daring rogue, who, low or high,
Comes forward with big words me to defy?
I'll beat him and smash him as small as a fly,
And send him to Mother Dorrity to make apple pie.
I'll grind him and grind him as small as the dust,   310
And send him to old Father Christmas to make apple-pie
    crust.

Slasher
Oh-ho! I dare thy challenge to defy,
And soon thy ugly carcase low at my feet shall lie.

*They fight and dodge round. The Giant hits a tremendous blow
and misses and loses his balance. Slasher runs him through.
He falls.*

Slasher (spurning him)
So perish all who dare with me to fight.

Retires. Enter Father Christmas and Dame Dorrity

Dame
Oh! here's a purty state of things. Oh my! Beelzebub's
   dead.   *315*

Father
Then let him die!

Dame (strikes him)
You old rogue, don't you see he'll pay us well if we cure
   him?
Here's more work for the doctor.

Father
Here's more work for the carpenter. I don't like the
   doctor's fees.
We owe him five pounds.   *320*

Dame
Then charge this man twenty. I'll fetch the doctor.

Fetches him. Enter Doctor.

Father
Here's a case for some of thy pills
That cures a man of all his deadly ills.
Call this man to life again,
And then of pounds we'll give thee ten.   *325*

Dame (beats him)
No! No! Five. That's the doctor's charge. Now then,
   doctor, get about it, get about it.

Doctor
Come, take my pills; they cure all ills,
Past, present and to come.
Take a little of my niff-naff
Put it down thy tiff-taff
Rise up and fight again.   *330*

Giant (rises, rubs his eyes)
'Tis wondrous strange again to rise,
And feel once more the strength that in me lies.

Dame
Now, Mr Beelzebub, you've got to pay the doctor.

Father
Yes! Yes! Pay the doctor! I'll take the money.   *335*

Giant
How much?

Father
Twenty pounds in gold.

Doctor
My fee is five.

Dame
He's a rich old gentleman and can pay more.
It's nought to him to have to pay a score.   *340*

Doctor
And what am I to have?

Dame
You shall have your five.

Father
Yes, you shall have your five, and perhaps a farden
   more.

Doctor
Not I forsooth. I'll have the score or none.

Dame and Father (striking him)
Then take the pay in knocks and get thee gone.   *345*

They drive him out with blows.

Both (to Giant)
Now then the money, the money.

Giant
Best take your pay in knocks, so get you gone.

Drives them out
Now will I face St George or any knight.
Come one, come all, and meet me in my might.

Enter St George

St George
To meet thee, swaggering tyrant, I come in   *350*
And over thee the victory will quickly win.

They fight. The Giant is killed.
Bearers, this carcase foul at once remove.

*St George retires. Father Christmas, Dame Dorrity and
Mummers enter and drag Giant off right.*

All (singing)
Old Jan Page is dead and gone. Oh! Oh! Oh!

*Enter Tom Bowling with Mummers, Father Christmas and
Dame Dorrity*

Tom Bowling
Here's me, a man o' war,
Just come ashore,   *355*
In hope to beat eleven score.
We'll hoist the guns aboard of them,
And make a terrible noise;
We'll make the King jump over his throne,
And all the people shall rejoice.   *360*

Cheers. Dance. To the others.
Now who do you think in this ship of mine
Came over the sea this Christmas time?

Father
Who was it?

Dame (beats him)
Get thee away, thee inquisitive old rogue,
Here, who cam'd over in thee ship?   365

All gather round Tom Bowling

All
Yes, who was it?

Tom
A champion bold whose name's well known
In this our Minehead town.

All
Come, tell us who did you bring?

Tom
King John. *(Cheers)*   370
He's lately come from the wars in Spain;
He's fought the French with might and main,
But now no longer will he tarry
For he's come back his love to marry.⁴

King John
Here come I, King John.   375

Queen Susan
Here come I, Queen Susan.

King
Madam, to you I bow and bend.

Queen
Stand off, sir, I take you not to be my friend.

King
For why, Madam, did ever I to you do harm?

Queen
Yes, you saucy coxcomb, get you gone.   380

King
Coxcomb, indeed, is not my name,
Were other lips than thine to say such words,
I'd stab such a saucy dame.

Queen
Stab, indeed, is the least I fear,
Appoint a place and I'll meet you there.   385

King
I'll cross the water at the hour of five,
And meet you there if I'm alive.

Queen
I'll meet you there at the hour of ten,
And meet you there with 20,000 men.

King, is going
Why, the man's going, upon my life!   390

Goes after him
Stop, stop, sir, do you want a wife?

King
Not such a saucy dame as thou, upon my life!
Why we'd tipple and nipple over an orange.

Queen
Such trivial things with us shall not make strife.

King
Fair dame, I think a fickle mind thou hast,   395
But loving thee, I'll fearless take the chance.

Take hold round her
So we'll appoint the day of marriage.
Music play up merrily and we'll have a dance.

Dance. Duet

King
Long time I courted you, miss,
I'm just returned from sea.   400
We'll make no more to do, miss,
But quickly married be.
        Sing ri-fal-the-diddle-al-the dee,
        Ri-fal-the-diddle-al-the-day.

Queen
I never did wed a tar, sir,   405
Deceitful as yourself.
It's very plain you are sir,
A good-for-nothing elf.
        Sing ri-fal, &c.

King
It's useless to contend, miss,   410
So let the storm subside,
Our courtship's at an end, miss,
Thou ne'er shall be my bride.
        Sing ri-fal, &c.

Queen
False man, you courted Sally,   415
With vows you filled her head.
And Susan of the valley,
You promised her you'd wed.
        Sing ri-fal, &c.

King
Now, dearest girl, surrender,   420

Queen
Yes, love, I'll be your wife;

King
And I'll be your defender,

Queen
And I'll be true for life.
        Sing ri-fal, &c.

Dance. Enter Mummers

Mummers
Music, play up merrily.   425

*Song, during which the various characters enter, beginning
with St George.*
Music, merrily play,
And cannons loudly roar.
You're welcome home, St George } *bis*
Home to your native shore.

79

Oh the next we do call in,
It is our noble King;
He's lately come from the War,
Glad tidings he doth bring.   } bis   430

Oh, the next we do call in,
It is the Squire's Son.
It's all because of his love
Because he was so young.   } bis   435

Although I've been in the wars,
It's not for any harm;
It's all for the sake of my love
Because I was so young.   } bis   440

Oh! divers⁵ is the next,
And misers you shall see;
In spending all their gold
Now they're come to poverty.   } bis

Hodge-bodge, I have forgot,   445
He's one of all our crew;

And if I must tell you plain,
My dear, I'm in love with you.   } bis

Oh! Music, change your tunes,
And play right merrily,   .
That we may have a dance,
For to please our company.   } bis   450

Dance

Footnotes to Minehead Text
1. The meaning of this phrase is not clear.
2. Ask.
3. Farthing.
4. Thirteen lines have been deliberately omitted from this point onwards, since the publishers state that they were not in the traditional version and were inserted 'for completeness'.
5. Dives.

Iping, Sussex, Tipteerers, Play. Hero-Combat

Vaughan Williams Memorial Library Collection

This version is typical of Sussex. On to a normal Hero-Combat action are grafted carols and the dialogue from the *Ombres Chinoises* as part of the *Quête*. The latter puppet play must have been popular in Sussex for it to have been added to the ceremonial action. There are several champions but only one fight. Whether there were other combats at one time is unknown, but as the action stands now, it is complete. Johnny Jack, who introduces the action, is normally a *quête* character, but his place has been usurped by more attractive features. The costume is more traditional than any of the versions so far noted here, and is again typical of the county. It is interesting that the decoration on the swords was often found on the sticks carried by Cotswold Morris dancers.

Leader (Doctor) carries a cow's horn on which he announces the approach of the Tipteerers. They file into the room and form into a ring and sing:
'Twas sweet and delightful on a bright summer's morn,
When the fields and the meadows, they were cover'd
   with corn,
And the blackbirds and thrushes stand on every green
   tree,
And the lark, he sang melodious at this dawn of the day.

As a sailor and his true love were a-walking one
   day,   5
Said the sailor to his true love, 'I am bound far away.
I am bound for the Indies where the loud cannons roar,
I must go and leave my Nancy, she's the girl I adore.'

Then a ring from her finger she instantly¹ drew,
Saying, 'Take this, dear sweetheart, that your heart may
   prove true'
And whilst he was embracing her, the tears from her
   eyes fell,   10
Saying, 'May I come along with you?' 'O no, my love,
   farewell'.

'O now, my dearest Nancy, I no longer can stay,
For their topsails are hoisted and their anchors aweigh,
And the good ship lies a-waiting for a full flowing tide,
And if ever I return again, I'll make you my
   bride.'²   15

Little Johnny Jack, with three dolls sewn on his back, comes in and walks up and down, saying
In comes I, Little Johnny Jack,
With my family up my back.
Though my family be but small,
I can scarce find bread and cheese for them all.
Christmas comes but once a year,   20
And when it comes it brings good cheer.
Roast beef, plum pudding, mince pie,
Who likes these any better than I?
Christmas fare makes us dance and sing,
Money in the purse is a capital thing.   25
Ladies and gentlemen, give what you please,
Old Father Christmas will welcomely receive.

Old Father Christmas comes forward and walks up and down saying
In comes I, Old Father Christmas, welcome or welcome
   not,
Sometimes cold and sometimes got,
I hope old Father Christmas will never be forgot.   30
Although we've come, we've but a short time to stay,
But we'll show you sport and pastime before we go
   away.
Room, room, Ladies and gentlemen, though, I pray,
I am the man that leads the Noble Captain and all his
   men this way.

The Noble Captain comes forward and walks up and down saying
In comes I, the Noble Captain, just lately come from
   France,   35
With my broadsword and jolly Turk I'll make King
   George to dance.
And I had him here, I wonder what would appear?
I'd cut him up as small as mint dust

And send him to Old Father Christmas to make a pie
    crust.

King George comes forward and walks up and down saying
In comes I, King George the Fourth,   40
From England I did spring;
With some of my wondrous works
Now I'm going to begin.
First in a dungeon I was shut up and left on a rocky
    stone,
That's where I made my sad, dismal moan.   45
I fought the fiery dragon through,
And brought him to great slaughter,
And by some of those wondrous works
I won Queen Alice's fairest daughter.

*The Turkey Snipe[3] comes forward and walks up and down
saying*
In comes I, the Turkey Snipe,   50
Just come from the Turkish land to fight;
I'll fight King George with courage bold,
If his blood's hot, I'll make it cold.

King George
Down under thee I'll never bow nor bend,
I never took thee to be my friend.   55

Turkey Snipe
For why, for why, sir, did I ever do you any harm?

King George
You saucy man, you ought to be stabbed.

Turkey Snipe
Stab for stab, that is my fear,
Appoint me to the place, and I'll meet you there.

King George
My place is pointing to the ground,   60
Where I mean to lay your fair body down.

Turkey Snipe kneels on one knee and guards saying
Then on my bended knee I pray
All for to be a Turkish slave.

King George
Arise, arise, you Turkish Knight,
Go unto your Turkish land to fight;   65
Go unto your Turkish land to tell
What people there is in Old England dwell.

Turkey Snipe
Across the water I'll defy,
I'll meet you there if I'm alive,
Pull out your sword and fight,   70
Pull out your purse and pay,
For one satisfaction I will have
Before I go away.

King George
No money will I pull out nor pay
But you and I will fight this battle most manfully. 75

Gallant Soldier comes forward and walks up and down saying
In comes I, the Gallant Soldier, 'Bold and Slasher' is my
    name,
Sword in hand to guard my knucklebones, I am for to
    win this game.

My head is made of iron, my body lined with steel,
    And brass unto my knucklebones, I'll fight you in this
      field.
Stand off, stand off, you noble Turk, or by my sword
    you shall die,   80
I'll cut your driblets through and through, I'll make your
    buttons fly,
I've travelled o'er England, France and Spain,
And many French dogs, in my time, I've slain.
For what our King shall have his right,
The Turkey Snipe I'll fight.   85

They fight. The Turkey Snipe falls and the Gallant Soldier says
Behold, behold, what have I done?
I cut him down like the evening sun;
And ten more of such men I'll fight
For what our king shall have his right.

The Noble Captain comes forward and says
Indeed, indeed, my Turk is slain,   90
Between two arms his body's lain;
For what some doctor must come and see
Where my man lies bleeding at his feet.
O! is there a noble doctor to be found
To raise this dead man from the ground?   95

Father Christmas comes forward and says
O yes, there is a noble doctor to be found
To raise this dead man from the ground.
So step in, doctor.

Doctor Good comes forward and says
In comes I, Doctor Good,
With my hand I can stop the blood.   100
I can stop the blood and heal the wound
And raise this dead man from the ground.

Father Christmas
What can you cure, doctor?

*If this is acted out of doors when the ground may be wet or
muddy, the Turkey Snipe is supported between two of the
players, instead of falling on the ground.*

Dr Good
I can cure the hipsy, pipsy, peasy, palsy or the gout,
Strain within and strain without.   105
If the man's neck's broke, I'll set 'un again or
Else I won't have one farthing for my fee.

Father Christmas
What is your fee, Doctor?

Dr Good
Ten pound.

Father Christmas
Can't pay no such money as that.   110

Dr Good (turning away)
Saddle my horse, Jack, I'll be gone.

Father Christmas
Stop! Stop! doctor. I've a jackass you can ride.
What is your lowest fee, Doctor?

Dr Good
£9.19.11¾d, and that's a farthing under price
Because you're a poor man.   115

Father Christmas
Better try your skill, doctor.

Dr Good
Now, you see, Ladies and Gentlemen, I've got a little
    bottle in my pocket *(showing it)* called the Golden
    Slozenger Drop, and a box of pills.

Kneels by Turkish Knight and suits actions to words
I puts a drop in his temple and a pill in his mouth, I strike
    a light on his whole body, and he'll move one leg   120
    already.

Turkey Snipe moves one leg slowly.

Father Christmas
So he did, Doctor.

Dr Good
You see, Ladies and Gentlemen, I ain't like one of these
    quack doctors goes about from house to house telling
    people a passel o'lies.   125
But I can raise the dead before your eyes,
And so you all shall see. Rise up, young man,
And see how boldly you and I can walk and sing.

Turkey Snipe rises up and he and the Doctor sing[4]
Good morning to you, gentlemen,
The sleep that I have had   130
And now I am awaking,
I can no longer stay.
I beg as a favour of you all
The doctor's bill to pay.

*The Turkey Snipe retires and the Noble Captain and the Doctor
come forward to sing, crossing and hitting their swords at the
words marked ***

Noble Captain
I *am the blade   135

Dr Good
That *drives no trade,
Most people *do *adore *me.
I *will you *heat and I *won't you *cheat,
And I'll *drive you *all before *me.

Noble Captain
My *new silk bows,   140

Dr Good
My *square topped[5] shoes,

Both
For I can *love to *act and *swear of *wagger,
And *every *champion *I do *meet
I'll *push him *with my *dagger.

Noble Captain
And *now I have   145

Dr Good
Spent *all my gold

Both
Among you *wretched *fellows.
And *if we *are *condemned to *die,
We'll *die *upon the *gallows.

*There follows a dialogue between the Doctor and all the rest
who chant the answers in chorus*

Dr Good to the Noble Captain
Hip, Mr Carpenter, Hallow Sir, I've got a little question
    to ask you:–   150
How far is it across the river?

All
When you're in the middle you're halt way over,
Fol the riddle ido.
When you're in the middle you're half way over,
Fol the ri the ray.   155

Dr Good
I know, when you're in the middle you're half way over,
    but that
wasn't the question I asked ye.

*The Noble Captain turns away and the Doctor prods him with
his sword and says*
Hip, Mr Carpenter, I've got another little question to ask
    ye. How deep is the river?

All
If you throw in a stone it will go to the bottom, &c.

The whole business is repeated, the next question being

Dr Good
How do you get across the river, &c.   160

All
The ducks and the geese they all swim over, &c.

And repeat asking
Whose house is that over yonder?

All
It is not yours but it is the owner's etc.

Next question
How strong is the beer they sells?

All
If you drink too much it will make you tipsy, &c.   165

At the end of the last refrain they go on with
This ends the play; all form in a ring again and sing the carol:[6]
The moon shone bright and the stars gave a light
A little before it was day,
When the Lord our God, he called on us all
And he bade us to wake and to pray.

Awake, awake, good people all,
Awake and you shall hear   170
How Christ our Lord, He died on the Cross,
And for us whom He loved so dear.

So dear, so dear, as Christ loved us,
And for our sake He was slain;
We must leave off our wicked wickedness   175
And turn to the Lord again.

Our song is done, and we must begone;
We can tarry no longer here.
So God bless you all, both little, great and small,
And God send you a happy New Year.   180

82

Costume

Dressed in overalls and tunics, some of gay chintz or cretonne, some of white calico, covered all over with patches and adornments of cloth, silk, velvet &c., cut into fantastic shapes and sewn on, and hanging in strips and ribbons from various places. Hats as fantastic, of brilliant colours, decorated with flowers, streamers, &c. Gallant Soldier wore a red coat and round forage cap with imitation medals and badges. All have wooden sword painted in stripes of red and blue running diagonally round the swords, except Father Christmas, who carries a long staff painted in the same way and decorated with hanging ribbons and a huge bunch of holly and mistletoe at the top.

Footnotes to Iping Text

1. Pronounced 'instant*lie*'.
2. The music is not given, but the whole text is virtually identical with that from Chithurst in the same county, where the music was collected. See Alex Helm: *Five Mumming Plays for Schools*, 1965, 19–29.
3. Turkish Knight.
4. Music not collected.
5. (?) square-toed.
6. As fn. 2.

Dorchester, Dorset, Mummers' Play. Hero-Combat

B.B.C. Recording 14th December 1936

This version, recorded during an actual performance in Dorchester Town Hall, is more puzzling than many. It seems to fall into two parts, one where there is a parade of purely historical characters, ending with the defeat of Napoleon, but without a cure, and the second a traditional version with the death and cure of Tommy the Pony. Interspersed throughout both parts are irrelevant songs, and one is left with the impression that it was a special performance arranged for the B.B.C. with a strong bias towards entertainment. The first part has some affinities with the Wexford, Ireland, versions, if only in the parade of famous characters. The death and cure of Tommy the Pony is found in other Dorset versions, but normally it occurs after combats between champions as at Symondsbury. Sometimes the Pony is revived by the laying on of hands, so that their warmth will restore him, but the blowing of air into him is not uncommon.

The text was taken from the B.B.C. recording, and sometimes it was impossible to decide who was actually speaking. No costume details were given, but elsewhere in Dorset, the disguise consisted of streamers flowing over ordinary clothes.

The dialogue suggests that some parts have extended. The Jonah and the Whale speech of Father Christmas is unusual, occurring nowhere else so far as has been noted, and quite irrelevent here. Indeed, of all the action, only the final cure of the Pony is completely traditional in the area, but nevertheless, the action has the necessary elements for revitalisation.

The final song was sung in harmony, but at some places either it was in unison, or the lower part was not picked up on the recording. Such harmony is rare in English folk songs, the most noted of the few exponents being the Copper family of Rottingdean in Sussex. The words of this song are similar to those of the final song of the Revesby Play.

Unnamed Character
Room, room, gallant room, give me room to render.
I've come to show you sport to pass away the winter.
If you don't believe what I say,
Step in Old Father Christmas and boldly clear the way.

Father Christmas
'Ere comes I, wold Father Christmas, welcome or
   welcome not,   5
And I hope wold Father Christmas will never be forgot.
Christmas come but once a year,
And when it come it bring good cheer,
Wi' a pocketful of money and a zellar full of beer.
I was over there just now and now I be come back over
   yere   10
And I'd like to taste a drop of true Christmas beer;
If it be a pot of best, may your soul in heaven rest.
But if it is a pot of small,
Well, that's better than none at all.
And if you don't believe what I say,   15
Step in my son, young Father Christmas, and boldly
   clear the way.

Young Father Christmas
Here am I, young Father Christmas, welcome or
   welcome not,
And I hope young Father Christmas will never be forgot.
Although you call me young Father Christmas, my name
   is John Bull,
And I'm here tonight to present you with, my humble
   servant, Tom Fool.   20

Tom Fool
Here am I, Tom Fool. Haha! Is Mr Bull in?

John Bull
Yes, Tom, what may you want of him?

Tom Fool
I've come to tell you that Buonaparte's just come from
   France
With twenty, hundred, thousand French.

John Bull
Never mind him, Tom, nor all his army too,   25
Give me and my men the battle, we'll show them a
   British rattle.

Tom Fool
Rattle! Rattle! That will not do,
Where there's rattling there must be fighting as well as
   rattling too.
Therefore I must see what I can do –
But Hark! I think I hear them coming.   30

Buonaparte
Here am I Buonaparte, lately come from France
To pay John Bull a visit, and teach him a new dance.
Such a dance that has never been taught before my boys,
    by any man but me;
I'll strike fire in all you hearts and make you Britons flee.

Tom Fool
Ha! when the French do come to England they do come
    without their hearts,   35
Therefore tonight Mr Bull and I will try to upset proud
    Buonaparte.
And show, tyrant Buonaparte, I hope for to lay down
And with good sword in hand tonight to lay thee on the
    ground.

John Bull
Be silent, Tom, don't interrupt that noisy fellow's breath;
Be as it will, although Tom Fool, thou shall be that
    tyrant's death.   40

Buonaparte
Don't talk to me of fools, nor yet of death,
But learn this warlike dance;
For the time shall quickly come
When I am free in France.
Come on, my bold hero.   45

Prince Galore
Here am I, Prince Galore, from Flanders lately come,
Where the cannons they do rattle and sound the warlike
    drum.
With my true courage I followed Boney,
Slow to your land to fight for Buonaparte,   50
Which is my whole delight.
Likewise you British dogs, I will defeat this night.

Duke of York
Here am I, the Duke o' York, standing all on British land,
Proud Buonaparte I do defy and all his daring band.
With British troops I've been my boys,
Through Holland, France and Spain,   55
And will this night with sword in hand,
Face Buonaparte again.

Prince Beelzebub
Here am I, Prince Beelzebub, Buonaparte's own dear
    friend,
That I did place ten votes to one to make Buonaparte a
    king.
And when Buonaparte and I do meet we'll lay our two
    heads together,   60
So take in hand whate'er you will is my advice for ever.
Buonaparte was a brave scholar when he came to my
    school,
And 'twould take one of the best men in John Bull's
    troops
Buonaparte to fool.

Lord Wellington
Here am I, Lord Wellington,   65
By the Duke of York I fought full fifteen days
With my broadsword that shines so bright.
When I was in Flanders the other day,
Where I first began my warlike play,
I threw my guns into their flank   70
To see my two brothers cut through their rank.
We turned their front ranks to their rear

Although their army hadn't been there;
They turned their backs and ran away,
And on their baggage we did make our prey.   75
Out of old England I've now come,
You dirty French dogs, to give your doom;
And as for Beelzebub and Buonaparte, this night
I'll cut them to the heart.

Prince Witzenburg
Here I am, Prince Witzenburg, come to your land to
    fight;   80
To fight for Boneyparte which is my true delight.
I'll fight for Boneyparte as long as I am able
To make John Bull obey.
And when I can no longer fight,
I'll turn my back and run away.   85

Buonaparte
Behold, behold, my valiant soldiers are all come in!
Prepare for war! Let us begin!
Form up your ranks, see all things clear,
And of these British rascals never fear.

John Bull
Boys be bold, but not too bold!   90
Until to you these articles I unfold.
Kill or be killed! No quarter give!
Don't suffer one of these dirty French dogs to live.

Fight

Tom Fool
To hit the first blow, Mr Bull, is half the battle,
Buonapart's new-fashioned dance and John Bull's British
    rattle.   95

Fight
Cheer up! Cheer up! my lads again,
For champion Bull he is not slain,
But only falls to rise again.
And I'm an Englishman true blue
Will soon make Buonaparte to roll. To it again!   100
Have at thee, Boney! Deliver thy sword to me!

Buonaparte
Alas! Alas! What am I now?

Tom Fool
Why! a prisoner sure!

John Bull
Well done, thou good and faithful servant Tom!
A gold chain thou shalt have before 'tis long   105
For saving me from that fatal blow.
£10,000 is yours also besides a valiant soldier too.

Tom Fool
Well, Mr Bull, what shall be done with the body of
    Buonaparte?

John Bull
That's your proposal, Tom?

Tom Fool
Take him through the towns and villages of England and
    make a show of him.   110

84

John Bull
No! Stay! I've a letter in my pocket I had from Squire
    Greaves the other day,
He wants an old horse for his dogs – so take him away.
Dog's meat! Dog's meat!

Buonaparte
Although you Britons thought to have me killed,
Yet I am come before you with all my men to yield.   115
Although they were so scandalous to run away,
They come before you now to reverence and obey.

All (sung)

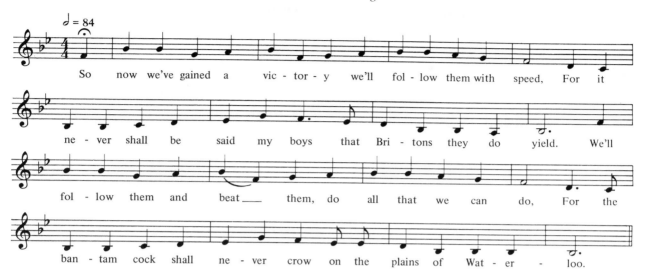

So now we've gained a vic-tor-y we'll fol-low them with speed, For it
ne-ver shall be said my boys that Bri-tons they do yield. We'll
fol-low them and beat ___ them, do all that we can do, For the
ban-tam cock shall ne-ver crow on the plains of Wat-er - loo.

We'll send him to some hisland that is so far away,
And hope that they will keep him there for ever and a
    day;
And not let him return again to do as he did before,
But keep him is some prison strong, and the wars will
    soon be o'er.   125

Oh! now unto old England we shall return again;
A health there is to drink to Great George who is our
    king.
Likewise unto Lord Wellington and all his armies too,
For if Boney lives for a hundred years, he'll remember
    Waterloo.

Father Christmas
Aye, I should think I would remember such a time as
    that. I know I should.

?
Yes, I should think so too, Father. But we want you to
    give us a song now if you will be good enough.

Father Christmas
Well, my lads, I'll **try**, but I can't sing like I could sixty
    year ago. I must **sit down**, 'cos I be wold and stiff, and
    you, Garge, must help me in the call box.

George
Yes, Father, we'll help you in the chorus.   135

Father Christmas (sung)

So I had a lit-tle cow and he had a lit-tle calf,
CHORUS **Quicker**
thought I had a bar-gain but I lost one half Wim wam
wad-dles, Jack stick swad-dles, Roz-a-bo, Roz-a-bo way went the broom.

Father Christmas (sung)
So I sold my little cow and bought a little dog,
A pretty little creature to keep off the mob.   140

Chorus (all)
Wim wam waddles, . . .

Father Christmas (sung)
So I sold my little dog, and bought a little goose,
He walked so many miles that his legs got loose.

Chorus (all)
Wim wam waddles, . . .

Father Christmas (sung)
So I sold my little goose and bought a little cat,
A pretty little creature to keep off the rats.   145

Chorus (all)
Wim wam waddles, . . .

Father Christmas (sung)
So I sold my little cat and bought a little mouse,
Finally his tail set fire to my house.

Chorus (all)
Wim wam waddles, . . .

Father Christmas
There, my lads, how will that do for thee?   150

?
Very good, Father, very good indeed. And now we'll
give you one of your old favourites.

Father Christmas
Aye, so do, me lads!

All (sung)

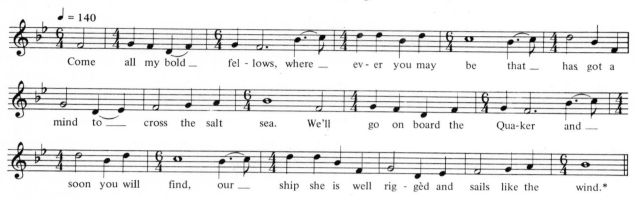

Come all my bold fel-lows, where ev-er you may be that has got a
mind to cross the salt sea. We'll go on board the Qua-ker and
soon you will find, our ship she is well rig-gèd and sails like the wind.*

* Pronounced to rhyme with "find."

Our ship's built up like waxwork in every degree,
Our ship she is well riggèd and fitted for the sea.
With five hundred and fifty bright seamen so bold,
And by those blooming French dogs we'll never be
    controlled.   160

We fought them for hours till they **could no** longer stay,
While big guns and small guns **sweetly** did play.
Till the dead lay on our decks, boys, most kind to
    complain,
And the blood rushed through the scuppers like showers
    of rain.

So now the war is over and homeward we do
    steer   165
Unto our wives and sweethearts and the girls we love so
    dear.
And this is my good health, boys, to the girl that's stout
    and true
Likewise unto Lord Nelson, the best of all our crew.

Father Christmas
Well! What a noise to be sure!
Come! I want my 'oss to go to market!   170
Come, groom! Be quick about it!

Groom
Yes, Father, I won't be long.
Hahaha! You're be going there a Christmas coming.
With a pretty little horse.

Father Christmas
Whoa, there! Stand still, can't 'ee?   175
Let's see, what be 'is name?

Groom
Ball, Father.

Father Christmas
Paul, do 'ee say?

Groom
No! Ball, Father.

Father Christmas
Oh! Ball! I do see.   180
Well, gie I the reins and hold his head while I do mount.

Groom
Come on, old Father, thee's had plenty of practice at
    getting on a horse! Casn't thee get on any better than
    that? Cock thy leg up over him, can't 'ee?
Are you hurt, Father?   185

Father Christmas
Hurt? I 'low I be, and now I'll hurt 'ee.

Groom
Don't 'ee hurt yer horse too much mind, Father. When
    he's not yet in mind. Where's your horse then, Father?

Father Christmas
My horse forty miles away drowned in a dry ditch.

Groom
Well, Father, you'd better go back and try to find
    him!   190

Father Christmas
Try to find him? Not I, unless, well, will you help me?

Groom
Yes, of course I will, Father.

Father Christmas
Well, then, see you go thick way and I'll go these.

86

Groom
No, Father, you know this part of the country better than
   I do,
So you go that way and I'll go this.   195

Father Christmas
Oh aye! Left I the longest way, of course.
Young folks be terrible slack now-a-days.

Groom
Oh, Father, don't 'ee keep on grumbling like that.
The result 'tis Christmas time. You want to be merry
   then.

Father Christmas
A good she-bear! A good she-bear!   200

Groom
Where, Father?

Father Christmas
Why, there!

Groom
Why, that's your horse, Father.

Father Christmas
My horse? No, my horse got white legs.

Groom
Yes, and so has this one.   205

Father Christmas
Aye, so 'ee have. 'tis my horse right enough!

Groom
Why, it's dead, Father!

Father Christmas
How can he be dead if I drowned him?

Groom
Well, Father, if you drowned him 'ee must be dead. But
   you'd better get a doctor as soon as you can to see if
   anything can be done.   210

Father Christmas
Doctor! What good's a doctor if he's dead? Better get a
   spade and put 'un underground.

Groom
Oh! I don't know, doctors can do lots of wonderful
   things now-a-day, you know, Father.

Father Christmas
Aye, I suppose they can. Well, are thee going to look for
   one, or shall I?   215

Groom
You'd better go, I think, Father.

Father Christmas
Aye, well, I suppose I shall then.
Is there a doctor to be found,
And to be found this night,   220
To cure my poor little suckling colt and make him stand
   upright?

Doctor
Yes, Father, there is a doctor true to be found,
And to be had this night
To cure your rib of a horse and make him stand upright.

Father Christmas
What's that you called my horse?   225

Doctor
Suckling colt, Father.

Father Christmas
That's better, certainly; but what's thy fee?

Doctor
My fee is £20, ready money paid down;
But since 'tis for your majesty,
From thee I'll take but ten.   230

Father Christmas
That's a lot of money that is to make a hoss stand
   upright.
What can'st cure?

Doctor
I can cure the Hip, the Pip, the Palsy and the Gout,
Pains within and pains without;
And if Old Harry's in your horse,   235
I'll very soon turn 'im out.
I have a bottle in my pocket called the Golden 'ospital.
   Touch nipper napper. Rise, Jack, and make the old
   cripple dame dance a monkey's hornpipe.

Father Christmas
Aye, thee'st one of the clever sort, I can hear.   240
More talk than do about thee, I'm thinking.
But come, if thou'st going to the job,
Zee about it! How art going to cure 'er?

Doctor
Give him a ball, Father!

Father Christmas
Beat his head up against a wall? I'll soon do that!   245

Doctor
No, Father, that would kill him if he ain't dead already!
I said give him a ball.

Father Christmas
Oh! Give him a ball, eh?
Well, go on then!

Doctor
Fetch me a pretty sized pill. What's it going to
   give?   250

Groom
Why! 'tis as big as a cricket ball!

Father Christmas
There! I know thee wasn't so clever as thee's made out.
   What else art going to do?

Doctor
Bleed him, Father!

Father Christmas
Bleed 'im where to?   255

Doctor
In the eye vein.

Father Christmas
Well, thee 'old the flame, and I'll 'it 'im.

?
Haha! Dost thee think tha's going to 'it 'im?

Father Christmas
Dost thee call thyself a doctor?
Call that the eye-vein of a 'oss?   260
This is where I'd a-call the eye-vein of 'ee.

?
What's going to happen then?

Father Christmas
There, I know thee wasn't going to cure 'im!

Doctor
There's one more thing we can do, Father!

Father Christmas
What's that?   265

Doctor
Blow wind into him, Father!

Father Christmas
Blow wind into him, eh? Well, blow away, then!

Doctor
No, you blow, Father, while I watch the dust come out of
    his ears.

Father Christmas
Look here, young man, my groom's too particular as all
    that to
left any dust in his earholes, and I bain't going to blow
    doing   270
thy work and thee take the money.

Doctor
Oh! we'll go shares, Father.

Father Christmas
Well, I don't mind if thee's go halves!

Blows
Rise, Ball!

?
Ah! him's come around, Old Father. I zeed him move a
    little bit.   275
Doesn't see his eyes blinking?

Father Christmas
Halloa, my horse is coming round. Groom! Come here!
    Sharp! My horse is cured.

Groom
Yes, Father!

Blows

Father Christmas
Rise Ball!   280

?
Ah! Second time were better than the first, wold Father.
    He's like to have a good blow – mind doesn't bust
    second time!

Blows
Rise, Ball!
Ah! He's comed right up, Father! That were a good blow
    that time!
Thy horse is cured.

Father Christmas
Take him away! Take him away!   285

?
Were you hurt much, Father?

Father Christmas
Yes! Knocked all to pieces! I can't never ride any more.
    But come, my lads, see if you can't give us a song now
    after all I've been through.

?
Why don't you sing us one now?   290

Father Christmas
No! I can't sing no more tonight; my voice has got hoarse
    with keeping you lads in tune.

?
Well, then, tell us one of your old yarns about when you
    went to sea and got shipwrecked.

Father Christmas
Aye, well! I don't mind doing that. Let's see, I must
    collect my brains a bit. Well, my lads, years and years
    and years ago, when I was quite a young man – and a
    smartish looking chap I was in they days. Well, as I was
    a-saying, I took a ship and went to sea. Well, we sailed
    about three parts of a chain, what we used to call a
    cable's length, when it come on to blow a girt well.   300

?
Gale, you mean, Father.

Father Christmas
Aye, or a girt boy, one of it, but if you be going to spin
    these yarns, zay zo, or else bide quiet. Well, as I were
    a-zaying, it come on to blow and blow, till
    last of all, I was washed overboard and swallowed up
    in the belly of a girt whale. Well, I seemed to be in a   305
    comfortable kind of house enough, but I didn't know
    what to do about grub but I thought I'd have a smoke
    and think it over. So I lighted my pipe and blew a little
    large cloud of smoke out of the whale's nostrils. Well, I
    began to think and think and think, and at last of all I
    took out my penknife and stuck 'un into the whale's   310
    gall, and then I had plenty of salt provisions and a
    zellar full of drink. Well, I bed there altogether about
    three months, happy as a king, and couldn't want to be
    more comfortable, when the whale washed hisself
    ashore and I cleared out, and I can tell 'ee my lads, I   315
    was glad to be out in the open air again. For 'twas
    terrible close copped up in there for so long together.
    Well, I looked about me and found I was landed at a
    place called Ivory Lane, and one by the name of Mrs
    Tiddleywinks kept it then. I daresay some of you can
    mind her?

Eddie Duff
Yes, John.

Father Christmas
What, you rascal, Eddie Duff? Nothing but plain John
this Christmastime?

Eddie Duff
Sir John!

320 *Father Christmas*
That's better manners, sure!
Well, my lads, there's my yarn and now give us one
    more song, and then we must move on.   *325*

?
We'll sing one more, Father, if you will help us.

Father Christmas
Aye, Aye, so I will, my lads! I'll come in the call box
    along wi' ye.

All sing

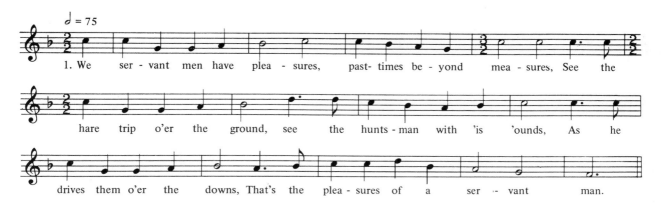

Father Christmas (spoken)
I do think my pleasures better than all that. I do like to
    zee my oxen grow up wi' girt rolls of fat, travelling o'er
    the land so strong. I can reap and I can mow, I can
    plough and I can sow, and I do like to see my corn grow.
    That's the pleasures for a wold husbandman.   *335*

All sing

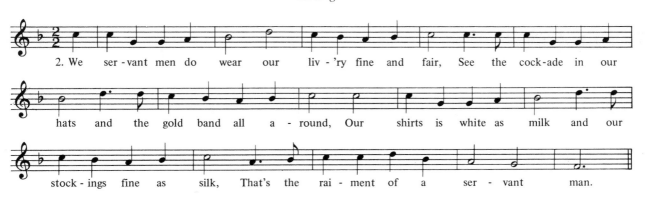

Father Christmas (spoken)
Don't tell I about thy silks and satins. That won't do for
    us to wear all through the bushes and briars. Gi' I my
    leathern and a pair of buckskin breeches. That's the   *340*
    raiment for a wold husbandman.

All sing

cock, goose, ca-pon and swine, _____ Af-ter lord and la-dy
dine we drink strong beer ale or wine, That's the di-et of a ser-vant man.

Father Christmas (spoken)
Dost want to make I bad? Gi' I a hunk o' brown cheese and
a horn of thy home-brewed ale and a gad of bacon hung
up in the chimney corner.

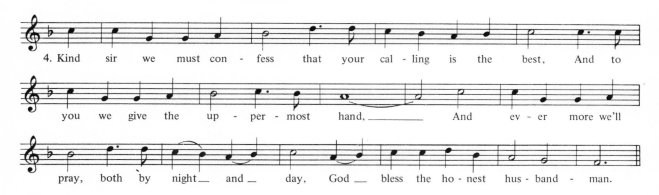

4. Kind sir we must con-fess that your cal-ling is the best, And to
you we give the up-per-most hand, _____ And ev-er more we'll
pray, both by night__ and __ day, God __ bless the ho-nest hus-band - man.

Father Christmas (spoken)
That's I that is! I known thee's had to gi' in to I at last.
But come, dress up there, my lads! Now then, miss
attention, there! Ready! Draw! Shoulder arms! Right
about turn! Left wheel! Quick march! *355*

All sing

Our time is come, we must be gone, We'll stay no lon-ger here, God
bless you all, both great and small, And send you a hap-py new year.

Hawick, Roxburghshire, Scotland, Guisards' Play. Hero-Combat

John Young Scott: The Scotsman, *2nd January 1889, 6g*

This is a typical version of a Scottish action performed in the early nineteenth century. There is no mention of St George as a champion and he is replaced by Sir William Wallace, a Scottish hero. Golaschin is a typical champion, always defeated, and has a variety of spellings of name. The first character, Sir Alexander, has lines reminiscent of the earliest chapbooks, but after the opening speech the resemblance ends. The Farmer's Son could belong to the East Midlands as far as his name goes, and he begins by seeming to be the combatant but is replaced at the last minute by Wallace. Then comes a passage reminiscent of the Bouphonia, but not carried to the normal conclusion. The action eventually dwindles into a normal Hero-Combat cure and *quête* with very little to show that this is a Scottish version other than the names of the characters. If anything, there has been more influence from the north-east of England than any other area.

90

Enter Sir Alexander
Silence! Silence! gentlemen, and on me cast an eye,
My name is Alexander, I'll sing you a tragedy.
My men they are but young, sir, they never fought
    before,
But they will do the best they can, the best can do no
    more.
The first I call in is the Farmer's Son.   5

Farmer's Son
Here comes I, the Farmer's Son,
Although I be but young, sir,
I've got a spirit brave
And I will freely risk my life
My country for to save.   10

Golaschin
Here comes I Golaschin – Golaschin is my name
My sword and pistol by my side,
I hope to win the game.

Farmer's Son
The game, sir! The game, sir! it is not in your power.
I'll cut you into inches in less than half an hour.   15

Golaschin
My body's like a rock, sir.
My head is like a stone.
And I will be a Golaschin till I am dead and gone.

Wallace
Here come I Sir William Wallace Wight,
Who shed his blood for Scotland's right.   20
Without a right, without a reason,
Here I draw my bloody weapon.

They fight and Golaschin falls.

Farmer's Son
Now that young man is dead, sir,
And on the ground is laid
And you shall suffer for it,   25
I'm very sore afraid.

Wallace
It was not me who did the deed,
I don't know how he was slain.

Farmer's Son
How can you thus deny the deed?
As I stood looking on.   30
You drew your sword from out its sheath
And slashed his body down.

Wallace
Well, well, if I've killed Golaschin, Golaschin shall be
    cured in the space of half an hour.

Dr Brown
Here come I, old Doctor Brown,
The best old doctor in the town.   35

Wallace
What can you cure?

Dr Brown
I can cure all diseases.
I've travelled through Italy, France and Spain,
And I've come to Scotland to raise the dead again.

Wallace
How much would you take to cure this man? Would £5
    do?   40

Dr Brown (turning away)
£5! No, £5 would not get a good kit of brose.
Jack would come over the bed and sup them all up.

Wallace
Would £10 do?

Dr Brown
Well, £10 might get a little hoxy-croxy to his nose and a
    little to his bum.
Rise up Jack and fight again.   45

Golaschin rises up and sings
Once I was dead,
But now I am alive.
O blessed be the doctor
That made me to revive.
O brothers, O brothers,   50
Why threw you your sword to me?
But since I am revived again,
We'll all shake hands and gree.

All four
We'll all shake hands and gree,
And never fight no more,   55
But we will be like brothers
As we were once before.
God bless the master of this house,
The mistress fair likewise,
And all the pretty children   60
That round the table flies.
Go down to your cellar
And see what ye can find.
Your barrels being not empty,
We hope you will prove kind.   65
We hope you will prove kind
With some whisky and some beer;
We wish you Merry Christmas,
Likewise a Good New Year.

After this was sung, another appeared to make the collection
Here come I, old Beelzebub   70
Over my shoulder I carry a club;
And in my hand a dripping pan,
And I think myself a jolly old man.
I've got a little box which can speak without a tongue,
If you've got any coppers, please to pop them in.   75

Lislane, Londonderry, Mummers' Play. Hero-Combat

Ulster Folk Museum Archives

This Irish Hero-Combat version contains all the elements
of those in England, but with an entirely Irish overlay to
them. The champions are unusual. Prince George has
replaced St George and is killed by Oliver Cromwell,
normally a *quête* character. Beelzebub has moved also
from the end of the action and has become part of the

Presentation, the final characters being entirely Irish. Jack Straw, with his riddle rhyme, and Johnny Funny with his plea for money are not found normally in England. The Doctor's cure is worth noting. It retains the form of the English versions but its ingredients are typically Irish. It is a version stripped of all non-essentials, unless these have been forgotten along with the costume details. Nevertheless, it is clear that the version, typical of others in Northern Ireland, is of a common stock with those of England, even though it has developed its own characteristics.

Speaker
Room, room, my gallant boys,
And give us room to rhyme.
We'll show you some activity
About this Christmas time.
Active young and active age,   5
The like of this was never acted on a stage
Before, nor never will again.
And if you don't believe me what I say,
Enter in Beelzebub, and he'll soon clear the way.

Beelzebub
Here comes I, Beelzebub,   10
Over my shoulder I carry my club
And in my hand a graip and pan,
I count myself a jolly wee man.
And if you don't believe me what I say,
Enter in Oliver Cromwell, and he'll soon clear the
    way.   15

Oliver Cromwell
Here come I, Oliver Cromwell, with my long copper
    nose,
I've conquered many nations as you may well suppose,
The Spanish for to tremble and the British for to quake,
I fought the jolly Dutchman until his heart did ache.
And if you don't believe me what I say,   20
Enter in Prince George, and he'll soon clear the way.

Prince George
Here come I, Prince George, newly come from Spain,
A man like me you've never seen before, nor never will
    again.
I fed your horse on oats and hay, for seven years and a
    day,
After that he jumped the ditch and ran away, sir.   25

Oliver Cromwell
You're a liar, sir!
Pull out your sword and try it, sir.
I'll run my rusty weapon through your heart
And make you die away, sir.

Oliver and George fight, George falls

(Voice)
Five pounds for a doctor!   30
Ten pounds for a good Doctor!
Is there not a doctor to be found,
To cure this deep and deadly wound?

Doctor Sure
Yes! Here come I, Doctor Sure.
With my medicine I can cure.   35

(Voice)
What can you cure?

Doctor Sure
I can cure the plague within the plague, the palsy or the
    gout,
Where there's nine devils in, I can kick ten out!

(Voice)
What's your medicine, sir?

Doctor Sure
The sip, sag, the wild goose's egg,   40
The brains of a mouse, the tail of a louse,
And the heart's blood of a wee creepy stool.
Mix that up together with a black cat's feather,
Clap that to his sould, as hot as he can thole,
Three weeks before breakfast time and a month before
    sunrise.   45
Besides all this,
Bring me an old maid fourscore and ten,
Her nose and her toes both at the end!
I'll make her as neat and as straight as a maid of sixteen!
If that doesn't cure him, the Devil may cure him,   50
As long as I get my fee!
It's all done by a wee bottle I keep in the crown of my
    hat,
Some call it this and some call it that,
I call it hokus, pokus, Oliver's campain,[1] or Dr William's
    Pink Pills,
Take three drops of this, Prince George, and rise and
    fight again.   55

Prince George
Once I was dead and now I'm alive,
God bless the wee Doctor that made me survive.
If you don't believe me, then, what I say,
Enter in, Jack Straw Striddle, and he'll soon clear the
    way.

Jack Straw
Here comes I, Jack Straw Striddle,   60
Kiss the Devil's wife through a reel, through a riddle,
Through a sheep shank shin bone.
Through a bag of pepper,
Through a mill hopper!
And if you don't believe me, what I say,   65
Enter in, Johnny Funny, and he'll soon clear the way.

Johnny Funny
Here come I, Johnny Funny,
I'm the one collects the money.
All silver, no brass,
Bad coppers won't pass.   70
If I don't get that I must take less,
And afterwards a song.
We'll all join hands and we'll never fight again,
We'll be good as brothers as ever we have been.
With our pockets full of money and our barrels full of
    beer,   75
We wish you a bright and happy Christmas and a glad
    New Year.

Footnotes to Lislane text
1. Elecampane.

Bellerby, North Riding of Yorkshire. Sword Dance

M.K.: J.E.F.D.S., 2S, 1928, 35–42
(by permission of Dr. Karpeles)

The version was last performed in 1879 and was revived in 1926 when it was collected by Dr Karpeles. Performers are alive in the village who still remember the dialogue, and the text which follows contains lines recently collected by Miss B. G. Wilson. Both old and new costumes are shown on Plates 11 and 12. In recent years disguised men have been appearing at Whitsuntide to collect money, but without performing either dance or drama. Their costume is said to be exactly that of the old performers: on the white tunic and trousers are appliqued cut out shapes of animals, geometric patterns and faces. Colour photographs taken by Mr Tom Chambers show these clearly as well as three 'Females'. They now call themselves 'Guisers' and show no desire to revive the ceremony in full as it used to be performed, which is unfortunate.

The text received comment in the chapter on Sword Dance Ceremonies and needs no further comment here.

The players process in the following order and form up in a straight line facing the audience:
Drummer, Fiddler, Bessie with a clown on either side, King, Five dancers, one behind the other.
The performers, as they speak, leave the line and move forward.

1st Clown (walking round in a ring)
Gentlemen and ladies, I have sprung from a noble
　　knight;
I have come here to spill my blood for old England's
　　right;
Old England's right and a free goodwill;
Gentlemen and ladies, I'll sing be mesel'.

Sings[1]

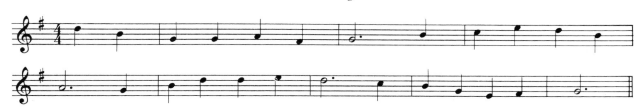

Oh, there isn't a family　　　　　　　　　　　　5
That can compare to mine,
My father he was hanged
For stealing of three swine.
O my father he was hanged,
And my mother was drowned in a well;　　　　10
Isn't I a bonny chuck
To be living by mesel'?

2nd Clown (spoken)
Rumble, rumble, here my brave lads
And give us leave to sport,
For on this ground I mean to resort,　　　　　15
Resort and play – show you many rhymes.
Gentlemen and ladies, this is Chris-a-mas time.
Cris-a-mas comes but once a year,
When it comes it brings good cheer.
Roast beef, bull beef, apple pie,　　　　　　　20
With very small shares for you and I, Bess.

Turns and taps Bess on the chest with his stick.
So mind, brave lads, what I do say;
My name is bold Hector, I've come to clear the way;
Hector, Hector, from Dulberry Bush,
The devil's own sister-in-law clothed in lamb's
　　wool.　　　　　　　　　　　　　　　　25
Our king stands waiting on this ground *(pointing to the
　　king with his stick)*
He swears and tears he will be in
To teach me of my skill.
He is some silly fool I vow.
He will say more in the burning of an inch of
　　candle　　　　　　　　　　　　　　　30
That he will perform in ten times ten pounds burning
　　out.

The Clowns walk about during the next part　　5

King
Hold, Hector, hold. Shall I wound thee on the leg,
Or wilt thou fall down on thy knees and beg?

2nd Clown
No. Neither for my hand nor my van;
Thousands have I slain,　　　　　　　　　　35
And here I've travelled to set old England right again.

King
I'm the king of the conquerors and here I do advance.

2nd Clown
And I the ragged clown and I've come to see thee dance.

King
Dance? Thou admits to see a king dance?
Dance? I am a king that's highly known.　　　40
I'll be very sorry to be offended by a saucy fellow, ragged
　　clown.

2nd Clown
Hearty good fellow, art thou a king?
Wasn't thou stealing swine last night?

King
Stealing swine?

2nd Clown
Tenting swine, perhaps I mean.　　　　　　45

King
My blood is raise, I swear and vow

I've been the death of many a man,
And I'll be the death of thou.
Young men, draw your shavers, and quit this scoundrel
    from my sight;
For if I stand to prate with him, he'll prate with me all
    night.   50

*From this point until the performance of the dance the words
are all sung*

1st Clown (walking about)
With your leave, kind gentlemen,
I've come to see a sport,
And likewise for to see
If a lady I can court.

But the lasses nowadays   55
They are so plaguey shy,
My clothing is so fine
They will not come me nigh.

Our king is coming in
Dressed in his grand array,   60
He'll call his young men in
By one, by two, or three.

Goes to one side.

King (walking round in a circle)
Spectators, silence keep,
And you will plainly see,
I'll call these young men in   65
Dressed in their grand array
By one, by two, or three. ²

Oh, the first is Mr Spark
Who's lately come from France
He's the first man in our list   70
And the second in our dance.

2nd Dancer (following King, walking behind him in a circle)
God bless your honour's fame
And all your young men too;
I've come to act my part
As well as I can do.   75

King
If thou wilt act thee part
And wil not from me flee
I'll call these young men in
By one, by two or three. ³

Oh, the next is Mr Stout   80
As you will understand;
As good a swordsman he is
As ever took sword in hand.

3rd Dancer (following 2nd Dancer)
My valour has been tried
Through city, town, and field;   85
I never met the man
That yet could make ye yield.

King (walking round in a circle)
O the next is Mr Wild
Who has travelled many a mile;
I'm afraid the worst of all   90
The lasses he'll beguile.

4h dancer (following 3rd dancer)
Although I've travelled the world
Not for any wrong;
It is for my false love
Because from me she's gone.   95

King
O the next he is a prince,
He is a squire's son,
I'm afraid he's lost his love
Because from me she's gone.

5th Dancer (following 4th Dancer)
Although I be too young,   100
I've money for to roam *(or, rove)*;
I'll freely spend it all
Before I'll lose my love.

King
Then in comes last of all,
Mount Zion is his name;   105
He's a worthy gentleman
And by birth of noble fame.

6th Dancer (following 5th Dancer)
My father's a metal man
And a tinker too by trade;
He never stopped one hole,   110
But two for it he made.

1st Clown (running after them)
Now, I'm the last of all
My name is Captain Tom.
If you've got fifty girls,
I'll kiss them every one.   115

2nd Clown
Cox Bobs, I'd like forgot;
I am one of your crew,
If you want to know my name,
My name is 'Love so True'.

King
So you've see us all go round,   120
Think of us what you will.
Music, strike up and play
A tune – just what you will.

*The Dance follows. At the end of the Dance Bessie comes
forward and stands in the middle of the dancers, they getting
into hilt and point position and walking round.*

King (sings)
Our lady she comes in,
She looks both pale and wan;   125
She's got a long beard on,
Just like a collier's man.

Dancers make Lock and hang it round Bessie's neck.

Bessie (sings, standing, dancers walking round)
Just now I'm going to die,
As you can plainly see;
These six fine glittering swords   130
Will soon put an end to me.
Farewell unto you all,
And my old father here,
Farewell unto you all,
And my old grannie dear.   135

Dancers draw swords and Bessie falls down and lies flat on her back. The Dancers continue marching round.

King (sings)
Our lady she is dead,
And on the ground she's laid;
We must all suffer for this,
Young men, I'm sore afraid.

2nd Dancer sings
I'm sure it's none of I   140
That did this awful crime;
It's the man that follows me,
He drew his sword so fine.

3rd, 4th and 5th Dancers sing in turn
I'm sure it's none of I
That did this awful crime;   145
It's the man that follows me,
I caught him in the act.

6th Dancer (sings)
Since I'm the last of all,
And I the blame must take,
Down on my bended knee   150
For pardon I must pray *(Bends knee)*

Yet I not daunted be,
Although I be the last,
Our king had done this crime
And laid the blame on me.   155

King (sings)
Cheer up, my lively lads,
And be of courage bold;
We'll carry her to the church
And bury her in the mould.

Dancers stand still. The following words are all spoken.

2nd Dancer
Bury her, bury her, where do you mean to bury her, and
    all these people standing round? How do you mean to
    escape a halter? Send for a doctor out of van. I've heard
    tell of a doctor famed far and near; if he'd been here he
    would have brought this queen to life again.   160

King
Send for a doctor.

2nd Dancer
Doctor, doctor, twenty pounds for a doctor.   165

Doctor (one of the clowns)
Here am I.

King
Hearty good fellow, art thou a doctor?

Doctor
Yes, I am a doctor.

King
What is thy name, doctor?

Doctor
My name is Evan Lovan rantantiser to a boarding
    master taught by twelve universals, fried balsam upon
                                                           170

balsam made of dead man's fat, rosin, and goose
grease – that's my name, doctor.

King
And a very curious name, doctor.

Doctor
Aye, Ah think so.

King
How far hast thou travelled, doctor?   175

Doctor
Travelled? I've travelled through Itty Titty, where there
    is neither house, land, nor city; wooden churches,
    leather bells, and black-puddings for bell-ropes.

King
Is that all doctor?

Doctor
No. I've travelled through England, Ireland, Scotland,
    France, and Spain   180
And here I've travelled to bring this old queen to life
    again.

King
Well done, doctor. What can you cure, doctor?

Doctor
Cure? I can cure the itch, the stitch, the ague, and the
    gout. If there be
nineteen devils in, I can bring one-and-twenty out. I can
    cure the whisky jade,
the smiling maid, I can make   185
the paper soak to crack, sir. I can make the deaf to hear,
    the dumb to speak, or the lame to walk or fly, sir.

King
Is that all, doctor?

Doctor
No. I can cure the maiden with a red pale face, I can do
    the like to a hare. Any maiden wishing to cure her
    sweetheart, I can tell her how she shall win. I can cure,
    aye, boys, aye. I once cured my old grandmother who   190
    had been dead two year, after which she lived three and
    brought forth two children.

King
Well done, doctor. What's thy fee, doctor?

Doctor
My fee is twenty pounds.

King
Far too much, doctor.   195

Doctor
Well, as it's thee, I'll take nineteen pounds, nineteen
    shillings, and elevenpence three farthings.

King
Fall to work, doctor. I will see thee paid, or unpaid, in
    the morning.

Doctor (going away)
Paid, the devil. One bird in the hand is worth two in the

bush. I've got my own old wife at home been dead a
fortnight – a far better job than that.   200

King
Fall to work, doctor. I'll see thee paid out of my own
    pocket.

Doctor comes back

Doctor
How did this old queen happen her misfortune?

King
She tumbled upstairs and broke her neck.

Doctor
Well done, stupid. I've heard tell of falling down.   205

King
Well, down, I mean.

Doctor (goes to Bessie's feet and lifts them up)
Her neck is broken.

Goes to her head and raises it.
Her things are out of joint and she is filling with wind
    causing her bowels to be in an uproar. She is in a very
    bad state indeed, sir. But I've got some pills in my
    pocket that will cure all ills, time present, time gone, *210*
    and time to come. If that won't do, I'll scour her over
    and up again till the spirit moves;

Doctor rubs Bessie's stomach and she arches her back.
and I've got a little bottle in my pocket called oakum-
    pokum pennyroyal.
Open thy niff-naff and I'll let it down thy chiff-chaff.
    Rise, old girl, and sing.   215

Bessie (sings, standing up)
Good morning, gentlemen,
A-sleeping I have been,
I've had such a sleep
As the like was never seen.

But now I am awake   220
And alive unto this day;
So we will have a dance
And the doctor must seek his pay.

*Dance performed as before, Bessie and Clowns fooling about.
The performers stand in two lines, facing audience, the two
Clowns in front with Bessie in the middle of them.*

All sing[4]
Gentry and sentry all stand in a row
I mean you no manner of ill;   225
But I wish you sweethearts
And our Clown a new coat,
So, ladies, I bid you farewell,
So, ladies, I bid you farewell.

*At the word 'farewell', they bow, singing swords down and
up.*
They march off in the order of coming on.

Footnotes to Bellerby text
1. This song tune was used throughout except for the
   last song.
2. Added from a version collected by Miss B. G. Wilson.
3. *ll.* 76–9 are added from the Miss Wilson version.
4. The music for 'Gentry and Sentry' was only imper-
   fectly remembered, and Dr Karpeles was unable to
   note it.

Hibaldstow, Lincolnshire, Ploughboys. Wooing

Mabel Peacock: 9 NQ, vii, 1901, 322–3.

The following version is an example of those which have
neither combat nor cure, but which are restricted to the
wooing only. The characters are typical of those in the
more complete versions, but whether the revitalisation
was deliberately omitted, forgotten, or never existed, is
now problematical. The number of versions reported,
largely without text, of this type, suggests that it did not
actually exist. The mention of the Boer War in the
Foreign Traveller's speech dates the version fairly
closely, but Miss Peacock gives no indication as to its last
date of performance. She does however say that the
North Lincolnshire 'plough-jags' have gone about from
'house to house this season fantastically attired' but is
not otherwise more specific about costume. The text is
reproduced as printed.

Clown, 1st (Actor)
Good evening, ladys and Gentlemen,
I am making rather a bole[1] call;
But Christmas time is a merry time,

I have come to see you all.
I hope you will not be offended
For what I have got to say:
Here is a few more jolly fellows
Will step in this way.

Soldier, No. 2nd
I am a Recruited seagant *(sic)*
        Ariving here just now;
My orders is to enlist all
Who follow the cart and plough.

Foreign Traveller, 3rd
O, endeed, mr. seagant,
As I suppose you are,
You want us bold malishal lads[2]
To face the Boer war.
Will boldly face the enemy
And do the best we can,
And if they dont prove civil
We will slay them every one.
I am a Foreign Traveller,
I have travelled land and sea,
And nothing do I want but a wife
To please me the rest part of my life.

Lady, 4th
I am a lady bright and gay,
The fortune of my charm,
And scornfully I am thrown away
Into my lover arm.

3rd (i.e., the Foreign Traveller)
I have meet my dearest jewel;
She is the comforts of my life,
And if she proves true to me
I entend her been my wife.

Farmer, 5th
Madam, it is my desire,
If I should be the man
All for to gain your fancy, love,
I will do the best I can.
I have got corn and cattle,
And everything you know,
Besides a team of horses
To draw along the plough.

Lady
Young man, you are deceitful,
As any of the rest;
So for for *(sic)* that reason I will have
Them I love best.

Soldier (sic)
Come, me lads, who is bound for listing,
And gan³ along with me:
You shall have all kinds of liquor
While you are in our company.

Indian King, No. 6
War out!⁴ me lads, and let me come in!
For I am the old chap called Indian King.
They all have been trying me to slay;
But you see I am alive to this very day.

Hoby Horse, No 7
In comes a four year old cout,⁵
A fine as ever was brought:
He can hotch and he can trot
14 miles in 15 hours just like nought.

Lady Jane, N.8
In comes Jane with a long leg crayn,⁶
Rambling over the midow;
Once I was a blouming young girl,
But now I am a down old widow.

N.2 (i.e., the Soldier)
Gentleman, and ladies,
You see our fool is gone;
We make it in our busines
To follow him along;
We thank you for civility
That you have shown us here;
We wish you a merry Christmas
And a happy new year.

Footnotes to Hibaldstow text
1. Bold.
2. martial lads.
3. Go.
4. Look out.
5. colt.
6. crane.

Sproxton, Leicestershire. Wooing Play

E. C. Cawte: Private Collection (© E. C. Cawte 1980)

The following text is the only one known which has been collected in full with the music for the songs. It has not however, the Bastard incident, but as the performances were by children in its final days, the passage may have been deliberately omitted. In the 1890s it was acted by adult farm labourers, and was taken up by the children between 1905-8. It was performed on 'Plough-boy Night' in early January, and for some weeks prior to the performance, they practised in a pig-sty with straw on the floor.

Fool
In comes I who's never bin yet
With my big head and little wit,
My head is large, and my wit is small,
I can act the fool's part as well as you all.
Okum, pokum, France and Spain,   5
Walk in Sergeant all the same.

Sergeant
In comes I the Recruiting Sergeant,
I've arrived here just now,
I've had orders from the King
To enlist all jolly fellows that follow the carthorse at
   plough.   10
Likewise tinkers, tailors, peddlers, nailers, all that take
   to my advance,
The more I hear the fiddle play, the better I can dance.

Fool
Faith lad, think I've come here to see a fool like you
   dance?

Sergeant
Yes Tommy, I can dance, sing or say.   15

Fool
If you can dance, sing or say, well I'll quickly march
   away.

Farmer's Man
In comes I the Farmer's Man
Don't you see my whip in hand?
When I go to plough the land I turn it upside down.
Straight I go from end to end   20
I scarcely make a balk or bend
And to my horses I attend
As they go marching round the end
I shout 'Come here, jee woah back'.

Lady

Be-hold a la-dy bright and gay, good for-tunes and sweet charms, How scorn-ful I've been thrown a-way right out of my true love's arms, He swears if I don't wed with him as we some day p'raps may, He'll 'list for a sol-dier and from me run a-way.

Sergeant

Come all you young fel-lows that are bound for 'list-ing, 'list and do not be a-fraid, you shall have all kinds of liq-uor, like-wise kiss that pret-ty fair maid.

Farmer's Man

Thank you sir, I like your of-fer, time and a-way do sweet like pass, Dash to my wig if I'll grieve an-y long-er For that proud and sau-cy lass.

Lady

Now since me lov-er's 'list-ed and en-tered vo-lun-teers, I nei-ther mean to sigh for him nor yet to shed one tear, I nei-ther mean to sigh for him but I'll give him for to know, I'll have a-no-ther sweet-heart and a-long with him I'll go.

Fool
Dost thou love me my pretty maid?

Lady
Yes Tommy, and to me sorrow.

Fool
When shall be our wedding day?

Lady

Tom - my love, to - mor - row.

All sing

We'll shake hands and we'll make bands and we'll get wed to - mor-row.

Fool
Stop stop stop to me old flip flaps. I want to ask some of
you old riff-raff to me and my old girl's wedding; what
you like best you'd better bring with you. I don't
know what you like best, some like fish, some like
flesh, some like fruit and frummity; what me and my
old gel likes best we're going to have.

One of the others
What's that Tommy?

Fool
A barley chaff dumpling buttered with wool, cut up in
slices fit to choke an old bull. If your saucy old flats ain't
satisfied with that, you'd better go without, so right
away lads, we'll get wed tomorrow.

All sing, as before
We'll shake hands, and we'll make bands, and we'll get
wed tomorrow.

Beelzebub
In comes I Beelzebub,
On my shoulder I carry my club,
In me 'and a drip leather pan,
Don't you think I'm a funny old man?
Any man or woman in this room dare stand before me?

Fool
Yes, I darest, 'cos me 'ead is made of iron   65
Me body's made of steel,
Me hands are made of knuckle bone
No man can make me feel.

Beelzebub
What? I don't care if your 'ead is made of iron,
Your body made of steel,
Hands are made of knuckle bone
I can make you feel.
I'll smish you, smash you small as flies,
Send you to Jamaica to make mince pies.   70

*Hits him with a club then. (Hits on shoulder, used to be on
head.) Fool falls on the ground as if helpless*

Farmer's Man
Oh Bellzie, Oh Bellzie, what hast thou done?
Thou's killed the finest man under the sun.
Here he lays bleeding on this cold floor

Faith never to rise no more.
Five pound for a Doctor.   75

?Beelzebub
Ten pound for him to stop away.
What's the good of having a doctor to a dead man?

Farmer's Man
Sixteen pound for him to come in.
Step in doctor.

The Doctor's at the door

Doctor
Whoa, boys, hold my horse's head by the tail and mind
he don't kick you, he's only a donkey. I'll show you the   80
bright side of a shilling when I come out again.
In comes I the Doctor.

Sergeant
You a doctor?

Doctor
Yes, I a Doctor!   85

Sergeant
How became you to be a doctor?

Doctor
I travelled for it.

Sergeant
Where did you travel?

Doctor
England, France, Ireland and Spain,
And I come back to old England again,   90
Just below York there I cured an old woman named Cork;
She fell upstairs, downstairs, over a half empty teapot
full of flour, and grazed her shin-bone above her right
elbow, and made her stocking leg bleed, I set that and
made it straight again.

Sergeant
What else can you cure?

Doctor
Ipsy pipsy palsy and gout,
Pains within or aches without,

99

Set a tooth or draw a leg,
And almost raise the dead to life again.

Sergeant
You must be a very clever doctor, you'd better try your
 experience on this young man.

Doctor
Just wait while I take off my big top-hat, kid gloves, and
 corduroy walking stick, and I'll feel this man's pulse.
Then he bends down to him, feels round him
This man's pulse beats nineteen times to the tick of my
 watch,
he's in a very low way indeed, couldn't be much lower
 without

digging a hole. He's been living on green tater tops for
three weeks all but a fortnight. This morning he tried to
swallow a young wheelbarrow for his breakfast. Tried to
 cut
his throat with a rolling pin. I'll stop him from all them
tricks. Give him some of my old riff raff down his chiff
 chaff,
that'll make him rise and fight. Also I'll give him some of
my epsy doansum pills, take one tonight, two in the
morning, and the box tomorrow dinner time. If the pills
don't digest the box will. If he can't dance, we can sing,
so let's rise him up and we will begin.

All sing

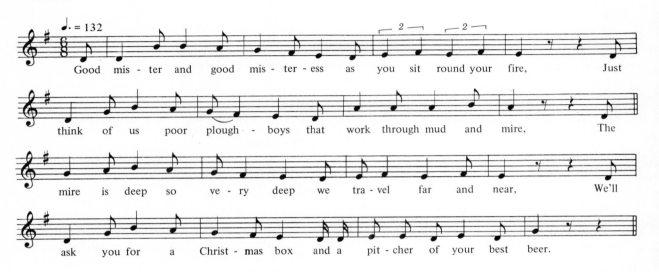

Good mis-ter and good mis-ter-ess as you sit round your fire, Just
think of us poor plough-boys that work through mud and mire, The
mire is deep so ve-ry deep we tra-vel far and near, We'll
ask you for a Christ-mas box and a pit-cher of your best beer.

Second verse to the same tune
We're not the London actors that act upon the stage,
We are just country ploughboys that work for little
 wage,
We're not the London actors, I've told you so before,
We'll wish you all goodnight friends, and another happy
 New Year.

Costume
Tom Fool   Dressed like a clown, conical hat ten inches
 high, no brim, one inch dark band at bottom. Print
 shirt, with baggy linen trousers striped blue and
 white, white face, red nose.
Recruiting Sergeant   Dressed as much like a Recruiting
 Sergeant as possible. Military cap and tunic, and
 sergeant's stripes on arms.
Farmer's Man   Working clothes, pale brown corduroy
 trousers, waistcoat, jacket (usually also corduroy),
 striped cotton shirt, handkerchief round neck, folded
 in two and knotted, the ends either loose or tucked
 into the shirt. Trousers tied with string below the
 knee, – these ties were known in the district as
 'Yorks'. Boots, cloth slouch hat set on one side.
 Carried a whip. Formerly he wore a smock.

Lady   Wide-brimmed hat about two feet across, frilled
 and maybe a veil, bright coloured blouse, woollen
 shawl (any colour), about two and a half feet square,
 folded in two diagonally, the right angle hanging
 down from the shoulders. Skirt padded at hips, and
 hanging nearly to ground, usually grey.
Beelzebub   Rough looking type. Black or dark fitting
 skull cap, dark coat like a windcheater. V-neck, striped
 cotton shirt, muffler, pale moleskin trousers, boots.
 Black face. Not stuffed with straw. Carried a club
 about 18 inches long, made of a woman's black stocking stuffed with straw, and a stick inside to stiffen it.
Doctor   Black top hat, gloves, swallowtail coat, white
 shirt, collar, long tie, riding breeches, tight at knee,
 riding boots, riding crop. Doctor's bag with pill box
 and medicine bottle of ordinary type and size.

The team was accompanied by a man in his ordinary
clothes who carried a box with a slit in the top. He
passed it round for the collection during the final song.

Footnote to Sproxton text
1. *ll.* 91–4 were spoken all at once in the style of a
 tongue-twister.

Bibliography and Abbreviations

A.B.: Communication to *The Lincoln, Rutland and Stamford Mercury*, The Prop., Stamford, 26th January, 1821, 4d.

ABRAHAMS, Roger D.: 'Pull Out Your Purse and Pay': A St George Mumming from the British West Indies' in *FL*, 79, The Folk-Lore Society, London, Autumn 1968, 176–201.

A.F.R.: 11 *NQ*, iii, 1911, 325.

ALPORT, Miss M. A.: Holograph letter to Rev. M. Noble, dated Halifax, Nova Scotia, 15th December 1811, in Bodleian Library MSS, Eng. Misc. d.162, f.23v.

ALFORD, Violet: 'The Basque Masquerade' in *FL*, XXXIX, 1928, 68–90; 'The Mummers' Play' in *The Proceedings of the Scottish Anthropological and Folklore Society*, IV, 1, Oliver and Boyd, Edinburgh, 1948, 29; *Sword Dance and Drama*, Merlin Press, London, 1962, 43.

ANDERSON, C. J.: *The Lincoln Pocket Guide*, Edward Stanford, London, 1880, 70.

ANON: 'October ye 20.1779. The Morrice Dancers (named in Dramatis Personae) acted their merry dancing &c. at Revesby . . .' in BM Add. MS 44870, 20.10. 1779.

ANON: *The Lincoln, Rutland and Stamford Mercury*, The Prop., Stamford, 12th January, 1844, 3d.

ARAM, C. H.: 'Ipsy, Pipsy, Palsy, Gout' in *The Nottinghamshire Countryside*, Vol. 17, No. 3, Nottinghamshire Rural Community Council, Nottingham, Winter 1956/7, 25–6.

ASWARBY Collection: 10/88/84 (Lincoln Record Office).

BAKER, Anne Elizabeth: *Glossary of Northamptonshire Words and Phrases*, II, John Russell Smith, London, 1854, 430–2.

BARLEY, M. W.: 'Plough Plays in the East Midlands' in *J.E.F.D.S.S.*, VII, 2, 1953, 68–95.

—, Private Collection.

BARLEY, L. B. and M. W.: 'Plough Monday Play from Branston near Lincoln' in *The Lincolnshire Historian*, 2, 4, Lincs. Local History Society, Lincoln, 1957, 36–43.

BASKERVILL, Charles Read: 'Mummers' Wooing Plays in England' in *Modern Philology*, XXI, No. 3, University of Chicago Press, February 1924, 225–72.

B.B.C.: British Broadcasting Corporation. B.B.C. Record No 14288, 14th December 1936.

BEATTY, Arthur: 'The St George, or Mummers', Play: A Study in the Protology of the Drama' in *Transactions of the Wisconsin Academy of Sciences, Arts and Letters*, Vol. XV, Pt. II, Democrat Printing Co., Madison, Wisconsin, October 1906, 273–324.

BELL, Robert; (ed.): *Ancient Poems, Ballads and Songs of the Peasantry of England*, Parker, London, 1857, 175–80.

BERNHEIMER, Richard: *Wild Men in the Middle Ages*, Harvard University Press, Cambridge, 1952, 1.

BERRY, C. J.: 'Mummers' Play is a Relic of Mediaevalism' in *The Andover Advertiser and Northern Hants Gazette*, No. 4936, Holmes and Son, Andover, 2nd January 1953, 3b–f.

BLAKE, Mrs Lois: Private Collection.

BM: British Museum.

BORLASE, William: *The Natural History of Cornwall*, W. Jackson (printer), Oxford, 1758, 299.

BOWER, H. M.: MS (Vaughan Williams Memorial Library).

BOYD, Arnold W.: Private Collection.

BRAND, John: *Observations on Popular Antiquities*, T. Saint, Newcastle upon Tyne, 1777, 175–6.

—, *Observations on Popular Antiquities*, ed. Sir Henry Ellis, I, Bohn, London, 1849, 213, 513.

BRECK, Samuel: *Recollections of Samuel Breck . . . (1771–1862)*, ed. H. E. Scudder, Sampson Low, London, 1877, 35–6.

BRICE, Andrew: *The Mobiad, or Battle of the Voice*, Brice and Thorn, Exeter, 1770, 90.

BRIERLEY, Benjamin: *Tales and Sketches of Lancashire Life*, John Heywood, Manchester, I, n.d. (1863), 113–14.

BRISCOE, John Potter: *Nottinghamshire Facts and Fictions*, Shepherd Bros., Nottingham, 2nd Edn., 1876, 6–7.

BROADWOOD, Lucy E.: Collection (Vaughan Williams Memorial Library).

BROADWOOD, Lucy E. and FULLER-MAITLAND, J. A.: *English County Songs*, Leadenhall Press, London, 1893, 22–5.

BROGDEN, J. Ellett: *Provincial Words and Expressions current in Lincolnshire*, Robt. Hardwicke, London, 1866, 151–2.

BURKETT, Anne R.: Collection.

BURKITT, C. E.: 'Wiltshire Mummers', Letter to *The Times*, No. 52517, Times Publishing Co., London, 12th January, 1953, 5e.

BURNE, Charlotte Sophia: *Shropshire Folk-Lore: a Sheaf of Gleanings, edited by Charlotte Sophia Burne from the Collections of Georgina F. Jackson*, Trübner, London, 1883, (–1886), 483–9.

BURTON, Alfred: *Rush-Bearing*, Brook and Chrystal, Manchester, 1891.

BURTON House, Household Accounts, Lincoln Record Office, 10/1A/3, 10/1A/6.

CAMERON, Hector Charles: *Sir Joseph Banks, K.B., P.R.S. The Autocrat of Philosophers*, The Batchworth Press, London, 1952, 264.

CAMPBELL, Marie: 'Survivals of Old Folk Drama in the Kentucky Mountains' in *Journal of American Folk-Lore*, LI, 199, J. J. Augustin Inc., New York, January–March 1938, 10–24.

CANTLE, James: A Christmas Play, MS in Collectanea Hunteriana, Popular Antiquities (collected by S. J. Hunter), n.d., BM Add. MS 24546, ff. 46r–47r.

CANZIANI, Estella: 'The Sword Dance of Fenestrelle' in *J.E.F.D.S.*, 2nd S., 4, O.U.P., London, 1931, 19.

CARY, Henry: *Memoir of the Rev. Henry Francis Cary, M.A. . . .*, II, Edward Moxon, London, 1847, 22.

CASSIE, Bill: 'Rapper Knots from High Spen' in *Folk Music Journal*, The E.F.D.S.S., London, 1965, 7.

CASTLE CARY VISITOR, II, No. 48, December 1899, 189.

CATHCART-SMITH, Catherine: 'The Soul-Cakers' Play' in *J.E.F.D.S.S.*, V, 2, 1947, 85–91.

CAWTE, E. C.: Private Collection.

—, 'The Morris Dance in Herefordshire, Shropshire and Worcestershire' in *J.E.F.D.S.S.*, IX, 4, 1963, 197–212.

CAWTE, E.C., HELM, Alex and PEACOCK, N.: *English Ritual Drama*, FLS, London, 1967.

CAWTE, E. C., HELM, Alex, MARRIOTT, R. J. and PEACOCK, N.: 'A Geographical Index of the Ceremonial Dance in Great Britain' in *J.E.F.D.S.S.*, IX, 1, 1960, 1–41.

CAWTE, E. C. and SOPER, C. J. F.: *The Rapper Dance as taught by the Lowerson Family at Murton*, The Guizer Press, Ibstock, 1967, 6.

CHAMBERS, E. K.: *The Mediaeval Stage*, I, Clarendon Press, Oxford, 1903, 214–16.

—, *The English Folk Play*, Clarendon Press, Oxford, 1933.

[CLARKSON, Christopher]: *The History of Richmond in the County of York. . . .* T. Bowman, Richmond, 1814, 296, 297.

CLARKSON, Christopher: *The History of Richmond in the County of York. . . .* The Author, Richmond, 1821, 290, 291.

COOK, T. D.: 'A Northumbrian Sword Dance' in *J.E.F.D.S.S.*, I, 2, 1933, 111–12.

CROKER, Thos.: Trinity College, Dublin, MS 1206, Chap. 9, ff. 11–12, *circa* 1800.

DARBY, H. C. (ed.): *An Historical Geography of England before A.D. 1800*, C.U.P., Cambridge, 3rd Edn., 1951, 472.

DAWKINS, R. M.: 'A Visit to Skyros' in *The Annual of the British School at Athens*, No. XI, Macmillan, London, 1904–5, 72–80.

—, The Modern Carnival in Thrace and the Cult of Dionysus' in *Journal of Hellenic Studies*, XXVI, Macmillan, London, 1906, 191–206.

DEAN-SMITH, Margaret: 'Folk-Play Origins of the English Masque' in *FL*, LXV, 1954, 74–86.

—, 'The Life-Cycle or Folk Play' in *FL*, 69, 1958, 249.

—, 'Disguise in English Folk Drama' in *Folk Life*, I, Folk Life Society, Cardiff, 1963, 98.

DOUGLAS, G. W.: *The American Book of Days*, H. W. Wilson, New York, 1948, 6.

DOUGLAS, Mona: 'Manx Folk Dances: their Notation and Revival' in *J.E.F.D.S.S.*, III, 1937, 114.

—, 'Folk Song and Dance in Mann' in *The Proceedings of the Scottish Anthropological and Folklore Society*, IV, 1, Oliver and Boyd, Edinburgh, 1949, 53.

DOWSON, Frank W.: 'Notes on the Goathland Folk Play' in *The Transactions of the Yorkshire Dialect Society*, Pt. XXVIII, IV, The Society, York, April 1926, 36–7.

ED&S: *English Dance and Song*, The E.F.D.S.S., London.

E.F.D.S.S.: The English Folk Dance and Song Society.

EGGAR, J. Alfred: *Remembrances of Life and Customs in Gilbert White's, Cobbett's, and Charles Kingsley's Country*, Simpkin Marshall, Hamilton, Kent, London, n.d. (1924), 27–32.

E.H.: 'Manners and Customs of Old Stockport: Peace Egging' in *Advertiser NQ*, [I], Advertiser Office, Stockport, 1882, 103–4 (Reprinted from *The Stockport Advertiser*, 9th July 1881).

EWING, Juliana Horatia: *The Peace Egg and a Christmas Mumming Play*, S.P.C.K., London, n.d.

FALLOW, T. M.: 'Yorkshire Sword-Actors' in *The Antiquary*, XXXI, No. 65, NS No. 186, Elliott Stock, London, May 1895, 138–42.

F.B.H.: 'Ickwell May Day' in *ED&S*, XXVII, 3, April 1965, 91.

FL Folk-Lore, 1890 – continuing. (1890–1912, published by David Nutt, London; 1913–1919, Sidgwick and Jackson, London; 1920 – continuing, Glaisher, London. After 1958 as *Folklore*).

FLS: The Folk-Lore Society.

FLETT, J. T. and T. M.: 'Some Hebridean Folk Dances' in *J.E.F.D.S.S.*, VII, 2, 1953, 115.

FRAZER, Sir James George: *The Golden Bough*, abridged edition, Macmillan, London, 1949, 1, 347.

FRIEND, Hilderic: 'Brackley Morrice-Dancers' in *The Midland Garner*, Vol. 2, 1st S., Guardian Office, Banbury, 1884, 23.

GAILEY, Alan: *Christmas Mummers and Rhymers in Ireland*, Guizer Press, Ibstock, Leicester, 1968, 23.

—, *Irish Folk Drama*, The Mercier Press, Cork, 1969.

GATTY, Ivor: 'The Eden Collection of Mumming Plays' in *FL*, LIX, 1948, 16–34.

GRANADA Television: Programme entitled 'Scene at 6.30', 6.30 p.m., 24th December 1964.

GRAY, Howard Levi: *English Field Systems*, Merlin Press Reprint, London, 1959 (First published 1915).

GROVE, Florence: 'Christmas Mummers' in *FL*, X, 1899, 351–2.

HALPERT, Herbert and STORY, G. M. (eds): *Christmas Mumming in Newfoundland*, Memorial University of Newfoundland, 1969.

HAMMOND, H. E. D.: 'Folk Songs from the Hammond Collection' in *J.F.S.S.*, No. 34, December 1930, 192–4.

HARDY, Thomas: *The Return of the Native*, Bk. ii, Chap. 3.

—, *Thomas Hardy's Notebooks* (ed. Evelyn Hardy), Hogarth Press, London, 1955, 37.

HARWOOD, H. W. and MARSDEN, F. H.: *The Pace-Egg: The Midgley Version*, Halifax Printing Works, Halifax, 1935, fp.1.

HELM, Alex: Private Collection.

—, 'The Lymm (Cheshire) Morris Dance' in *J.E.F.D.S.S.*, VI, 3, 1951, 100.

—, (ed.): *Five Mumming Plays for Schools*, E.F.D.S.S. and FLS, London, 1965.

—, *Cheshire Folk Drama*. The Guizer Press, Ibstock, Leicester, 1968.

HELM, Alex and CAWTE, E. C.: *Six Mummers' Acts*, The Guizer Press, Ibstock, Leicester, 1967.

HENDERSON, William: Very old MS copied 1788, quoted by Sir Walter Scott: *The Pirate*, 1821.

HIBBERT, Samuel: *Description of the Shetland Isles. . . .* Constable, Edinburgh, 1822, 554.

HIBERNICUS: *NQ*, vol. CLXXVI, 1939, 399–405.

H.N.: 'Sword Dancing in Loftus' in *Loftus Urban District Council Souvenir Coronation Year Book*, 1953, 26–9.

HOLE, Christina: *Traditions and Customs of Cheshire*, Williams and Norgate, London, 1937, 113.

HONE, William: *The Every-Day Book*, II, William Tegg, London, 1826, cols. 18–21, 122–6, 565, 1645–8.

HUNTER, S. J.: *Popular Traditions, Proverbs, Forms of Expressions, Words and other Antiquities of the Common People* (MS), 1822, in BM Add. MS 24542, f.13r (p. 25), f.25r (p. 49)–27r (p. 53).

IFCM: Irish Folklore Commission.

JACKSON, John: *The History of the Scottish Stage from its first establishment to the present time*, Peter Hill, Edinburgh, 1793, 409–11.

J.E.F.D.S.: *The English Folk-Dance Society's Journal*, The English Folk Dance Society, London, 1914–15 and *The Journal of the English Folk Dance Society*, O.U.P., London, 1927–8 and 1930–1.

J.E.F.D.S.S.: *Journal of the English Folk Dance and Song Society*, The Society, London, 1932–1964.

J.F.S.S.: *Journal of the Folk-Song Society*, The Society, London, 1899–1931. After 1931 amalgamated with J.E.F.D.S. (see above) and continued as J.E.F.D.S.S.

JONES, Edward: *Musical and Poetical Relicks of the Welsh Bards*, a new edition, doubly augmented and improved, The Author, London, 1794, 108, fn.9 (The 1st edn., 1784, contains nothing relevant).

JOHNSON, T. Osbourne: 'Ploughjags' Revenge' in *The Sunday Times*, No. 7742, 9th January 1966, 13c.

KARPELES, Dr Maud: Private Collection.

—, *The Lancashire Morris Dance*, Novello, London (*circa* 1930), 11–12.

—, 'The Abram Morris Dance' in *J.E.F.D.S.S.*, I, 1, 1932, 59.

KENDALL, Frank H.: 'A Calder Valley Custom', Communication to *The Yorkshire Evening Post*, No. 10088, The Yorkshire Conservative Newspaper Co. Ltd., Leeds, 20th January 1923, 4g.

KENNEDY, D. N.: 'The North Skelton Sword Dance' in *J.E.F.D.S*, 2nd S., 1, 1927, 27.

KENNEDY, Douglas: 'Observations on the Sword-Dance and Mummers' Play' in *J.E.F.D.S.S.*, 2nd S., 3, 1930, 17–20.

—, 'The Wooden Sword Dance' in *J.E.F.D.S.S.*, III, 4, 1939, 288–9.

[KENNEDY, Patrick]: 'Hibernian Country Pastimes and Festivals Fifty Years Since' in Dublin University Magazine, LXII, George Herbert, Dublin, July–December 1863, 584–6.

KIRKE, John: *The Seven Champions of Christendome*, Acted at the Cocke-pit, and at the Red Bull in St Johns streete, with a generall liking. And never printed till this Yeare 1638. Written by J. K. London: Printed by J. Okes, and are to be sold by James Becket at his shop in the Inner Temple Gate, 1638.

LARKE, Sir William: *The Steel Age*, British Iron and Steel Federation, London, July 1954.

LEE, Frederick George: 5 *NQ*, ii, 1874, 503–5.

LEYLAND, John: *Memorials of Hindley* (Preface dated 31st December 1878), 106.

—, *Memorials of Abram*, Manchester, 1882, 113–15.

LOCHLAINN, Colm O: 'Christmas Rhymers and Mummers' in *The Irish Book Lover*, XVI, The Prop., Dublin, Bound Edn., January–December 1928, 126.

MAGNUS, Olaus: *De Gentibus Septentrioanlibus*, Rome, 1555, l.xv., c. xxiii.

MANNING, P. J.: MSS, Bodleian Library, Oxford, Top. Oxon. d.199.

—, Letter to *Oxford Times*, 24th December 1898, 9e.

—, 'Some Oxfordshire Seasonal Festivals' in *FL*, VIII, 1897, 313–5, Pl.V.

MARRIOTT, R. J.: Private Collection.

MIDDLETON, Thomas: 'Rushbearing and Morris Dancing in North Cheshire' in *Transactions of the Lancashire and Cheshire Antiquarian Society*, LX, The Society, Manchester, 1948, 47–55.

M.K.: 'Some Fragments of Sword-Dance Plays' in *J.E.F.D.S.*, 2nd S., 2, 1928, 35–42.

MONSON Collection as under Burton House Household Accounts, *q.v.*

MORRIS, Oliver: 'The Old Broadway Mummers' Play' in *Evesham Journal and Four Shires Advertiser*, No. 5507, W. & H. Smith Ltd., Evesham, 24th December 1965, 8d–f, 9ab.

MORRIS, William: *Swindon Fifty Years Ago (more or less)*, Advertiser's Office, Swindon, 1885, 141–50.

NEAL, Mary (ed.): *The Esperance Morris Book*, Part 1, Curwen, London, 5th Edn., 1910, 4.

NEEDHAM, Joseph: 'The Geographical Distribution of English Ceremonial Dance Traditions' in *J.E.F.D.S.S.*, III, 1, 1936, 27.

NEEDHAM, Joseph and PECK, Arthur L.: 'Molly Dancing in East Anglia' in *J.E.F.D.S.S.*, I, 2, 1933, 79–85.

NORGROVE, Mrs: *Birmingham Weekly Post, NQ*, No. 1582, Jaffray, Feeney and Co., Birmingham, 4th October 1884, 1a.

NQ: Notes and Queries.

ORDISH, T. Fairman: Collection, FLS, University College London, Gower Street, London, N.W.1.

—, 'Folk Drama' in *FL*, II, 1891, 314–335.

—, 'English Folk Drama' in *FL*, IV, 1893, 149–175.

ORMEROD, George: *The History of Cheshire*, I, 1818, p.lxxix.

PARKER, Angelina: 'Oxfordshire Village Folk Lore, 1840–1900' in *FL*, XXIV, 1913, 86–7.

PASQUIN, Anthony (arranged and digested by) (pseud. for John Williams): *The Eccentricities of John Edwin, Comedian*, I, printed for J. Strahan, No. 67, Near the Adelphi, Strand (1791), 253, 255, 262–4.

PATERSON, T. G. F.: 'The Christmas Rhymers' in *Journal of the County Louth Archaeological Society*, XL, No. 1, 1945, William Tempest, Dundalk, 1946, 46.

PEACOCK, A. J.: *Bread or Blood: the Agrarian Riots in East Anglia; 1816*, Gollancz, London, 1963.

PEACOCK, Edward: *A Glossary of Words used in the Wapentakes of Manley and Corringham, Lincolnshire*, [EDS Vol. 15], Trübner, London, 1877, 173.

—, *A Glossary of Words used in the Wapentakes of Manley and Corringham, Lincolnshire*, 2nd Edn., revised and considerably enlarged, EDS Vol. 59, II, Trübner, London, 1889, 357.

PEACOCK, Mabel: 9 *NQ*, vii, 1901, 364–5.

PEACOCK, N.: 'The Greatham Sword Dance' in *J.E.F.D.S.S.*, VIII, 1, 1956, 29–39.

—, Private Collection.

PIESSE, G. W. Septimus: 2 *NQ*, x, 1860, 466–7.

PILLING, Julian: 'Morris, Nutters and Rushcart in Whitworth' in *ED&S*, XXVII, 5, October 1965, 142–4.

POTTER, Louisa: *Lancashire Memories*, Macmillan, London, 1879, 81.

PRIESTNALL, John and MITCHELL, William E.: *The Play of St George, the Knights and the Dragon*, compiled for private circulation, 1930.

PROTHEROE, A. M.: 'Scraps of English Folklore. X. Derbyshire (Repton)' in *FL*, XXXII, 1925, 83.

RAYNBIRD, William and Hugh: *On the Agriculture of Suffolk*, Longman, London, 1849, 307.

READER'S DIGEST: *Complete Atlas of the British Isles. . .*, Reader's Digest Association, London, n.d. (1965), 122.

REES, George Edward: *The History of Bagendon*, The Author, Bagendon, 1932, 124–5.

RICHARDSON, M. A.: *The Local Historian's Table Book, Legendary Division*, Vol. III, M. A. Richardson, Newcastle upon Tyne, 1846, 375–80.

ROBINSON, Mrs Jennifer: Private Collection.

R.S.: 'Origins of British Theatre' in *Theatre Notebook*, 7, No. 3, The Society for Theatre Research, London, April/June 1953, 58–60.

RUDKIN, Ethel H.: Private Collection.

—, 'Lincolnshire Folk Lore' in *FL*, XLIV, 1933, 289.

—, 'The Plough Jacks' Play' in *FL*, L, 1939, 201–4.

SAWYER, Fredrick Ernest: 'Sussex Folk Lore and Customs connected with the Seasons' in *Sussex Archaeological Collections relating to the History and Antiquities of the County*, XXXIII, Sussex Archaeological Society, Lewes, 1883, 256.

SCOTT, Sir Walter: *The Poetical Works of Sir Walter Scott, Bart.* III, Constable and Co., Edinburgh, 1822, Note III to Marmion, Canto VI;
Letter to Thomas Sharp dated 7th March 1826, bound in BM Add. MS 43645, f.346v.

SHARP, Cecil J.: *The Sword Dances of Northern England*, I–III, Novello, London, 1911–13.

—, *The Sword Dances of Northern England: Songs and Dance Airs*, III, Novello, London, 1913.

—, Field Note Books, Vaughan Williams Memorial Library.

—, MSS, Clare College, Cambridge (Microfilm Copy, Vaughan Williams Memorial Library).

SHARP, Cecil J. and MACILWAINE, Herbert C.: *The Morris Book. . .*, I, Novello, London, 2nd Edn., 1912, 23–4; *ibid.*, II, 2nd Edn., 1922, 23–4; *ibid.*, III, 2nd Edn., 74.

SHARPE, Sir Cuthbert: *The Bishoprick Garland*, Nichols and Baldwin and Cradock, London, 1834, 58–62 (Reprinted Frank Graham, Newcastle upon Tyne, 1969).

SHOEMAKER, Alfred L.: *Christmas in Pennsylvania: A Folk Cultural Study*, Pennsylvania Folklife Society, Kutztown, Pennsylvania, 2nd Printing, 1959, 21–3.

SMITH, Paul: Private Collection.

SMITH, Sidney: 'The Practice of Kingship in early Semitic Kingdoms' in S. H. Hooke (ed.): *Myth, Ritual and Kingship*, O.U.P., Oxford, 1958, 41–73.

SPOONER, B.C.: 'The Maypole' in *Old Cornwall*, II, No. 1, James Lanham Ltd., St Ives, Summer 1931, 21–2.

SWINBURNE, Dr W. H.: Contribution to *ED&S*, XVIII, 6, June/July 1954, 202.

TAYLOR, Antoinette: 'An English Christmas Play' in *The Journal of American Folk Lore*, XXII, No. LXXXVI, Houghton, Mifflin and Co., Boston, October–December 1909, 389–94.

THOMS, William: 'The Folk-Lore of Shakespeare' in *The Athenaeum*, No. 1036, John Francis, London, 4th September 1847, 937.

TIDDY, R. J. E.: *The Mummers' Play*, Clarendon Press, Oxford, 1923.

TINKLER, Rev. John: Letter sent to Cecil J. Sharp, 1912 (see MK: *J.E.F.D.S.*, 2nd S, 2, 1928, 33–4).

TOPLIFF, Robert: *A Selection of the Most Popular Melodies of the Tyne and Wear . . .*, R. Topliff. London, n.d. (BM copy dated 1815), 37, 42.

TUGWELL, George: *The North-Devon Scenery Book*, 2nd Edn., Simpkin Marshall, London, n.d. (1863), 110–13.

UFMA: Ulster Folk Museum Archives.

VAUGHAN Williams Memorial Library Collection.

VERNEY, Lady, Margaret Maria (ed.): *Verney Letters of the Eighteenth Century from the Manuscripts at Claydon House*, II, Ernest Benn, London, 1930, 41.

VUIA, R.: 'The Roumanian Hobby-Horse, the Calusari' in *J.E.F.D.S.S.*, II, 1935, 97–101.

WACE, A. J. B.: 'North Greek Festivals and the Worship of Dionysos' in *The Annual of the British School at Athens*, No. XVI, Macmillan, London, 1909–10, 232–53.

—, 'Mumming Plays in the Southern Balkans' in *ibid.*, No. XIX, 1912–13, 248–65.

WALLIS, John: *The Natural History and Antiquities of Northumberland*, II, London, 1769, 28.

WELCH, Charles E. Jr: ' "Oh Dem Golden Slippers," The Philadelphia Mummers' Parade' in *Journal of American Folk Lore*, University of Texas Press, Austin, Texas, 1966, 523–36.

WILLIAMS, Alfred: Collection (Swindon Public Library)

—, *Folk Songs of the Upper Thames*, Duckworth, London, 1923, 170–1.

—, 'A Wiltshire Mummers' Play' in *Wiltshire Gazette*, 30th December 1936, 3c–e.

WOLFRAM, Richard: 'Bergmännische Tänze' in *Der Anschnitt*, No. 1, 5, Bochum, April 1953, 6–10.

WOOD, James: Communication to *Manchester City News*, City News Office, Manchester, 11th March 1905, 2c.

WOOD, Melusine: 'Notes on Ritual Tools and Dances' in *J.E.F.D.S.S.*, IV, 6, 1945, 247–53.

WORTLEY, Russell: Private Collection.

W.R.: 6 *NQ*, v, 1882, 176.

YONGE, Charlotte M.: *The Christmas Mummers*, J. & C. Mozley, Paternoster Row, London, 1858, 79–99.

Notes

Foreword

1. Cawte, E. C., Helm, Alex, Marriott, R. J. and Peacock, N.: 'A Geographical Index of the Ceremonial Dance in Great Britain' in *J.E.F.D.S.S.*, IX, 1, 1960, 1–41.
2. Cawte, E. C., Helm, Alex, and Peacock, N.: *English Ritual Drama*, Folklore Society, London, 1967.

1. *Problems and Attitudes*

1. A bibliography to all these sources will be found in E. C. Cawte *et al.*: *English Ritual Drama*, 1967.
2. For the distinction between 'chapbook' and 'traditional' see Appendix One.
3. Ordish Collection.
4. The word is spelled thus in the MS. In its context it may be intended for 'deceased'; alternatively, it could be a mis-spelling of 'diseased'.
5. This, of course, should be Slasher.
6. John Kirke: *The Seven Champions of Christendome*, 1638.
7. As at Thame, Oxfordshire. See Chapter 6.
8. As at Rochdale, Lancashire, where the authors have based their version on eleven others and added a dragon for effect. (John Priestnall and William E. Mitchell: *The Play of St George, the Knights and the Dragon*, 1930).
9. E. K. Chambers: *English Folk Play*, 1933, 178.
10. J. Potter Briscoe: *Notts. Facts and Fictions*, 1876, 6.
11. As at Ripon, Yorkshire.
12. As at Symondsbury, Dorset.
13. At Bromborough, Cheshire, up to *circa* 1887 (Christina Hole: *Traditions and Customs of Cheshire*, 1937, 113) and Mullion, Cornwall, up to 1890–1 (Florence Grove: *FL*, X, 1899, 351–2), the ceremonies were still mimed. Neither is described with sufficient detail to be able to give a positive identification other than showing that they belonged to the actions under discussion.
14. Margaret Dean-Smith: *FL*, 69, 1958, 244.

2. *Literary Survey*

1. Thos. Croker: Trinity College, Dublin, MS 1206, Chap. 9, ff. 11–12, *c.* 1800.
2. Andrew Bryce: *The Mobiad or Battle of the Voice*, 1770, 90.
3. William Borlase: *The Natural History of Cornwall*, 1758, 299.
4. John Jackson: *The History of the Scottish Stage . . .*, 1793, 409–411.

5. Anthony Pasquin: *The Eccentricities of John Edwin, Comedian*, I (1791), 253, 255, 262–4.
6. BM Add. MS 44870.
7. Sir Walter Scott: *Poetical Works*, III, Note III to Marmion, Canto VI.
8. Edward Jones: *Musical and Poetical Relicks of the Welsh Bards*, 1794, 108 f.n. 9.
9. Samuel Breck: *Recollections of Samuel Breck . . . (1771–1862)*, 1877, 35–6.
10. Bodleian Library MS Eng. Misc. d. 162, f. 23V, 15th December, 1811.
11. Cecil J. Sharp: *The Sword Dances of Northern England*, III (1913), 50.
12. Frank W. Dowson: *Trans. of the Yorkshire Dialect Society*, Pt. XXVIII, IV, 1926, 36–7.
13. Henry Cary: *Memoir of Rev. Henry Francis Cary, M.A. . . .*, II, 1847, 22.
14. Sir Walter Scott: Letter to Thomas Sharp dated 7th March, 1826.
15. William Hone: *The Every-Day Book*, II, 1826, cols. 18–21.
16. William Thoms: *The Athenaeum*, 4th September, 1847, 937.
17. T. Fairman Ordish: *FL*, II, 1891, 314–335; *ibid.*, IV, 1893, 149–175.
18. Alan Gailey: *Irish Folk Drama*, 1969.

3. *The Wooing Ceremonies*

1. S. J. Hunter: Pop. Trads (MS), 1823, f. 25–27. This collection contains 'The Men's Play' and the 'Children's Play from Bassingham', three texts from Broughton – 'A Christmas Play', 'Broughton Play', and 'Broughton Xmas Play corrected by a recollection of 60 years'. These three are dated 1824. A further text is entitled 'The Recruiting Sergeant' with a wooing action and an abortive attempt at a combat which becomes a dance instead of a fight.
2. Throughout this study, this term is used to describe a man dressed as a woman. It is preferred to the customary 'man/woman' which suggests an hermaphrodite. This was not the intention of this character, either in the dramatic actions or anywhere else; for the purpose of his appearance he was a 'Female', a male character, who by adopting the dress of a woman, assumed the sex and fertility of a female.
3. See the Sproxton, Leicestershire, version, App. II.
4. Reproduced from the Vaughan Williams Memorial Library Collection.
5. 'Because of the difficulty of securing men for the regular army during the Napoleonic Wars liberal bounties were given to new recruits . . . The follow-

ing are the periods when the bounty was ten guineas:

	Cavalry	Infantry
Men and lads		8th May 1804– 16th June 1804
Boys under 16	14th December 1808– 1st May 1814	

Information from Mr D. W. King, Deputy Librarian, War Office Library, 7th July 1955.

The same promise of 'ten guines' is found in the text of 'The Recruiting Sergeant', and this can only be dated to 1824 roughly by its context with the other texts. The possiblity is that the inflated bounties attracted the attention of the country labourers who were normally the people who enlisted into the Regular Army to such an extent that the inducement was worth including in the ceremonials.

6. Coxcomb.
7. This is an example of the nonsense of the texts. The victim who was introduced as 'King George' has now become the King of Egypt. This may mean that formerly the latter character did appear in the action, but the passage of time had caused his part to be deleted.
8. The Men's version from Bassingham has:

> I can cure the Itch and the Veneral and the Gout
> All akes within and pains without

whilst the Children's Version has:

> The itch pox loosic palsy and the gout
> all agues and paines within and without.

The Doctor's lines have probably been bowdlerised for polite society more than any other.
9. Two weeks.
10. The invitation to the Fool's wedding is only found in these actions. It may be an indirect reference to a communal feast once the ceremony was over. This is still the practice in many Irish actions, though without any suggestion of a wedding feast.
11. Mr Fred Jacklin, from whom this version was collected, could offer no explanation of this word, but thought 'it might be Latin'.
12. According to Mr Jacklin, 'Child', if in respectable company'.
13. always.
14. Reproduced from M. W. Barley: Collection.
15. anecdote.
16. *ll.* 195–202 of the Branston version.
17. With the exception of one example from Treswell, Nottinghamshire, these are confined to Lincolnshire.
18. These too, are only found in Nottinghamshire and Lincolnshire.
19. e.g. the Swinderby version, Hunter Collection.
20. E. K. Chambers: *The English Folk Play*, 1933, 235.
21. At Ripon, Yorkshire, where the combatants used old bayonets instead of swords, the combat became so spirited on Boxing Day, 1964, that one of them was wounded and had to receive hospital treatment. (Inf. from Mr Tom Chambers.)
22. Monson Collection.
23. Aswarby Collection.
24. Edward Peacock: *Gloss. of Words used in the Wapentakes of Manley and Corringham*, 1877, 173.
25. *Edward Peacock: Gloss. of Words used in the Wapentakes of Manley and Corringham*, 2nd Edn., II, 1889, 357.
26. Mrs Ethel H. Rudkin: Collection.
27. For example, at Langworth, the Morris Dancers came round at Christmastime with Fool and Doctor, etc., and danced, sang and acted the Mummers' Play. (E. H. Rudkin: *FL*, xliv, 1933, 289). At Helpringham, the locals insisted that the ceremony was a morris dance (Vaughan Williams Memorial Library Collection), and at Frithville, both Morris Dancers and Plough Boys were remembered. (M. W. Barley: *J.E.F.D.S.S.*, 1953, 79).
28. This may be the explanation of 'Mr Rowley's, Mr Grundy's and Mr Crabtree's men' in 1775. See page 17.
29. M. W. Barley; *op. cit..*, 75.
30. At the County Fair at Swineshead, 1954, even so many years after the event, an argument about the right size for a gang became so heated that the supporters of the normal size gangs had to withdraw before violence broke out.
31. Mrs Ethel H. Rudkin: Collection.
32. M. W. Barley: *op. cit.*, 79.
33. At Kirklington, the character Eezum-Squeezeum was substituted for Beelzebub because the vicar of the time thought the latter not proper. The character still retained the Beelzebub lines with slight modification.
34. T. Osborn Johnson: *The Sunday Times*, 9th January 1966, 13c.
35. E. H. Rudkin: *FL*, L, 1939, 291–4.
36. M. W. Barley: *op. cit.*, 76.
37. L. B. and M. W. Barley: *The Lincs. Historian*, 2, 1957, 36–43.
38. M. W. Barley: *op. cit.*, 76.
39. It was customary for the gangs who had a plough with them to plough a furrow across the lawn of anyone who refused to contribute.
40. M. W. Barley: *op. cit.*, 76.
41. Ordish Collection.
42. C. H. J. Anderson: *The Lincoln Pocket Guide*, 1880, 79.
43. C. H. Aram: *The Notts. Countryside*, 17, No. 3, Winter 1956/7, 25–6.
44. Ordish Collection.
45. M. W. Barley: *op. cit.*, 88.

4. *The Sword Dance Ceremonies*

1. In some Long Sword dances the circle is broken and a longways set is formed. The No Man's Jig and The Roll at Sleights (Cecil J. Sharp: *The Sword Dances of Northern England*, II, 1912, 24–26) are good examples of this. Such figures are probably late developments when the inventiveness of the performers failed to devise other circular forms.
2. This description is not intended to refer to any Sword Dance in particular, but merely summarises general features. Details of particular methods of performance can be found in Cecil J. Sharp: *The Sword Dances of Northern England*, I–III, 1911–1913. A full list of locations together with a classification of each ceremony is given in E. C. Cawte *et al.*: *J.E.F.D.S.S.*, 1960, 1–41.
3. Cecil J. Sharp: *The Sword Dances of Northern England*, I, 1911, 82.
4. E. C. Cawte and C. J. F. Soper: *The Rapper Dance as taught by the Lowerson Family at Murton*, 1967, 6.
5. Sir William Larke: *The Steel Age*, 1954, 6. A patent was granted to Meysey and Elliott in 1614 for a process which was unsatisfactory and steel still had to be imported.

6. Pliable wood is possible however. The High Spen team of boys was initially trained in their Rapper dance by using such pieces of wood, because they could not afford the rappers. (Bill Cassie: *FMJ*, 1965, 7).

7. This is also true of some Long Sword implements. At Sleights these had a metal circle at the tip with a hole in the centre through which ribbons were fastened. (Cecil J. Sharp: *The Sword Dances of Northern England*, II, 1912, 13).

8. Miss Melusine Wood in *J.E.F.D.S.S.*, IV, 1945, 247–253, pointed out the similarity between a scutcher used in the preparation of flax and the implement used by the Flamborough sword dancers. Miss Wood was careful to point out that her notes were a suggestion for further study. Douglas Kennedy, writing in the same *Journal* (III, 1939, 288) and referring to previous correspondence with Miss Wood which had led him to follow up the suggestion, showed that the wooden 'sword' bore a stronger resemblance to the implement used by fishermen in repairing their nets.

9. There was until recently, in the collection of agricultural implements at the Queen's Head Inn, Burley, Hampshire, an implement in all respects like a rapper, but without a swivelled handle. It was called a 'Strapper' and was used, held bent, in the early years of this century in the same way as a currier's knife. (Inf. from Dr E. C. Cawte).

10. The Flamborough and Beadnell dancers were fishermen.

11. See the account of the Roumanian Calusari, page 46.

12. This was probably a late rationalisation to accord with the so-called 'Sword Dance'. At Kirkby Malzeard, the military costumes seem to have been devised for the Ripon Millenary Festival in 1886. (Bower MSS).

13. The Flamborough dance, with a reasonably long history of performance, is a typical example.

14. Most rapper dances can be described like this.

15. William Henderson: 'Very Old MS copied 1788' quoted by Sir Walter Scott: *The Pirate*, 1821.

16. Samuel Hibbert: *Description of the Shetland Isles . . .* , 1822, 554.

17. The text was first published by N. Peacock: *J.E.F.D.S.S.*, VIII, 1956, 29–39. The version printed here has additional material collected subsequently by Dr Peacock, by whose permission it is printed.

18. Hedgehog.

19. The revised MS has this sung by Mr Spark.

20. *cf. ll.* 11–14 of the Branston version, page 11.

21. Cuckold.

22. This is a parallel to the Greek 'Bouphonia', the ritual ox-murder where no-one will accept the blame for the crime, but eventually it falls on the axe which dealt the blow. This was connected with the worship of Dionysos. (Hibernicus: *NQ*, CLXXVI, 1939, 402).

23. See App. 2.

24. See E. C. Cawte *et al.*: *English Ritual Drama*, 1967, 79–80.

25. The two most accessible sources for this text are E. K. Chambers: *The English Folk Play*, 1933, 131–150 and Cecil J. Sharp: *The Sword Dances of Northern England*, III, 1913, 50–76. The latter gives instruction for the dance itself and there is discussion of the text in the Introduction, pp. 13ff. The music for the dance and songs is found in Cecil J. Sharp: *The Sword Dances of Northern England: Songs and Dance Airs*, III,

1913. The text is very literary, Part I being largely pieced together from Act III, Scene III, of Congreve's *Love for Love*, and the Fool's Wooing probably owing a debt to Lindesay's *Satyre of the Thrie Estaitis* dating from the early sixteenth century. (E. K. Chambers: *op. cit.*, 232).

26. BM Add. MS 44870. The text is more accessible to the general reader in Chambers: *op. cit.*, 104–123, where some discussion of the text from a literary point of view is given.

27. The fact that the Clown wears the Lock around his neck suggests that the links were rigid. This cannot argue that the form of the dance was similar to that now known as 'Long Sword'.

28. The 1849 edition of Brand contains a note that a Mr T. Park had inserted a comment, 'This is performed by the Morris dancers in the vicinage of Lincoln' against the description of north-eastern sword dances in his copy of the 1777 edition. A correspondent to the *Lincoln, Rutland and Stamford Mercury*, 12th January 1844, described the Plough Monday morris-dancers as 'ribbon-decked, sword-carrying buffoons and ruffians'. These may refer to sword dance ceremonies, but are too vague to be definite.

29. BM Add. MS 44870.

30. Hector Charles Cameron: *Sir Joseph Banks . . .* , 1952, 264.

31. The text contains passages from *Wily Beguiled* and *The Enterlude of Youth*, an early sixteenth century morality. It is furthermore comparatively free from any verbal or metrical irregularities.

32. Cecil J. Sharp: *The Sword Dances of Northern England*, I, 1911, 84–9.

33. *ibid.*, III, 1912, 22.

34. There is some affinity between these and those of the Pace-egg versions where the song is usually a variant of the folk song, 'The Seven Jolly Tradesmen' ('When Joan's Ale was New').

35. Cecil J. Sharp: *The Sword Dances of Northern England*, I, 1911, 42–3.

36. An 'Outsider' is a most unlikely victim, unless he was a 'plant' amongst the audience. Bell: *Ancient Poems, etc.* 1857, 175–80, gives a version containing a stage direction which says that the Parish Clergyman rushes in amongst the dancers and is killed. This unlikely variant owes its existence entirely to the fact that Topliff: *A Selection of the Most Popular Melodies of the Tyne and Wear . . .* , *circa* 1815, 37, 42, gives a Version which contains the line, 'Alas, our actor's dead'. The line was misquoted by Cuthbert Sharp: *The Bishoprick Garland*, 1834, 58–62, as 'Alas our Rector's dead', which gave rise to Bell's further misquotation. (Inf. from Dr E. C. Cawte). The likelihood is that Ampleforth's outsider owes his existence to something similar.

37. At Hunton, *circa* 1890, one of the Clowns was the Doctor (Dr Maud Karpeles: Collection). At Haxby, when the Clown was killed, the Betty came and picked him up. (Cecil J. Sharp: *Field Notebook*, I, Jan. 13th–Apr. 4th, 1913).

38. A woodcut of 1517–19 shows the Emperor Maximilian in full armour standing on a lock of swords laid on the ground. (Richard Wolfram: *Der Anschmitt*, 5, April 1953, 8).

39. Violet Alford: *Sword Dance and Drama*, 1962, 125.

40. *ibid.*, p. 91.

41. *ibid.*, 169.

42. Estella Canziani: *J.E.F.D.S.*, 1931, 19.

43. Olaus Magnus: *De Gentibus Septentrionalibus*, 1555, l.xv. c.xxiii.
44. John Wallis: *The Natural History and Antiquities of Northumberland*, 1777, 175–6, 177–8.
45. See page 9.
46. See Appendix 2.
47. Inf. From Dr E. C. Cawte.
48. Cecil J. Sharp: *The Sword Dances of Northern England*, III, 1912, 84.
49. Cecil J. Sharp: *ibid.*, III, 23–4.
50. At Gainford, the dance was described as 'no particular dance – something like a hornpipe in step and very quick'. (E. C. Cawte *et al.*: *English Ritual Drama*, 1967, 78).

5.   *The Hero-Combat Ceremonies*

1. The variations often appear on a regional basis. Appendix 2 contains a variety of Hero-Combat texts selected to illustrate the variations.
2. Reproduced from Alex Helm and E. C. Cawte: *Six Mummers' Acts*, 1968, 25–9.
3. It is difficult to see what these three crowns were intended to represent. Other variants include 'the eep, the sheep, the shamarocker' 'the He, the She, and the Shamrock'. Possibly, 'amma roceo' is an even more corrupt form of 'shamrock', but this does not explain the first two.
4. The source described this as meaning 'sword and buckle'.
5. These three parts have their parallel in the Court Masque, similarly divided into three parts, the Entry, the Main Dance and the Going Out, separated by speeches and music. See Margaret Dean-Smith: *FL*, LXV, 1954, 74–86.
6. See Appendix 2.
7. Armitage, Staffordshire (R. J. Marriott: Collection).
8. Chipping Norton, Oxfordshire (Mrs Norgrove: *Birmingham Weekly Post* NQ, 4th October 1885, 1a).
9. Cuddesdon, Oxfordshire (R. J. E. Tiddy: *The Mummers' Play*, 1923, 217–18).
10. Eccleshall, Staffordshire (C. S. Burne: *Shropshire Folk-Lore*, 1883, 483–9).
11. Norton Canes, Staffordshire (Alex Helm: Collection). This name was elaborated to Bold Rumour at Andover, Hampshire. (C. J. Berry: *Andover Advertiser*, 2nd January, 1953, 3b–f), and to Beau Roamer at Crondall in the same county. (J. Alfred Eggar: *Remembrances of Life and Customs . . .* (1924), 27–32).
12. See Antrobus, Cheshire and Greenodd, Lancashire, versions, Appendix 2, p. 000.
13. See Appendix 2.
14. At Islip, Oxfordshire, a stage direction reads, 'Decide which is to be dead and make a good fight'. (Ordish Collection).
15. There are isolated exceptions to this. On Holy Island up to 1956 at least, and possibly still, children simply recited their lines with no physical action of any kind. (Alex Helm *et al.*: *Six Mummers' Acts*, 1968, 23–4.) At Horsham, Sussex, the performers clashed their swords until the Turk died. (L. E. Broadwood: Collection).
16. The death was often symbolic. It was unnecessary for the victim to lie on the ground, and the prevention of wear and tear on a fragile disguise argued against him doing so, particularly when the ground was muddy. At Symondsbury, Dorset, the 'dead' champions simply knelt on one knee. (*See Walk in St George*, E.F.D.S.S. Colour film of the ceremony). At Ripon, Yorkshire, the victim merely dropped his head. The performer who called for a doctor put his hand on the dead man's shoulder and kept it there till the cure was effected. Information from Dr E. C. Cawte). Note also the stage direction following *l.* 103 in the Iping version, Appendix 2, p. 81.
17. *ll.* 36–8, Burntwood version, p. 28.
18. *ll.* 41–3, Antrobus, Appendix 2, p. 70.
19. *cf. ll.* 119–120, Syresham. How far the introduction of this character was influenced by the chapbook versions is uncertain. See Appendix I.
20. R. J. E. Tiddy: *The Mummers' Play*, 1923, 116, quoting the *Land of Cockayne* in an English MS *circa* 1305. A painting by Pieter Breugel the Elder dated 1567, entitled the Land of Cockaigne and depicting exactly the sort of scene described in the mummers' play, is in the Alte Pinakothek, Munich.
21. R. J. E. Tiddy: *op. cit.*, quoting *The Harangues, or Speeches of several celebrated Quack-Doctors in Town and Country . . .* , By Various Hands [London: Printed for J. Robinson, at the Golden-Lion in Ludgate Circus; and sold at the Pamphlet-Shops in London and Westminster. Price 6d.] cp. *ll.* 104–5, Iping: *ll.* 185–6, Minehead; *ll.* 61–2, Antrobus, &c. (Appendix 2).
22. Mrs E. H. Rudkin: Collection.
23. At Heysham, Lancashire, *circa* 1820, it was said that a doctor was introduced to effect the cure. This was an innovation borrowed from another set of performers who used to visit Heysham on Easter Monday from a village twelve miles away. (Lucy E. Broadwood and J. A. Fuller-Maitland: *English County Songs*, 1893, 22–5).
24. Jack Spinney at Islip. Here, Doctor and assistant appear to have coalesced.
25. Sometimes, as at Chadlington, Oxfordshire, the character is a 'Female' who insists on being called 'Miss Finney'. (Ordish Collection).
26. Douglas Kennedy: *J.E.F.D.S.*, 1930, 17–20.
27. Angelina Parker: *FL*, XXIV, 1913, 86–7.
28. This tallies exactly with the description given of the Doctor and his horse at Thenford, Northamptonshire. (A. E. Baker: *Glossary of Northamptonshire Words and Phrases*, II, 1854, 430–2).
29. Wm. & Hugh Raynbird: *On the Agriculture of Suffolk*, 1849, 307.
30. The Black Prince is normally a combatant who belongs to the main action, not the *Quête*.
31. Alex Helm: *Five Mumming Plays for Schools*, 1965, 16–18.
32. Fat Jack at Islip (*ll.* 60–4) has the Johnny Jack lines, but the latter character is a Presenter at Iping (*ll.* 16–27). (Appendix 2, p. 80).
33. Despite this, the lines appear in the song of the Greenodd version (*ll.* 100–4). (Appendix 2, p. 68).
34. R. J. E. Tiddy: *op. cit.*, 236.
35. At Minehead the version maintains the basic action, but the version is so elaborate that it has probably been rewritten. The characters from the *Quête*, Tom Bowling, King John, Queen Susan, &c., have accordingly been absorbed. The same is probably true of the Dorchester version.
36. R. J. E. Tiddy: *op. cit.*, 163–8.
37. Mrs Jennifer Robinson: Collection.
38. E. K. Chambers: *The English Folk Play*, 1933, 63–71.

39. E. K. Chambers: *The Mediaeval Stage*, I, 1903, 214, 215, 216.

40. Where a head was unobtainable, blocks of wood were used to form the upper and lower jaws, hinged at the back so that they could be made to open and shut. This was put down to the poverty of the performers at Guilden Sutton. (C. Cathcart-Smith: *J.E.F.D.S.S.*, 1947, 85–91 and communications to the author, 1950).

41. See *ll.* 112–148 of the Antrobus version (Appendix 2, p. 71). This particular section has much affinity with the 'Poor Old Horse' ceremonies of the Midland counties.

42. See Dorchester version, Appendix 2.

43. A similar hobby-horse, the Laare Vane, was connected with a Morris dancing ceremony in the Isle of Man, and gained the same gift after his revival from death. (Mona Douglas: *Proceedings of the Scottish Anthropological and Folklore Society*, IV, 1949, 53).

44. Pace-eggers.

45. John Leyland: *Memorials of Hindley* (preface dated 31st December 1878), 106. These are analogous to the white and grey hobby-horses of Burringham, Lincolnshire, page 18. See also the account of the La Soule ceremony, page 46.

46. At Stand, Lancashire, *circa* 1820, the dragon was described as having a horse's head. (Louisa Potter: *Lancashire Memories*, 1879, 81). The probability is that the so-called dragons were nothing more than hobby-horses, misunderstood by the spectators.

47. Christina Hole: *Traditions and Customs of Cheshire*, 1937, 113.

48. The regional chapbook versions of this same area are discussed in Appendix 1.

49. *ll.* 150–165 of the Iping Play (p. 000).

50. *ll.* 328–340 of the Dorchester version (Appendix 2, p. 83). The song may be more correctly entitled 'The Singing of the Travails' (R.S.: *Theatre Notebook*, 7, April/June, 1953, 58–60).

51. This is clearly shown on the film 'Walk in St George'.

52. The only exception to this is a Wooing Ceremony performed for a special occasion in Kentucky, U.S.A., *circa* 1860. (Marie Campbell: *J.A.F.L.*, LI, 199, 1938, 10–24).

53. The Irish ceremonies are fully discussed by Alan Gailey: *Irish Folk Drama*, 1969.

54. Mary Neal described the dance alone at Fishguard, South Wales, as being brought by two Irishmen as '. . . very like Shepherds Hay in form, . . . it was a war dance in connection with a mummers' play . . .', Patrick Kennedy: *Dublin University Magazine*, LXII, 1863, 584–6, writing of the period 1820, described the performers carrying out a 'kind of fencing with his vis-a-vis'.

55. The most complete collections of all these versions are in the archives of the Irish Folklore Commission and in the Ulster Folk Museum, Holywood, Co. Down.

56. Sir Walter Scott: *The Poetical Works of Sir Walter Scott, Bart.*, III, 1822, 87, note III to *Marmion*, Canto VI.

57. Alex Helm: Collection.

58 A suggested derivation is Galgacus, a chieftain who fought against the Romans. Another source is Goliath, who is actually named at Scremerston (see Appendix 2, p. 66).

59. Other versions from Newfoundland are from Change Islands and Salvage. The characters in these show not only an Irish influence, but also traces from the West Country and Cheshire. *See* Herbert Halpert and G. M. Story: *Christmas Mumming in Newfoundland*, 1969. More examples may come to light as the work of Dr Halpert and Professor Story proceeds.

60. Charles E. Welch, Jr: *J.A.F.L.*, 79, 1966, 523–536.

61. Alfred L. Shoemaker: *Christmas in Pennsylvania*, 1959, 21–3.

62. Marie Campbell: *op. cit.*, 10–24.

63. See f.n. 52. The other two versions are Hero-Combat; one from Gander had Dame Dorothy killed by Father Christmas, and included a character called Pickle Herring, who only appears elsewhere at Revesby.

64. And also in the Salvage version.

65. I.F.C.M.

66. J. T. and T. M. Flett: *J.E.F.D.S.S.*, 1953, 115.

67. Juliana Horatia Ewing: *The Peace Egg and a Christmas Mumming Play*, n.d.

68. A very unusual Old Tup version has been collected by Paul Smith in Mrs Ewing's village. After a normal Derby Ram song and killing, the Tup was revived in the Hero-Combat manner. It is possible that the performers joined existing Old Tup teams and produced a blended version rather than abandon the ceremony entirely.

69. Douglas Kennedy: *op. cit.*, 28.

70. Percy Manning: *Oxford Times*, 24th December 1898, 9e.

71. Anne Elizabeth Baker: *op. cit.*

72. This is not the version given in Appendix 2, but one reputed to date from 1780.

73. Margaret Maria, Lady Verney (ed.): *Verney Letters of the Eighteenth Century*, II, 1930, 41.

74. The late William Everett: Collection (1954).

75. This is borne out by the map from G. Slater: *The English Peasantry . . .*, 1907 as reproduced in H. C. Darby (ed.): *An Historical Geography of England before A.D. 1800*, 3rd Edn., 1951, 472.

76. Howard Levi Gray: *English Field Systems*, 1959.

77. *The Reader's Digest Complete Atlas of the British Isles*, . . . [1965], 122.

78. For example the Pace-egg and Chapbook actions of the north-west and the Souling versions of Cheshire.

6. *'Abnormal' Texts*

1. E. K. Chambers: *The English Folk Play*, 1933, 87–9.

2. The West Dorset versions are only abnormal because of their multiplied combats and the death and revival of Tommy the Pony. In the Dorchester version given in Appendix 2, the combats have been replaced by a very literary extract and the Tommy the Pony incident dominates the end of the action.

3. These versions have been influenced by the ballad of Robin Hood and Arthur a Brand. The outlaw characters contribute nothing to the action and appear to belong to a *Quête*. The ballad was probably interpolated as a literary device and was lost in its original form as memory faded.

4. G. W. Septimus Piesse: 2 *NQ*, x, 1860, 466–7.

5. F. G. Lee: 5 *NQ*, ii, 1874, 504–5.

6. The cures are described in four lines, two of them being the only familiar ones in the text:

   'I can cure the itch, the stitch, the pox, the palsy and the gout,
   All pains within and all pains without'.

7. The Escrick sword dance ceremony has a King and

Queen who appear arm-in-arm but who do not speak. Their lines were probably forgotten.

8. *Castle Cary Visitor*, II, December 1899, 189.
9. D. N. Kennedy: *J.E.F.D.S.*, 1927, 27.
10. There was an exception to this at Southery, Norfolk, where a Molly-dancing gang did admit women to the team as of right. This particular gang was noted for its rough, lawless behaviour and the women were said to have been as bad as the men in this respect. (Inf. from Miss E. M. Porter).
11. Hunter Collection, ff. 14R–47R.
12. Alfred Williams: *Wiltshire Gazette*, 30th December 1936, 3c–e.
13. Alfred Williams: Collection.
14. Alfred Williams: *Folk Songs of the Upper Thames*, 1923, 170–1.
15. Antoinette Taylor: *J.A.F.L.*, XXII, 1909, 389–394.
16. Oliver Morris: *Evesham Journal*, 24th December, 1965, 8d–f, 9ab.
17. Sabra.
18. See also *ll*. 155–163 of the Syresham version (p. 3) and *ll*. 54–60 of Iping (p. 81).
19. The extract exists independently as the folk song 'Good Morning, Moll', a dialogue song or two-part acting game. (*J.F.S.*, VIII, 1930, 192–4). Versions have been noted from Berkshire and Wiltshire (Alfred Williams: *Folk Songs of the Upper Thames*, 1923, 120–1) where the last verse was repeated as a duet whilst the singers bumped their backs together at the close as a sign of mutual repulsion.
20. Vaughan Williams Memorial Library: Collection.
21. The basic lines are common (see *ll*. 376–389, Minehead, and *ll*. 54–61, Iping) and are a common feature of the standard chapbook texts, but the 'Female', B, is not retained as such, 'Master' being more normal than 'Madam'.

7.   *The Disguise*

1. G. W. Douglas: *The American Book of Days*, 1948, 6.
2. Alan Gailey: *Christmas Rhymers and Mummers in Ireland*, 1968, 23.
3. At Offenham, Worcestershire, coloured calico replaced ribbons for dressing the maypole garlands whenever the latter could not be afforded. (Cecil J. Sharp: MSS, Folk Dances, vol. 2, p. 152).
4. Information from Crown Wallpapers, Holmes Chapel, Cheshire.
5. S. J. Hunter: MSS, 1822, BM Add. MS 24542.
6. T. Fairman Ordish: Collection.
7. *ibid*.
8. M. W. Barley: *J.E.F.D.S.S.*, 1953, 76.
9. The 'devil disguise' is found elsewhere. At Chesterfield, Derbyshire, Beelzebub wore horns in his hat and had a red tunic and trousers (Fig. 7), and Devil Doubt also wore a black hat with red horns. (Vaughan Williams Memorial Library Collection).
10. J. Ellet Brogden: *Provincial Words and Expressions current in Lincolnshire*, 1866, 151–2.
11. Mabel Peacock: 9 *NQ*, vii, 1901, 364–5.
12. Mrs Ethel H. Rudkin: Collection.
13. M. W. Barley: *op. cit.*, 89.
14. T. Fairman Ordish: Collection.
15. M. W. Barley: *op. cit.*, 89.
16. Margaret Dean-Smith: *Folk Life*, 1963, 98.
17. M. W. Barley: *op. cit.*, 76. As at Plumtree, Nottinghamshire.

18. As at Hibaldstow and Scawby. (T. Fairman Ordish: Collection).
19. M. W. Barley: *op. cit.*, 76.
20. N. Peacock: *J.E.F.D.S.S.*, 1956, 30. The Doctor is always dressed in character. This offers some support for the belief that he was a late introduction to the ceremony.
21. Cecil J. Sharp: MSS, Folk Dances, vol. 2, p. 175.
22. Cecil J. Sharp: *The Sword Dances of Northern England*, II (1912), 13–16.
23. Cecil J. Sharp: *op. cit.*, III (1913), 51. This attempt at realism was also found amongst the 'Females' of the East Midlands Wooing Versions.
24. T. D. Cook: *J.E.F.D.S.S.*, 1933, 111–12.
25. Rev. John Tinkler: Letter sent to Cecil J. Sharp, 1912.
26. [Christopher Clarkson]: *The History of Richmond, . . . 1814*, 296, 297. Compare the 1750 description given by John Jackson, page 7.
27. Cecil J. Sharp: *op. cit.*, III (1913), 31.
28. *ibid.*, 10, 19, *et seq*.
29. Cecil J. Sharp: Field Note Books, i, Jan. 13th–Apr. 4th, 1913.
30. Cecil J. Sharp: MSS, Folk Dances, vol. 3, p. 131.
31. H.N. [Harry Norminton]: *Loftus Urban District Council Souvenir Coronation Year Book*, 1953, 27.
32. Vaughan Williams Memorial Library Collection.
33. G. E. and W. H. Hadow: *The Oxford Treasury of English Literature*, II, 1908, 288–294.
34. Frank H. Kendall: *The Yorkshire Evening Post*, 20th January 1923, 4g.
35. Anne Elizabeth Baker: *Glossary of Northamptonshire Words and Phrases*, II, 1854, 430–2.
36. Lucy E. Broadwood and J. A. Fuller-Maitland: *English County Songs*, 1893, 22–5.
37. T. G. F. Paterson: *Journal of the County Louth Archaeological Society*, XL, 1945, 46.
38. Granada Television: Programme, 24th December 1964.
39. Frederick Ernest Sawyer: *Sussex Archaeological Collections*, XXXIII, 1883, 256.
40. C. E. Burkitt: *The Times*, 12th January 1953, 5e.
41. George Edward Rees: *The History of Bagendon*, 1932, 124–5.
42. H. W. Harwood and F. H. Marsden: *The Pace Egg. The Midgley Version*, 1935, 7.
43. William Hone: *The Every-Day Book*, II, 1826, cols. 122–6.
44. Bk. ii, Chap. 3.
45. *The Christmas Mummers*, 1858, 79–99.
46. Thomas Hardy: *Thomas Hardy's Notebooks* (ed. Evelyn Hardy), 1955, 37.
47. E. K. Chambers: *The English Folk Play*, 1933, 84–5.
48. Richard Bernheimer: *Wild Men in the Middle Ages*, 1952, 1. This book is not a study of folk elements but is concerned with 'art, sentiment, and demonology'. It contains some excellent illustrations in black and white of various aspects of the Wild Man.
49. *ibid.*, 52.
50. *ibid.*, 63.
51. *ibid.*, 94.

8.   *Abroad*

1. This is very similar to the Cotswold Jack Finney episodes which are not carried to the same conclusion however.
2. In the Padstow Hobby-horse ceremony, the horse

'dies' and comes to life again many times during its annual appearance on May Day. During the 'revival' the Clubman thrusts his club under the skirts of the recumbent horse, an action which is now apparently meaningless, unless it is the remnant of a forgotten gelding. Although no record of anything like this has survived in Padstow, the whole ceremony may be one of the most primitive revitalisation ceremonies in England.

3. I am indebted to Violet Alford: *FL*, XXXIX, 1928, 68–90 for this account.
4. Violet Alford: *The Proceedings of the Scottish Anthropological and Folklore Society*, IV, 1, 1903, 29.
5. cp. Askham Richard cure, p. 26.
6. E. K. Chambers: *The Mediaeval Stage*, I, 1903, 185.
7. Up to 1837 a similar Hunt occurred every Ascension Day at Combe Martin in Devon. (George Tugwell: *The North-Devon Scenery Book*, 2nd Edn. (1863), 110–3. The hunted character was called the Earl of Rone; he wore a grotesque mask, a smock frock stuffed with straw and a string of hard sea-biscuits round his neck. With him were a Fool, a Hobby-horse, a real donkey decorated with flowers and a similar sea-biscuit necklace, and a troop of Grenadiers, armed with guns and tall paper hats decorated with bunches of ribands. The Earl of Rone was caught, mounted on the donkey facing backwards, and led to the village. At certain stages in the villages the Grenadiers fired a volley, the Earl fell to the ground, was lamented by the Fool and Hobby-horse, and the latter revived him.
8. E. K. Chambers: *op. cit.*, 185.
9. *ibid.*, 185. cp. the cure of Tommy the Pony in the Dorchester version.
10. The most apposite example in England was the Jack in the Green who appeared on May Day with his entourage of dancing chimney sweeps. This could well be the most primitive example of the so-called 'Morris' in England.
11. R. Vuia: *J.E.F.D.S.S.*, II, 1935, 97–107.
12. A copy of the film is in the archives of the Vaughan Williams Memorial Library, but it is not clear if it is complete. Some of the details known to have existed are not on the film, and it is believed that part of the original was in colour whereas the library copy is entirely black and white.
13. The Wild Man in its later stages was often shown as a Bear.
14. Sidney Smith: 'The Practice of Kingship in early Semitic Kingdoms' in S. H. Hooke (ed.): *Myth, Ritual and Kingship*, 1958, 41–73.
15. R. M. Dawkins: *The Annual of the British School at Athens*, No. XI, 1904–5, 72–80; *Journal of Hellenic Studies*, XXVI, 1906, 191–206.
16. A. J. B. Wace: *The Annual of the British School at Athens*, No. XVI, 1909–10, 232–53; *ibid.*, No. XIX, 1912–13, 248–65.
17. The double gangs of the East Midlands Wooing Ceremonies must almost certainly have had their origin in something similar, and the duplicate characters could well have been used in the same way.
18. Arthur Beatty: *The Transactions of the Wisconsin Academy of Sciences, Arts and Letters*, XV, Pt. II, October 1906, 292–321.
19. Sir James George Frazer: *The Golden Bough*, Abr. Edn., 1949, 1.
20. The priests of this religion regularly castrated themselves on entering the service of the goddess Cybele (Frazer; *op. cit.*, 347).
21. Frazer: *op. cit.*, iii, 195ff. saw this similarity in the Christian religion as being one of the reasons for its rapid spread in Western Asia. The death and resurrection of a god was already a belief in earlier religions so that no new fundamental change was required.
22. E. C. Cawte et al.: *English Ritual Drama*, 1967, 29.
23. Wace: *op. cit.*, 1909–1910.

9. *The Fragmentation of a Ceremony*

1. Joseph Needham: *J.E.F.D.S.S.*, III, 1, 1936, 27.
2. *ibid.*, 28.
3. T. Fairman Ordish: Collection.
4. N. Peacock: Collection.
5. Joseph Needham: *op. cit.*, 20.
6. E. K. Chambers: *The Mediaeval Stage*, I, 1903, 214–6.
7. R. J. E. Tiddy: *The Mummers' Play*, 1923, 79.
8. Hilderic Friend: *The Midland Garner*, 2, First Series, 1884, 22–3.
9. The term 'Maid Marian' is often used in early accounts to describe a 'Female' in the Morris. The label springs from the belief that essential characters in the dance were the Robin Hood characters, but it is unlikely that the name was anything more than a means of identification to describe something familiar.
10. Thomas Middleton: *Transactions of the Lancashire and Cheshire Antiquarian Society*, LX, 1948, 47–55.
11. Maud Karpeles: *The Lancashire Morris Book*, n.d., 11–12.
12. The only full account of rush-bearing is given in Alfred Burton: *Rush-Bearing*, 1891.
13. Julian Pilling: *ED&S*, XXVII, 5, October 1965, 142–4.
14. Alex Helm: *J.E.F.D.S.S.*, VI, 3, 1951, 100.
15. Maud Karpeles: *op. cit.*, 7.
16. Cecil J. Sharp and Herbert C. MacIlwaine: *The Morris Book*, III, 2nd Edn., 1924, 74.
17. E. C. Cawte: *J.E.F.D.S.S.*, IX, 4, 1963, 197–212.
18. E. C. Cawte: Collection.
19. *ibid.*
20. This information is based on two sources: E. C. Cawte: Collection, and Cecil J. Sharp: Field Note Book, i, Jan. 1st–May 10th, 1910.
21. Maud Karpeles: *J.E.F.D.S.S.*, I, 1, 1932, 59. This could well have been a portable Maypole. Where a Morris existed, it was invariably present when the Maypole was raised. Dr Karpeles also draws attention to the similarity between the Bagillt branch and the garland or bush carried at Abram, Lancashire.
22. *Wald und Feldkulte*, I, 1904, 156.
23. Often in the rushcart procession were 'green groves' decorated with fruit under which little girls walked.
24. Mona Douglas: *J.E.F.D.S.*, 1928, 18.
25. Joseph Needham and Arthur L. Peck: *J.E.F.D.S.S.*, I, 2, 1933, 79–85.
26. W.R.: 6 *NQ*, v, 1882, 176.
27. Russell Wortley: Collection.
28. A. M. Protheroe: *FL*, XXXII, 1925, 83.
29. T. Fairman Ordish: Collection.
30. On one occasion at Ducklington, Oxfordshire, the dancers forgot this ritual. An old inhabitant who saw the omission threatened to chop down the maypole before they returned in the evening, whereupon the dancers corrected their error. (Cecil J. Sharp and

Herbert C. MacIlwaine: *The Morris Book*, I, 2nd Edn., 1912, 23–4.)

31. Percy Manning: *FL*, VIII, 1897, 313–15.
32. A.F.R.: 11 *NQ*, iii, 1911, 325 quoting Hist. MSS. Commission, Cecil MSS, VIII, 1899, 201–2.
33. B. C. Spooner: *Old Cornwall*, II, No. 1, Summer 1931, 21–2.
34. Arnold W. Boyd: Collection.
35. Quoted J. Brand: *Observations on Popular Antiquities*, I, 3rd Edn., 1849, 213.
36. William Hone: *The Every-day Book*, I, 1826, col. 565.
37. Percy Manning: *op. cit.*, 308.
38. F.B.H.: *ED&S*, XXVII, 3, 1965, 91.
39. Dr W. H. Swinburne: *ED&S*, XVIII, 6, 1954, 202.
40. Mrs Loïs Blake: Collection.
41. Rushbearing and the north-western Morris are obvious exceptions, but there is reason for thinking that their date of appearance had changed to conform with the date of the local patronal festival of the church. There is also some reason for believing that the rushbearing replaced bringing in the May in this area, partly because the Wakes was the annual holiday period and partly because May is an uncertain period for weather there.

Appendix 1: Chapbook Texts

1. 'Chapbook' is a modern word, but it is derived from 'chapman', the man who sold them. In Old English he was 'céapmann', derived from 'céap', barter. The chapman became a pedlar who travelled from place to place.
2. ? Slasher.
3. These are almost exactly those given for the character B in the unlocated Kent Play, page 37. Alexander declines a wife because 'he loves a learned scholar, but not a learned wife'.
4. The whereabouts of copies of Nos 1 and 2 was discovered by the detective work of Dr E. C. Cawte.
5. Bodleian Library: MS Top Oxon d. 199 ff. 333–9.
6. John Brand: *Observations on Popular Antiquities*, 1777, 175–6.
7. A footnote given in the text explains this as 'all the night long'.
8. Colm O Lochlainn: *The Irish Book Lover*, XVI, Jan.–Dec. 1928, 126.
9. M. A. Richardson: *The Local Historian's Table Book*, III, 1846, 375.
10. Benjamin Brierley: *Tales and Sketches of Lancashire Life*, I [1863], 113, 4.
11. James Wood: *Manchester City News*, 11th March 1905, 2c.
12. Bodleian Library: *op. cit.*: T. M. Fallow: *The Antiquary*, XXXI, No. 65, NS No. 186, May 1895, 138–42.
13. William Morris: *Swindon Fifty Years Ago (more or less)*, 1885, 141.
14. A. J. Peacock: *Bread or Blood: the Agrarian Riots in East Anglia*, 1816.
15. Benjamin Brierley: *op. cit.*
16. Roger D. Abrahams: *FL*, 79, Autumn 1968, 176–201.

Index

For locations in Great Britain the County (England) or the Region (Scotland) is given in brackets, followed by the National Grid Reference. Where boundary changes were made under the Local Government reorganisation of the mid-1970's, the County or Region to which a place is attributed in this index may differ from that given in the text, where the Counties referred to were those existing prior to 1970.

For locations in Ireland, the County is given in brackets, followed by the Irish Grid Reference.

(T) indicates that the whole, or a substantial part, of the play text is given.

Alex Helm's study of the folk play in England was based on extensive and detailed surveys of the available material, including the geographical index of surviving customs, published as *English Ritual Drama*, which he compiled with E. C. Cawte and N. Peacock.

The English Mummers' Play is a detailed discussion of the connection between these various customs, and starts from the premise that these 'plays' are not drama in the literary sense, but a ceremonial, involving death and resurrection. Once they are seen as ceremonial re-enactments of a rite, many of the problems of text and characters disappear, and a tentative classification can be made, into wooing plays, sword-dance plays and hero-combat plays. Disguise is an important element in the plays, and this is discussed in a separate chapter, while analogies from other countries are also examined.

The appendices include a notable collection of texts of twelve plays from throughout the British Isles, several of them printed for the first time, and many of them including musical examples. The book as a whole is a most important contribution to the history of drama, and its study of the play as ritual or ceremony will be of interest far beyond the immediate sphere of folklore studies.